GUMPTION

GUMPTION

Relighting the Torch of Freedom with

America's Gutsiest Troublemakers

NICK OFFERMAN

DUTTON
— est. 1852 —

DUTTON
— est. 1852 —

An imprint of Penguin Random House LLC
375 Hudson Street
New York, New York 10014

Copyright © 2015 by Nick Offerman

DUTTON—EST. 1852 and DUTTON are registered trademarks of Penguin Random House LLC

LIBRARY OF CONGRESS CATALOGING-IN-PUBLICATION DATA
has been applied for.

ISBN 978-0-525-95467-5

Printed in the United States of America

1   3   5   7   9   10   8   6   4   2

BOOK DESIGN BY ALISSA ROSE THEODOR

For Cathy and Ric Offerman—my dear mom and dad—who first taught me the ways of gumption; and for Mike Schur, for teaching me that we can still be very funny while saying "I love you."

CONTENTS

PART 2
IDEALISTS

PART 3
MAKERS

To succeed in life, you need two things:

ignorance and confidence.

—MARK TWAIN

INTRODUCTION

How does one compile a list of great Americans? It's an embarrassment of riches. To narrow the field, I decided to begin with my choice for number one. I imagine, or at least I would hope, that most of our citizenry would agree by an overwhelming percentage that the first person landing upon that list is—no, not Ray Kroc, the progenitor of the McShit sandwich. No, not Miley Cyrus or Beyoncé Knowles, or even Oprah Winfrey. Jesus! Goddamn. No, people, not Jesus! Yes, he was reportedly a supercool guy, but he just doesn't qualify as an American. I am referring, of course, to George Washington. The father of our country. I want to note that, of all the possible subjects, he easily sprang to mind first, based merely on my foggy grade school knowledge of his life's achievements in helping to create our republic and then sticking around to lead it as our nation's first president. Plus, he had wooden teeth! I'm a woodworker! Slam dunk—a sports metaphor, specifically basketball, meaning that the point(s) has (have) been scored emphatically!

I then began a list of other possible great Americans, basing my selections upon achievements of one kind or another that I considered to be "great" in scope. Leaders of men and women. Leaders of 4-H clubs. Activists, artists, zealots. Woodworkers, boatbuilders, farmers. Musicians. Priests. Muckrakers. Stoners. Hillary. Because after all, for the purposes of my examination, what exactly constitutes a "great" American? Runs batted in? Military victories? Humanitarian efforts? Amassing wealth? Collecting scalps? A number one single on the Billboard charts? A larder full of bacon? Ford F-250 in the barn? Well, duh.

While I continued to compile a roster of potential icons and discuss the book's overall direction with my great American editor, Jill, I began to read anew about Washington and the birth of our nation. I was powerfully stricken when I contemplated the actual situation in which our Founding Fathers found themselves, well, foundering: faced with the choice of either a continued subservience to an overweening Mother England or a gathering of their colonial brass balls in their mitts with which to cast off the taxing yoke of England's imperial control. Years earlier, when I learned all this history as a lad in school, I suppose the full implications of the events were lost on me, as I was not yet wielding a complete grasp of adult responsibility or governmental culpability as it applies to our daily lives.

The magnificent sons of bitches who founded our United States truly brandished a courage that is hard to fathom and a serving of foresight that very well beggars my modern imagination. Washington, Thomas Jefferson, Benjamin Franklin, Alexander Hamilton, James Madison, and the like saw the extremely rare opportunity to create a new "American experiment," one in which the best organizational techniques and brewing methods could be retained from the old-guard European governments, while discarding all the more unsavory trappings (clotted cream) of the monarchies and oligarchies they'd left behind "on the continent." These forward thinkers envisioned a nation ruled "by the people, for the people," founded on notions like "liberty and justice for all." Now all they had to do was liberate themselves from the iron grip of the military equivalent of Dwayne "the Rock" Johnson that was eighteenth-century Great Britain.

As I will explore in the coming pages, our country's inception had a lot of heroic nobility deservedly draped about its innovative framework, but it was also a series of events conducted by human beings, and so the intrepid experiment could not help but display some flaws as well. Not only were our fledgling American government and society crafted by human beings, but further, it must be noted with appropriate gravity, by all white dudes. With no small irony, the Declaration of Independence was composed, ratified, and signed by several Caucasian men, some of whom owned a great many slaves. If that wasn't bad enough, the Native American tribes in the Ohio Country were being mercilessly murdered and/or driven off their ancestral lands so that "we" could eventually build the pastoral suburbs of Cleveland, an assemblage of neighborhoods that, it must be noted, really are quite leafy and serene, but are they worthy of genocide? That is precisely the stripe of conundrum I hope to probe in the following pages.

In their inaugural documents, our Founding Fathers framed a somewhat malleable structure as a means by which the population could govern itself, truly remarkable in its place and time, which allowed the citizens of the United States to set about building, in rather short order, the most prosperous and powerful nation in the world. The seemingly limitless wealth of natural resources in our stretch of North America allowed our predecessors to excel in many fields of industry and artistry, soon surpassing the manufacturing capabilities of their European fathers and the world at large. Our young society flourished, exhibiting a gaiety and "rascally" nature that the rest of the globe found (very) briefly adorable. This was our puppy phase. In many ways, an attitude of "free-thinking" grew fulsome and took root in the burgeoning states, finally logging some long-overdue advances in civil rights for every person residing under the Stars and Stripes. Or so we proclaimed, anyway.

This writing will endeavor to examine some examples of the ways in which we as Americans have used the powers of freedom bestowed upon us to become more decent as a people, which I believe was loosely the idea when the whole shebang got started. This book will also strive to cast a light on some instances in which we have not used our powers for good and have most assuredly *not* become more decent.

Beyond the inspiration of my chosen historical figures (who set the bar very high for us indeed), I will illustrate for you a group of idealists who have continued to pay homage to America's foundational principles. In their varied lives of rigorous employment, these high-minded individuals have set a further fine example of just how much good may be accomplished with active eyes and loving observation. On many levels, this collection of visionaries has inspired me with selfless choices made for the good of all the people—not just the white guys—but I don't want to get ahead of myself.

Bringing up the back of the bus are some pretty cool kids, all of whom make things like music, furniture, poetry, art, and laughter. In many ways, their creations enkindle within us the flames of gumption, as we seek each our own path to lead lives that enlarge and also depend upon the lives of others in America and beyond. Please enjoy my mixtape of great Americans, twenty-one in number, whom I sincerely hope will affect you like they do me—in a way that makes you examine your own God-given gumption and react accordingly, so that we may all end up with a little more decency and several more chuckles.

PART 1

FREEMASONS

1

GEORGE WASHINGTON

Before I began reading about Washington in preparation for this book, I had a loose idea of his life and achievements based upon a mixed bag of remembered stories and images. The Emanuel Leutze painting of Washington's historic crossing of the Delaware River on the night of December 25, 1776, has always stuck with me as a clear representation of his military chutzpah. Having rowed a lot of boats in my day, I was astonished to see these men rowing in a river full of large chunks of ice, which would obviously be incredibly uncomfortable and difficult, especially long before the advent of "boat fuel" (canned beer).

It was that image that cemented in my child's mind the hardships that this man endured in the securing of our original freedoms, because if you had to row across an icy river at night, it meant that shit was pretty rough. Besides that noble image, I have always appreciated the two most well-known stories about Washington, which are the chopping down of the cherry tree and the story of his wooden teeth. Long before I knew that wood, especially American cherry, would play such an important role in my own life, I was charmed, along with the rest of the suckers, by the tale of Washington's famous honesty in the great cherry tree caper.

The story has it that as a young boy, Washington was given a new hatchet. Now, I can tell you from experience that there is really nothing more fun for a young person who likes to spend time in the woods than either a sharp knife, for obvious reasons, or, just as obviously, a hammer, and by crikey, a hatchet combines the two into one devastating tool of destruction. There are very few surfaces inside the house or out that cannot be thoroughly butchered with an energetically brandished hatchet.

Our little George knew what he was about—he set to chopping everything within reach with his new hatchet, including his father's favorite cherry tree. When questioned on the subject, George answered truthfully, "I cannot tell a lie. I chopped down the cherry tree." His father was reportedly so moved by his son's integrity, he chose not to punish him, stating that "honesty is worth much more than any number of cherry trees." 'Twas a winning anecdote, however apocryphal, displaying Washington's pith from the get-go, written well after his death as part of a lionizing tribute to the great man.

Now, in hindsight, I could have shot holes in this story all day long. First of all, for a cherry tree to develop enough character, size, and, presumably, fruit yield to make it anybody's "favorite" would take many years, with said tree developing a trunk that would be much too thick and sturdy to fall easy prey to a boy's hatchet, no matter how robust the lad.

Second, the father of our country exhibited an adherence to the principles of gentility and politeness just about as soon as he could pee standing up (three months of age, legend has it). Little George would have known better than to destroy a fruit tree near the house, particularly one to which a family member had taken a shine. With his trademark good sense, he would have simply detoured several yards to the left of the cherry tree in question, entered the nearby forest, and made vast piles of wood chips with the chopping action of his hatchet upon any number of forest trees, deciduous or conifer, and nobody's feelings would have been bruised in the least. I consider this particular tall tale debunked.

Now on to those storied wooden teeth. Everyone knows George Washington had terrible dental trouble, and so he had dentures made of wood, right? Wrong! Our first president did have a terribly rotten set of original teeth—while they lasted, that is, because he had lost them all by late middle age. His final lower molar served as the anchor for a full set of hinged dentures, upper and lower, until it, too, finally fell victim to the barber's pliers, rendering our finest statesman completely toothless. As an avid eater of foodstuffs who loves to masticate red meat, not to mention the occasional churro, I shudder to imagine the complete loss of my chewing tackle.

Dentures of the period were often constructed of hard materials such as hippopotamus ivory, bone, or even actual human teeth, often "purchased" from slaves. Some of the organic materials used in eighteenth-century false teeth are suspected to have stained in a grainy pattern similar to wood, which seems to be the detail from whence that "wooden teeth" rumor sprang. More aggrandizing!

Whatever the story's origin, I have to wonder why we would ever even begin to feel the need to mythologize this man, whose real-life accomplishments were so goddamn impressive that I wet myself seven times reading Ron Chernow's amazing, Pulitzer-winning biography, *Washington*. I suppose this is how we as a society end up remembering these larger-than-life figures, tucking them neatly into a file drawer using landmarks like "wooden teeth"—Hoover: "wore a dress"; Woody Allen: "played clarinet"; Margaret Thatcher: "had three testicles"—satisfying a need to make these historical characters more iconic. In the case of George Washington, such embroidery was entirely unnecessary, as the reality of the complex and emotional man behind his steely visage was much more engaging than a mere accessory like false pearly not-so-whites.

As a teenager, young George transcribed, as a writing exercise, some 110 "Rules of Civility & Decent Behaviour in Company and Conversation." I dislike very much the contrast of this task with the diversions I see pursued by modern sixteen-year-olds. That accusation includes myself, by the way. As a teenager, I didn't have a video game in my pocket but instead ran obsessively to the bowling alley or the pizza parlor, where stood the noisome machines of escapism with names like *Donkey Kong* and *Frogger*.

Instead of burying his attention in his smartphone or video-gaming system, our nation's future father sat laboriously scribing phrases like "3d. Shew Nothing to your Freind that may affright him." (Translation: "Don't freak me out, dude.") "35th. Let your Discourse with Men of Business be Short and Comprehensive." ("Wrap it up, asswipe.") "54th. Play not the Peacock, looking every where about you, to See if you be well Deck't, if your Shoes fit well if your Stokings sit neatly, and Cloths handsomely." ("This ain't a fashion show, brah.") "56th. Associate yourself with Men of good Quality if you Esteem your own Reputation; for 'tis better to be alone than in bad Company." ("Steer clear of the mall.") "89th. Speak not Evil of the absent for it is unjust." ("Why'n't you say that to my face, Chad?") "92. Take no Salt or cut Bread with your Knife Greasy." (I believe this one to be a sexual euphemism.) "101st. Rince not your Mouth in the Presence of Others." ("Say it, don't spray it.")

I mean, come on! Those are amazing and also chock-full of terrific advice. Since I read these, my wife, Megan, has commended me on keeping my "knife" much less "greasy." My own parents did an excellent job of teaching me good and decent manners, despite my irrepressible desire to this day to lie back on a table or car hood, legs in the air, and light up a fart in a most bewitching fireball. Still, I can't help but think that we could all benefit from having to write out these simple but effective phrases, to better commit them to our respective remembering parts (noggins).

Had Washington lived in our era, he would have undoubtedly been the leader of a troop of elite Eagle Scouts as well as the star of the local football team, with a side business building post-and-beam barns. He was a renowned physical specimen in his young manhood, often impressing his family and friends with feats of incredible strength and fortitude, whilst training for a career as a surveyor of land.

The journeys he would undertake for the purpose of land speculation, sleeping on little more than a handkerchief, truly entailed the most badass of arduous outdoor living, a full century before the Thermos bottle came onto the scene with its savory payload of hot stew.

He and his peers were rugged, far beyond any toughness we might imagine today, sitting in our air-conditioning, whining about how long it's taking Zappos to deliver our new UGG slippers from Australia. A strapping man jack like Washington would have shot and cleaned a buck, cured its hide, and sewn himself two pairs of boots in the time it would take us to update our credit card information on Amazon.

In the journal he kept of his journey over the mountains, floridly entitled *Journal of My Journey over the Mountains*, George Washington firmly established his lifelong habit of chronicling the important events of every campaign to which he applied his considerable energies. The sheer volume of written correspondence he produced in his lifetime is staggering, especially to the urbanized inhabitants of this modern age, to whom handwriting letters seems as farfetched as scraping leather out in the tanning shed for harnesses, belts, and shoes.

The University of Virginia houses a program entitled the Papers of George Washington, which will inventory more than 135,000 documents, a project so vast they don't expect to be done collating and annotating it until 2023! If Washington started writing the day he leapt from his mother's womb, that would have been five-and-a-half letters a day over his sixty-seven years of life. That magnificent bastard could write, and he did so centuries before there was a Bic to click. No, nor roller-ball, felt-tip, Sharpie, or even that old standby, the Ticonderoga no. 2 pencil!

George scribbled those many thousands of letters and journal pages with a quill and ink, folks. And not only was his body of work prolific, but he was quite the wordsmith as well. As I perused selections of his letters, I was delighted by adjectives such as *scurrilous*, *acidulous*, *obdurate*, *opprobrious*, *contumelious*, and *vituperative*, almost all used to exclusively criticize or dress down others who had fallen short of his high standards on the battlefield or in the statehouse.

I, for one, greatly enjoy stumbling upon such colorfully descriptive wordings (even when they're directed at me), because they require me to seek out their meanings and pronunciations in the dictionary. (This is how I had learned, by the ripe age of seven, words like *misconduct*, *shenanigans*, *insubordination*, and then as a result of those, the subsequently juicy *confiscation*, *misdemeanor*, *castigation*, *retribution*, and, finally, *paddle*, *bludgeon*, or *glory-board*.)

As mentioned earlier, his manners were impeccable, as he strove to succeed not only among his Virginian neighbors and peers but in the eyes of the British Crown as well, since King George still controlled the activities of his colonies from across the wide ocean. Knowing no other governmental entity in his life, our young protagonist naturally aspired to impress the Crown in hopes of rising to a place of esteem. Unbeknownst to either party, the fates were crafting in George Washington the perfect weapon to be brandished against Britain herself in the impending, inevitable war for America's freedom.

In 1753, Washington was thrown into the fray in a very substantial way. Colonial France and England were both laying claim to the enormous Ohio Country (modern-day Ohio, Indiana, and parts of Pennsylvania and West Virginia), desiring not only to claim the land but also to secure the lucrative fur trade with the Native Americans.

An order came to the colonies from none other than King George II himself, calling for a valiant envoy to hustle west to see if the French were building forts where they shouldn't be. If so, the bearer of the orders was instructed to ask them to peacefully depart. Makes sense, right? "Oh, apologies, monsieur. We did not realize zat you British fellows would like zis land. Allow us to just collect our accoutrements and we will scoot along, begging your *pardonnez-moi*."

In the quite likely event that the French would not just meekly vamoose at the invitation of the British colonists, the envoy was then instructed to "drive them off by force of arms." As you may have surmised, these orders fell to none other than our virile, vigorous hero, who was a mere twenty-one years of age. Can you imagine the weight of this responsibility? I cannot. I am forty-four at the time of this writing; I like being trusted by my superiors (my wife, my director, my publisher) with responsibility, and I can't begin to fathom it. At twenty-one, I was impressing my playmates by successfully discerning between my butthole and a sizable gopher hole in the ground, say, four to five out of seven tries on the average.

Remember, at the time, Washington's superiors were the British royalty. He had no inkling that he was soon famously to become the loyal servant of the citizens of a fledgling country. It's difficult, if not impossible, to fathom the complications involved in the settlement/conquering/theft of North America by the three main European strengths—England, France, and Spain—with the added factions of myriad indigenous tribes trying their level best to literally hold their own against the avaricious white newcomers.

Washington's ability to navigate these treacherous hinterlands successfully and arrive safely back on the East Coast gave the strapping young buck a galvanized, heroic sheen, which played no small part, one assumes, in his subsequent appointment to command the Virginia regiment in the French and Indian War, part of which was known as the Seven Years' War. Washington distinguished himself as a leader of men, not so much through any one clear performance but more through his perseverance and discipline, costing the Virginia settlers less in casualties than the other colonies. It was during this conflict that he began to accumulate knowledge of British military maneuvers, information that would serve him very well in the coming Revolution.

It also didn't hurt his chances of landing a choice, wealthy bride in the form of one Martha Custis. Given our country's current population, I suppose I would have surmised that the colonists were not opposed to procreating, or "cultivating tubers," but I was not prepared for Chernow's report of an early mail order made by the newly wed Washingtons to a London apothecary: four ounces of Spanish fly! Also recorded in their possession were the books *Conjugal Lewdness: or, Matrimonial Whoredom*, by Daniel Defoe, and *The Lover's Watch: or, The Art of Making Love*, by Aphra Behn. Right on, George and Martha! Spill the wine!

Sadly, these titillating helpmeets did nothing to aid the Washingtons in producing any offspring of their own. A 1751 bout with smallpox is thought to have possibly rendered the baby-maker of our country's father ironically sterile. It certainly could not have been for lack of desire upon the part of George, since he could not have spoken of Martha in a more lascivious manner than he did in this favorite

phrase of approbation: "Virginia ladies pride themselves on the goodness of their bacon." I don't know about you, but I can think of few
more boner-inspiring turns of speech.

In any case, Washington was by now one of the most well landed
of the Virginia elite, with a young family and a plantation to manage.
These responsibilities must have weighed quite heavily when he was
called upon to serve in the growing conflagration of the Revolution.
Sure, he had political aspirations, but the fact that he left his wife and
their collective household of children from her previous marriage, as
well as other family strays, not to mention the thousands of acres of
farmland in his care, impresses deeply. Martha's ability to remain
steadfast as well, during all of Washington's extremely dangerous
campaigns into the woods or onto the battlefield, is equally laudable.
There must have been gumption in the Mount Vernon water supply.

Upon reexamination, the overall cause of the Revolutionary War
is one of the aspects of Washington's history that struck me in a much
more resounding way. These colonists under British rule, on a new
continent some thirty-four hundred miles from England, were receiving news and commands from England that were three months old
by the time they hit their front porches, which would have been frus-
trating in the kindest of circumstances, and these were anything but.

Let me just nutshell where we're at for you: In the early 1770s the
asses of the thirteen American colonies were growing unbearably
chapped thanks to the taxes being imposed upon them by the British
Parliament. I suppose England, wielding the strongest military on
the planet at that time, thought little to nothing of possible repercus-
sions to their bullying. After all, what were the colonies going to do,

put together a ragtag bunch of militiamen and throw a tiny revolt? How precious!

In what has to be one of the most infamous cases of royal myopia on record, Mother England lost her opportunity to count the Grand Canyon, the Walmart and Sam's Club empires, and the Disney theme parks among her holdings. If King George had only been able to quell the British ego just enough to deal reasonably with the colonists instead of electing to suppress them like an insubordinate child, then instead of delicious coffee-based drinks and jazz-compilation CDs, all those lucrative Starbucks franchises would likely be serving tea and crumpets today.

When our Congress elected to form a Continental army and unanimously agreed to post George Washington at its head, they undertook what was, on paper, an incredibly foolhardy quest. With very little budget and no training, our forefathers had decided to fight their way clear of England's tyranny—or die trying. The catalyst that led to this unlikely and dangerous course of action was the simple realization of undeniable human rights that had occurred to these great thinkers in what has come to be known as the Age of American Enlightenment. The self-evident truths of an individual's right to "life, liberty, and the pursuit of happiness" that these trailblazers had apprehended would no longer let them rest under the onerous hand of monarchist rule. This, to me, is the moment in our history when the corncrib of gumption was fully stocked. I am so grateful that these farseeing men had the temerity to make this moral choice even when the life-threatening odds were stacked against them.

Washington himself was scared shitless by the task in front of him, and with good reason. Just because he was the clear choice in the colonies to lead a military force doesn't mean the population as a whole had any business engaging in a war with an accomplished international power like England. Nonetheless, lead them he did.

It was at this juncture in Chernow's biography that I was struck with an intense feeling of empathy for Washington, perhaps because he was approximately my age, forty-four, when the conflict began, or perhaps because Chernow had imbued him with such a textured humanity. Having been a sometime leader of men and women myself by now (in a much, much tinier way), as a director or producer or supervisor of a team of carpenters for the stage or a shopful of woodworkers, I was able to imagine myself much more effectively in his shoes thanks to the explicitly described conditions of the conflict.

Speaking of shoes, frequently Washington was the only one wearing any at all, as his troops were so underfunded as to exist in constant want of the bare minimum of clothing and footwear. Despite his consistent hectoring for funds, Washington received only very rare aid from the citizenry whose freedoms he was sworn to defend. To add to this indignity, many of the colonists sold their food or offered their lodgings to the British troops, because the lobsterbacks had hard cash with which to purchase such luxuries. And this wasn't just through one winter, folks. This deplorable treatment lasted for several winters. Nature's four seasons can be beautiful on the East Coast, but they're lovelier by far if one is wearing pants.

When the details of this situation settled upon me, my once distant and cold admiration for our first president was refueled with a strong sense of the here and now. If I consider the dilemmas that face our modern populace, it's hard to reconcile any degree of complaint with the hardships that these brave and long-suffering soldiers endured. Sure, it sucks when your airplane sits on the tarmac for an unexpected forty-five minutes, making you late to Austin, meaning you'll miss the eight fifteen showing of *The Hobbit: The Battle of the Five Armies* at the Alamo Drafthouse, where you can enjoy a pint of Guinness and a sausage with your film. It sucks big time, I agree, but compared to sleeping in the wintry elements with little on your back but a potato sack, and an empty belly to boot, it seems rather bearable.

The Revolutionary War was filled with occasions of fortune's ebb and flow, but my adulation for Washington was most replenished by this turn of events: In the fall of 1776, the American troops were badly defeated by British general William Howe in his successful campaign to capture Manhattan. Washington managed to limp away across New Jersey with his life intact, but the coming winter and recent string of defeats had the future prospects of the Continental army looking rather bleak. Despite the idealistic goals of the dwindling American forces, surrender must have been looming heavily as the only remaining recourse for our George.

Fortunately for us, George had another idea. He and his men staged a surprise attack on Christmas Day of 1776, stealing across the Delaware River to whup the Hessian army stationed in Trenton, New Jersey, capturing a thousand Hessians. Thus, the historical image to which I had clung, of those redoubtable wildcats rowing their boats across the icy river, turned out to be damn accurate as a representation of the unquenchable spirit of American gumption!

As you may have by now gleaned, we won. Washington realized

going into the war that he had one hell of a tough row to hoe, and so he masterfully created in himself an heroic figure behind which the colonists could rally. As the author and journalist Garry Wills has noted, "Before there was a nation—before there was any symbol of that nation (a flag, a Constitution, a national seal)—there was Washington." According to Chernow, as Washington arrived at each town, he would exit his carriage and climb astride a horse, knowing that the people wished to picture him upon a horse, lending a little bit of theater magic to his creation of, really, our first superhero.

Naturally, when we emerged from the other side of this long and bloody conflict as the victors, Washington was fully deified and likely could have written his ticket to claim whatever power he chose as the clear "King of America." Certainly no one expected his next move, which was to *resign* his commission as commander in chief in order to return to his home at Mount Vernon. Trying to imagine another political leader before him or since who would hand over the keys to the kingdom just as his or her greatest power was realized is pretty impossible. For this, especially with the winning reason of returning to his farm and family, I am quite gratified in my choice of Washington for this first chapter. King George III agreed with me, when he exclaimed upon hearing the news of this noble demurral, "If he does that, he will be the greatest man in the world."

As our rough-and-tumble American forces were eventually handing the British their finely candied asses, the nuances of the Constitution—the document which would provide the cornerstone of our new government's foundation—were also being hammered out. In his lifetime, Washington frequently voiced his consternation over the conundrum that slavery embodied and how the language about the freedoms of the individual that fills the Constitution was obviously hypocritical. He was aware, fully aware, that all slaves deserved to be freed, on principle, but was unable to bring such a liberation to fruition in the chaotic morass that was our fledgling United States. His own household, if not his state of Virginia, and really the whole enchilada, his misgivings assured him, would come to crumbling ruin if he freed his slaves.

The Marquis de Lafayette was instrumental in voicing this particular complaint, urging the new American government to enact a manumission setting free all those held in slavery. His passion went a long way toward inspiring the leaders of America's Revolution, for he had determined, as he wrote to his wife, that "the happiness of America is intimately connected with the happiness of all mankind."

Despite the number of esteemed thinkers who shared his enlightened view, it proved to be more than two generations before the Emancipation Proclamation would be enacted. Washington was the only significant slaveholder among the Founding Fathers to grant his slaves their freedom in his will upon the occasion of his wife's death. While this act deserves credit, it also strikes me as passing the buck to his inheritors; the problem was too messy for him to tackle, but here you go, kids. Good luck! Despite the apparent deflection of responsibility, I suppose it was better done than not.

The stark division of opinions over the issue of slavery was only one of the many issues on the table for the crafters of the Constitution, which makes its ultimate completion and subsequent ratification all the more miraculous. Again, I point to the example of modern legislation, wherein it seems to take years just to craft a clause about one small tax law in one obscure bill. The fact that all the politicians from all thirteen of the colonies were able to agree *enough* to set this ship a-sail is simply astonishing. As Washington himself averred, "It approached nearer to perfection than any government hitherto instituted among men."

Another quality I have come to admire more and more in George Washington is the near-perfect neutrality that he exhibited over the course of his political career. He was known for patiently hearing out, sometimes to the point of infuriating his peers, each side of an argument until he felt that he could draw his own considered opinion. Certainly he would have had his own agenda, as would any human being, but more often than not his intentions seemed to rest in whichever direction was best for the common good. Regarding the Constitution, as he told James Madison, "the appearance of unanimity . . . will be of great importance."

So adept was he at satisfying all sides of the issues at hand that Washington remains our only president to date who has received 100 percent of the electoral votes, on the occasion of each of his two terms. To imagine a modern president tallying even 75 percent of those votes today is purely unfathomable. Even in these early days of America's inception, Washington was surrounded by virulent politicking on the parts of Madison, Jefferson, Monroe, Hamilton, and anyone else who could get a leg up. There was plenty of dirty pool being played, including backdoor deals and smear campaigns in the press, even then. It seems to me that without Washington's impartial demeanor, this great "American experiment" could well have foundered on its moorings before it ever left the harbor.

Thinking about his approach points out to me my own extreme laziness in scrutinizing political issues. My attitude to begin with—that most politicians are full of shit—doesn't help, but it's a hard piece of information to get around and impossible to disprove. For candidates to achieve any high office in our state or federal legislature, they are required to make loud, ambitious public promises during their campaigns, which can never be completely fulfilled, even by the greatest humanitarian intentions. Therefore, we're starting off our relationship with each prospective leader on the wrong foot, a foot of mistrust.

This insubstantial beginning is then quickly exploited and exacerbated by the sources from which most of us derive our news of the world, be it politics or foreign policy or which teenage pop star had her bikini on backward yesterday, "news items" that have all come to hold equal weight in today's media. In any given election, when I'm on top of it, I talk to my friends about the bullet points and I look up information online to inform myself about bill initiatives, and I usually end up very confused. Few bills or amendments are ever so cut-and-dried as to lend themselves to a clear "right" or "wrong" answer. (And this is the best-case scenario, when I'm not buried under a writing deadline, or twelve-hour shoot days, or both, in which case I lazily just leave it all until the last minute.)

Once my confusion is firmly established, I can then simply turn to one of the handy consumer channels we've been provided to tell us what we think. Depending upon my leanings, I can flip on Colbert, Stewart, or the new hottie John Oliver, or conversely I can tune in to Rush Limbaugh or Bill O'Reilly or any other personality on the Fox News marquee. In any given circumstance, they will leave me no doubt whatsoever as to who is deserving of my vote and who is an asshole. Although I initially appreciated this convenience, much the same as I appreciated the Big Macs of my teenage years, I have come to wonder indeed, in both instances, what are the ingredients that go into the sandwich?

Without George Washington's inaugural acumen for nonpartisan governance, I am convinced that we would be sunk even deeper in "policy" than we now find ourselves. It's telling that the scholars all seem to agree that we have never seen another of his ilk in the White House and are not likely to going forward. At great personal cost, this excellent "first American" set our country sailing on as even a keel as he could manage, sails billowing, full speed ahead upon the winds of gumption.

OFFERMAN WOOD SHOP

G

Gumption

2

BENJAMIN FRANKLIN

Benjamin Franklin was never president of our country, and yet his likeness adorns the most substantial denomination of our paper currency in circulation, the one-hundred-dollar bill. I find it appropriate, by the way, that George Washington graces both the one-dollar bill (aka "bob," "buck," or "single") and the quarter (aka "two bits"), as they have been the most hardworking and honest forms of currency in my lifetime. Many of my earliest wages were paid in quarters, which worked out just fine since I turned right around and funneled them into *Galaga* and *Joust* video game machines and then occasionally into washers and dryers at the Laundromat. In college, there was a perfect storm of a Laundromat that had washers, dryers, and *Galaga*, the allure of which kept me coming back with a frequency that kept my clothing smelling very pleasant indeed. Washington most likely would have approved of his likeness representing simple, honest lucre, as he was comfortable with his reputation as the go-to guy for all your cash needs, but James Madison would most certainly not have liked the fact that he landed upon the five-thousand-dollar bill (which is no longer in circulation). The Mad Jam was not given to the fancier things in life, nor was he one to seek the spotlight, so such a display of his visage, while understandable to us, would have undoubtedly caused him consternation.

The hundred-dollar bill seems fitting for our man Benjamin, since he had the knack of pulling himself up by his bootstraps and engaging in admirably top-drawer activities, whether he was inventing some clever new innovation, seducing foreign powers with his skills of diplomacy, or disseminating wisdom and humor with his *Poor Richard's Almanack*. (For these reasons and more, he is considered to be the father of American Freemasonry. In fact, he was instrumental in the initiation of George Washington into that secret society. This is all I am allowed to reveal.) I am powerfully enamored of Mr. Franklin for the achievements he crafted in his life, fueled primarily by an insatiable sense of curiosity.

As a boy, Ben Franklin loved to swim, and he was fascinated by the physics of the tangible world, that is, the way things operated chemically and mechanically, so he naturally invented flippers to help him swim more expeditiously. He found himself in a burgeoning new society, and he explored every avenue by which he might have a positive effect. He established the first library in Philadelphia; he established the US Postal Service, no big deal; and he touted reading above all other diversions. A lifestyle that I still consider to be the most attractive and profitable, if one can just avoid all the distractions of technology and other media channels. He was so devoted to reading as a pastime, he invented a reading chair equipped with a foot-powered fan as well as a handy ladder, so when the chair was flipped open, one could climb it to reach a book on a high shelf. The man invented bifocals; he greatly improved the science of burning wood to heat one's home by inventing the Franklin stove, which was exponentially more efficient than the popular open fireplaces of the day; and, of course, he famously discovered electricity and thereby the electric battery. Without this man and his creativity, our dildos would remain silent and lifeless to this day.

Now, as I have learned the hard way, accomplishing any achievement worth crediting in this life usually requires a few important missteps before one can discern the path to success. In my own case, naturally much less impressive than his, that means that I ruined a good deal of expensive white oak in joinery mistakes before finally succeeding in executing a respectable trestle table in the style of Gustav Stickley. If you were as profound and prolific an inventor as Benjamin Franklin, it only stood to reason that you would also invent some folly. My favorite example of this would have to be Franklin's "air bath." This technique entailed sitting completely naked in a room with all its windows thrown open, so that a person could "bathe in the pure, fresh air." Before I too readily enjoyed a chuckle at the expense of this idea, I thought I had better try it out for myself. While I did find the experience to be enervating and even slightly titillating, I couldn't in all honesty say that I felt any cleaner after thirty minutes of air bathing. I'm glad I tried it, although I can't say the same for the rest of the people at the coffee shop. Personal experience is the surest method by which one can determine the truth of a supposition, no matter how reputable the reporter, since so many experiences are subject to individual proclivities.

A lifetime of deep thinking and subsequent tinkering was fostered partially by Franklin's father, who would take him on walks around the Boston of his boyhood, to witness "joiners [carpenters], bricklayers, [wood] turners, braziers [brass workers], etc. at their work." Franklin stated that ever since then, it had been a pleasure to see good workmen handle their tools and that he had learned enough to allow him to construct little machines for his experiments. This episode moved me, as I had a similar but less intentional experience with my own dad. Among him and my uncles and grandfathers, not to mention our neighbors, I witnessed, and even got to take part in, carpentry, paving, roofing, gardening, animal husbandry, sewing, painting, boating, and mechanical work on engines large and small. None of these trades struck me particularly on their own, but I was quickly enthralled by the world of tools and materials and, most important, hardware.

Trips to Mel Phillips's True Value Hardware in Minooka bore the savory fruit of working-class camaraderie in addition to row after row of magical implements with which one might plumb running water into one's home or wire electricity to one's tree house. There was real wizardry in those mom-and-pop hardware stores, delivered with a personal, avuncular touch and a free cup of coffee. Not every youngster is going to end up a woodworker, but some trips to the hardware store or a craft fair might go far in igniting a creative spark in your own little Ben or Betty Franklin. Many of Franklin's projects were contrived by simply walking down the sidewalk or sitting at a café, observing the man-made systems around him. He noticed that the oil-burning streetlights would rapidly grow dark with accumulated soot, so he invented a new design with improved airflow, then added more streetlights and night watchmen to make the Philadelphia streets safer at night.

His desire to devise implements by which our lives would be improved was bolstered by his interest in what he called his list of "virtues." Much like his younger friend George Washington, Franklin wrote out a list of the ethical ideals to which he hoped to measure up. They were temperance, silence, order, resolution, frugality, industry, sincerity, justice, moderation, cleanliness, tranquility, chastity, and humility. Franklin began to keep a tabulation of the instances in which he would transgress these virtues, and he said he was "surprised to find myself so much fuller of faults than I had imagined; but I had the satisfaction of seeing them diminish."

To me, this sort of self-evaluation is most inspiring, as I find it all too easy to waltz through life lazily maintaining a minimum display of decency, which must necessarily register to others as a mediocre effort. Just go ahead and read through that list once again, and if you're anything like me, two or three (or six or seven) of the virtues will jump out as areas that might like a bit more attention. We're human and therefore flawed by design, so it's a test we can never ace, but as the man himself puts it, "I never arrived at the perfection I had been so ambitious of obtaining, but fell far short of it, yet I was, by the endeavor, a better and a happier man than I otherwise should have been if I had not attempted it." The notion gives me comfort—that if I simply *pay attention*, then I should end up a better and happier man.

This introspection no doubt played an important role in fueling Benjamin Franklin's most consistently sagacious and hilarious journal, entitled *Poor Richard's Almanack*. Self-published for twenty-seven years, from 1732 to 1758, this periodical was loaded with a mix of sound advice and jocularity. Authoring famous adages like "Early to bed and early to rise makes a man healthy, wealthy and wise" brought to Franklin a level of celebrity heretofore unknown in the colonies. Considered the first American humorist, Franklin regaled his readership with a constant stream of raillery over the years, uproarious yet redolent of horse sense. Within his *Almanack* and without, he is credited with such gems as:

> Three may keep a secret, if two of them are dead.
>
> The greatest monarch on the proudest throne, is oblig'd to sit upon his own arse.
>
> He that falls in love with himself, will have no rivals.
>
> He's a fool that cannot conceal his wisdom.
>
> Serving God is doing good to man, but praying is thought an easier service, and therefore more generally chosen.
>
> There will be sleeping enough in the grave.

To wit, this last phrase seems an accurate depiction of Franklin's own practice, as a neighbor described him to be nothing if not industrious: "For the industry of that Franklin is superior to anything I ever saw of the kind; I see him still at work when I go home from club, and he is at work again before his neighbors are out of bed." Time after time I am reminded by my heroes, from Ben Franklin to my wife, Megan, that great achievements require more than just talent and skill and super-foxy good looks. If a person wants to succeed, he or she must work his or her cute little tail off.

Additionally, many of the subjects I chose for this book seem to prefer reading books to all other forms of diversion, which I understand. Watching a television show or playing a few hands of euchre, or even indulging in a video game, can certainly be most enjoyable, and it surely passes the time. The catch is that those activities do little else than divert my attention, while a well-chosen book can actually concoct a stew of betterment within me. Whether I'm reading the excellent nonfiction of a John McPhee or an Elizabeth Gilbert or the narrative stories of a Donna Tartt or a Patrick O'Brian, I have cultivated the opinion that a certain alchemy occurs up in my math-can that is unmatched in its potency by any other form of recreation. This is why I always prefer the book to the movie; even if Peter Jackson has spent considerable millions embroidering the astonishingly real world of Middle-earth, it cannot compare in verisimilitude to the Shire I imagine within my own cerebral laboratory.

In the Philadelphia library that he had established, Benjamin Franklin spent "an hour or two each day, and thus repar'd in some degree the loss of the learned education my father once intended for me. Reading was the only amusement I allow'd myself. I spent no time in taverns, games, or frolicks of any kind." Now, I know what you're thinking: Isn't this the guy who said, "Beer is proof that God loves us and wants us to be happy"? Well, not exactly. This quote has been somewhat paraphrased and hijacked by many of our nation's craft breweries, and rightly so. It may be revisionist writing, but I for one am okay with it. What Franklin did write was, "Behold the rain which descends from heaven upon our vineyards, there it enters the roots of the vines, to be changed into wine, a constant proof that God loves us, and loves to see us happy." Beer, wine . . . come on. Six of one, etcetera. He also coined the euphemism for drunkenness

"Halfway to Concord," which tickles me to no end. That, my friends, is fun with words.

I myself think that taverns, games, and especially frolics are very important activities in which to engage as well, but in moderation. For every four nights in the library, I would like to feel I've earned one night in the tavern, or at least half a frolic, if Megan is up for it.

Despite the rather puritanical tone of his guidelines, Franklin was still a lot of fun. I mean *a lot* of fun. I am heartened by his advice to set up an orderly, structured, and productive life, and then fuck around within that framework, ensuring that you engender mirth whilst remaining optimally productive. For Pete's sake, he wrote a scientific letter to the Royal Academy of Arts of Brussels suggesting that research be undertaken to explore methods of improving the odor of human flatulence, a letter that later came to be entitled "Fart Proudly." If there had been any question up to this point that Ben Franklin was my kind of guy, this one piece of writing would extinguish all doubt. I could well have been his muse, had we shared a more contemporary time line.

From his vast, golden canon of wise scribblings and witty sayings and treatises on both foreign policy and breaking wind, there are two sentiments that appeal to me above all others. The first could well serve to mirror the main theme of my own book, and it looks like this: "We must, indeed, all hang together, or most assuredly we shall all hang separately." Franklin made this statement just before signing the Declaration of Independence, giving us a clear indication that (a) he was hilarious even in the face of such a momentous occasion, and (b) the assembled statesmen were not remotely all in accord with the document at hand.

The year was 1776, and the aforementioned king of England, a somewhat addled chap by the name of George, had refused to answer yet another petition from the colonies to redress his aggressive taxation. The publicly chosen leaders of the colonies likely could have argued amongst themselves for decades about the issues at hand, but they did not. They recognized that despite many differences of opinion, whether they preferred the thin New York–style pizza crust or the clearly superior Chicago-style deep-dish version, they must leave those common sources of rancor at the door and behave as one united front. To my way of thinking, this is, and always will be, our task as the human race on this planet.

We'll never settle this pizza debate, for after all, when weighing the advantages of either crust style or pan depth, they're both fucking pizza, for crying out loud. The answer to the question of which style is better is simply, "Yes," but as James Madison adroitly pointed out, human beings can never rest in such agreement, at least not for very long. There are many sections of the world's population that might admonish us, saying, "Why are you arguing about this minor detail? There is pizza that we can eat. We're hungry, you assholes!" This sensibility brings me to a follow-up quote by Franklin, from Paris after signing the peace treaty in 1784, again searingly on point: "Thus the great and hazardous enterprise we have been engaged in is, God be praised, happily completed. . . . A few years of peace, well improved, will restore and increase our strength; but our future safety will depend on our union and our virtue. . . . Let us, therefore, beware of being lulled into a dangerous security; and of being both enervated and impoverished by luxury; of being weakened by internal contentions and divisions."

Right? Is it just me, or is this statement alarmingly prescient? I suppose it was not at all ambiguous to a thinker with such a clarion comprehension of human nature that given an inch of slack, we Americans would then take mile after mile. We engaged in the bloodiest of battles to gain the individual freedoms of our citizens (that is, our white citizens who owned property), and once that was achieved we effectively put our feet up and began to obstinately enjoy our *Real Housewives* television programming and our Twinkies. I feel this profoundly, for I love a Twinkie.

We have been occasionally made, with reluctance, to pause the programming of luxury long enough to look out the window and witness some persevering injustice or other, which is a total pain, right? We've been made to acquiesce the right to vote in our elections to people like ladies and also dark-skinned people. Ugh, fine. Can we please get back to *The Dukes of Hazzard* now? This episode is amazing—they jump the General Lee over three creeks *and* Sheriff Rosco P. Coltrane's police cruiser! Plus, that lady has an amazing butt, so successfully exploited that tiny denim shorts came to be known as Daisy Dukes! This diversion is top-drawer!

I think we can hold as self-evident the truth that Ben Franklin, having been shown to possess a love of humor as well as a fascination with farts, would have been a great fan of my television program *Parks and Recreation*. I believe, furthermore, that he would have enthusiastically approved of modern viewing systems, by which we can watch the programming of our choosing at whatever time we prefer. This luxury allows me to budget my time accurately, allowing for one or two hours in an evening devoted to *Downton Abbey* or

Jimmy DiResta videos on YouTube. Unlike the TV viewing of my youth, I am no longer required to watch anything I don't fully choose. If I wanted to watch *Happy Days* at eight and *Three's Company* at nine, I had to sit through some bullshit called *Laverne & Shirley* at eight thirty. That's not the best example, since *Laverne & Shirley* was fantastic, but you get the idea.

I believe that Mr. Franklin would have enjoyed the small percentage of television programming that is not garbage, much as I do. Particularly if he had taken some beer onboard, transporting himself "halfway to Concord," for he takes a very inspiring position on the topic of leisure versus laziness. Bear witness: "Employ thy time well, if thou meanest to gain leisure. . . . Leisure is time for doing something useful; this leisure the diligent man will obtain, but the lazy man never."

I believe the difference in the two conditions described above, leisure and laziness, is one of intent. Franklin is instructing us to live diligently, working at our vocations to raise an income in such a way as to leave a remnant of time for more leisurely pursuits. In my own life, these pursuits can include hiking, woodworking, television, reading for pleasure, walking by the ocean with my wife, playing with our dogs, listening to records, playing my guitar, etcetera. These are all activities for which I earmark periods of time, as opposed to just randomly thinking, "Hmm, I have three hours to kill; what should I do now?"

Conversely, I feel like laziness requires a strong inclination to passivity. I know that among my human attributes I definitely have the potential for laziness. That's when we think, "Ugh, this bed feels so nice. I don't want to do *anything*." The trouble with this human inclination is that, as Poor Richard says, "The sleeping fox catches no poultry." A refrain I have heard from young people my whole life, usually delivered in a plaintive whine, has been, "I'm bored! There's nothing to do!"

Franklin's guidance is precisely apposite to this particular complaint, as he is counseling us to fill our time with "something useful," which to me means that, if I know I'm going to ride a train for four hours, I bring a book. If I finish a project at the woodshop a few hours ahead of schedule, I try something new on the lathe or ride my bike to Griffith Park, whose mountainous roads are a useful workout indeed. I have learned to use foresight whenever possible to preemptively fill my time so that none shall be wasted. Sometimes I stumble in this effort, but sometimes I am successful, and I know well by now that I will go to bed much better satisfied if I have filled the day's time with productivity instead of the diversions of a lazy person.

Positively occupying one's time is also a matter of health, both physical and mental. We must avoid sloth, Franklin adds, for "Sloth, like rust, consumes faster than labor wears; while the used key is always bright, as Poor Richard says." When I have sometimes indulged in sloth, I can in hindsight identify how quickly I became depressed, which I "solved" by overindulging in intoxicants, namely, weed and bourbon. I have learned that by budgeting my "tavern time" just as punctiliously as I do my work and leisure times, then the libation of my choice (single-malt Scotch these days) becomes a temperate dose of medicine against the stress of the week rather than a constant dulling agent.

There's a great anecdote in Franklin's autobiography about one of his first jobs working at a London printing press as a young man. The work was incredibly physical, as I would imagine, hauling heavy trays of type to and fro, upstairs and downstairs. Franklin explains that he drank only water, as he was quite aware of the strenuousness of the exercise involved, while the other workers, the Brits, guzzled beer all day. He was able to carry one tray per hand, while the Englishmen would bear only one tray in two hands, causing them to marvel and dub him the "Water-American"! They wondered how he could appear stronger than they, drinking only water, while they consumed strong beer. Our young American explained to them that there was far more sustenance in a penny's worth of bread than in all that beer, but they would not be convinced.

To give you an idea of the quantity and consistency of this consumption, Franklin wrote, "My companion at the press drank every day a pint before breakfast, a pint at breakfast with his bread and cheese, a pint between breakfast and dinner [lunch], a pint at dinner, a pint in the afternoon about six o'clock, and another when he had done his day's work."

Using my ineluctable powers of arithmetic, I have tabulated that bar tab at six pints a day. Now, I don't know about you, but when I'm working hard at physical labor, I can handle a refreshing pint with my lunch, so long as I'm not required to perform any activities requiring precision or finesse. That's one pint. The second pint certainly feels good going down, but then the pleasing effect of the elixir's alcohol turns the idea of going back to work to one of misery. That's two pints. Six sounds like a possible problem was at hand.

The periods in my life when beer at lunch was de rigueur included my work on a blacktop crew, framing houses, and building scenery for larger Chicago theaters. All jobs as a member of a labor crew, some requiring more skill than others but as much muscle as anything else. Frequently, some of my fellow laborers would consume beer (or weed or vodka or all three) with a thirst to match Franklin's printing-house compatriots, which I found a bit alarming. Some of them were clearly alcoholics to the point where we'd stop at the bar on the way to work at six A.M. so they could slam a double vodka and fill a cooler with Miller Lite.

I tried to join in on this apparent good time, and on much more than one occasion. We managed to get through those years without anybody losing a finger or an arm or a life, but that's just luck and dumb animal fortitude. It turned out that I could haul plywood and framing timber and drive nails in a perfectly acceptable fashion after a couple of one-hitters or a few beers. It was also clear that I needed to lie down in my truck and sleep for three hours immediately after getting off work. I'd find a shady spot behind a barn, open the doors for the breeze, and pass out from exhaustion.

This seemed fun maybe the first or even the second time it happened, before I slowly discovered that my days were, on the whole, exceedingly more enjoyable if I *wasn't* shitfaced while performing extreme feats of physical strength in the hot sun for eight to ten hours. I suppose this was my first lesson in moderation, when I began to work sober and then enjoy the drinking only after work so much more. Youth was an important ingredient for me in this high level of consumption, and so as my years have progressed, so has my tolerance decreased, a statistic which I find to be comforting.

One reason I was able to identify the folly, eventually, in such a lifestyle was that it occurred to me that my coworkers had given up. They had resigned themselves to the fact that they would be merely brute laborers for the remainder of their able-bodied lives. Now, this isn't to say that one can't have a rewarding and admirable life pouring concrete or shingling roofs; in fact, I know a great many such tradespeople to whom I look up for doing just that. I often envy these men and women their lives of staunchly task-oriented schedules requiring only a pickup truck, a set of dependable tools, and some quality materials. I find an undeniable nobility in the men and women who build our houses and buildings and roads and bridges.

These particular fellows, however, had thrown in the towel, reducing their aspirations in life to simple dreams of a nicer, slightly less used Camaro or maybe an extra week at the Wisconsin Dells. I suppose what I'm driving at is this: If you're having drinks on your lunch break from work, you might be in the wrong job. Or you might be in the best job you can lay your hands on, in which case you might be neglecting the time and love you could be spending on your spouse/kids/pets. Working as an artist onstage or on-camera or making objects of wood in my shop, I flatly need every bit of sharpness and focus that I can muster. When I am lucky enough to be engaging in the work I love, the last thing I want to do is put on a buzz, which would serve only to cloud my abilities and desecrate my experience.

Ben Franklin wrote that "when men are employ'd, they are best content'd; for on the days they worked they were good natur'd and cheerful . . . but on our idle days they were mutinous and quarrelsome, . . . which put me in mind of a sea-captain, whose rule it was to keep his men constantly at work; and when his mate once told him that they had done everything, and there was nothing further to employ them about, 'Oh,' says he, 'make them scour the anchor.'" To clarify, scouring the anchor of a ship is a perfectly unnecessary activity, but given the choice between that and having a workforce stand about idling, a good administrator will always set the crew to a task. You'll see this refrain again before my book is done: Find good work to do, and get to it.

I mentioned earlier, you may recall, having two favorite statements from Benjamin Franklin. The second of the two is not funny at all, but it is the lesson of his that moves me the most to emulation. As a young man returning from England, he wrote out a moral code for himself, which included this: "I resolve to speak ill of no man whatever."

Among all of Franklin's advice, I found this instruction to be the most profound, perhaps because it is the simplest. Of course, my mother had said to me as a lad, "If you can't say something nice about a person, don't say anything at all," and of course that stuck with me, as did a great deal of my mother's beautiful teaching. However, since I can be described as the duplicitous mess known as a "human mammal," my nature will, on occasion, steer me in directions that blatantly disagree with my parents' gentle wisdom. Often, I am able to pull out the map that my mom drew and find my way through the underbrush of my ego back to the path of decency, but having that tutelage reinforced from out of the blue, by an American Founding Father no less, about whom I was reading simply because I knew there would be some talk of farting and electricity, has been stirring.

Like anybody, I am susceptible to insecurity or paranoia upon any given day. When I examine my professional choices, for example, good or bad, or even just a quote in a magazine or a review, I can, if I'm not careful, dive down a rabbit hole of self-doubt. What did that reporter mean by "bravely quirky"? Was I wrong to have passed on that crime teen drama? Is *ursine* a compliment?

But in the end, we're all Americans, and it's been said that we had better hang together or we shall most assuredly hang separately, or something like that. Beyond that, even, we're all earthlings. I'm afraid that eventually we're going to have to admit that we're all in *that* together as well and that Franklin's words hold true on a worldwide level. He knew this when he penned a letter home from Paris in 1777: "It is common observation here [Paris] that our cause is the cause of all mankind, and that we are fighting for their liberty in defending our own."

A Parisian contemporary of Ben Franklin's paid him this compliment: "He knew how to be impolite without being rude." I love that distinction powerfully. To me, that's one of the most important aspects of working as a giggle-pusher, and I know my personal technique still requires some improvement. I hereby vow to maintain this course of study so that I may one day also aspire to "Fart Proudly."

The Scrivener

3

JAMES MADISON

Beyond masters Washington and Franklin, the list of luminaries and firebrands comprising and surrounding the Founding Fathers is loaded with characters who exhibited a substantial deal of gumption: John Jay, of course, the "hot one"; John Adams, roundly admired for his marriage to Laura Linney; Alexander Hamilton, who famously attended every meeting with his fly "accidentally" wide-open; even the influential French aristocrat Gilbert du Motier, commonly known as the Marquis de Lafayette, or "Stinky Pierre," incessantly suggesting that heavier sauces be served with meat dishes (to the great chagrin of colonial chef Dieter Puck, ancestor to Wolfgang); and let's not exclude Thomas "Juicy Low-Hangers" Jefferson, whom I sincerely revere as a vocal proponent of an agrarian society (not to mention everyone knows he smoked a preponderance of his own homegrown "hemp"). These are just some of the marquee players on the scorecard of our nation's formation, but the list of qualified personages goes on at quite some length, if the main qualification is gravel. The bench is awfully deep, as it were, with shrewd thinkers and irascible orators who each brought their own individual flavor packet to this ideological melting pot. That said, it may then come as a surprise to the reader that I have chosen one of the *least* outwardly colorful, or "pimpin'," Founding Fathers to round out my initial threesome: James Madison, our fourth president, who is considered the father of the Constitution. He also authored a little brochure known as the Bill of Rights.

The primary reason I am drawn to Madison is that, while all these other great scholars and elocutionists were battling out the issues at hand, he was the one writing it all down and personally weaving all these innovative philosophies into the documents that continue to shape and protect our rights as Americans today. Most of the other valuable players were brandishing a powerful complement of charisma in the meeting halls, expressing with eloquence and volume their opinions and policies, which James Madison would then fairly weigh and curate in his writing. To my way of thinking, it was his even-keeled approach and his consummate reportage that allowed the explosive and exciting ideals of our newly hatched country to be most effectively incorporated in a documented way—that managed to take root and blossom, even while withstanding the clamorous rancor of opposing viewpoints.

A diminutive fellow, tipping the scales at a hundred pounds and boasting a mere five feet, four inches from crown to toe, Madison brings to my mind the legendary character actor Bob Balaban, who in every role seems quietly dismissible at the get-go but then proves to carry a presence of magnitude by the time the credits roll. Lacking the height and lung power to perform respectably in a shouting match with his contemporaries, James Madison instead relied upon an unwavering work ethic and commitment to neutrality in his summations.

When the blustering had subsided at any constitutional meeting, and the participants, heaving from exertion, (undoubtedly) leaning upon a handmade walnut tea table with meticulously carved ball-and-claw feet, regained their respective winds enough to ask, "Did anybody write that down?," Madison was able to relieve the room by reporting that yes, he had recorded every snatch and rejoinder, and then some. His participation went so far as to resemble that of the "great and powerful Oz," navigating machinations from behind his "curtain" for some of our government's greatest initial dramas. For example, when George Washington was elected our nation's first president, Madison wrote his inaugural address, as well as the House of Representatives' congratulatory reply to Washington's address, as well as Washington's reply to the House's reply! (Imagine how much less ignorant so many of the Bush boys would have appeared if they'd only had "Jimmy Madness-son" spinning the rhetoric for both sides of their presidential debates!) In much the same sensibility with which they trusted only George Washington to steer the newly launched schooner of American government, the Founding Fathers preferred only James Madison to write up both the captain's orders and the owner's manual.

Our fourth president, as we like to bandy in my scholarly circle, was "hella smart." In layman's terms this means he was smart as shit, "as shit" being rather incongruously employed here as a compliment. (Huh. That's not very good writing. Let's examine: Etymologically, I am inclined to think that this rather clumsy usage can likely be traced to the much more accurate phrase "slick as shit," an apt simile comparing a given condition, object, or person favorably to the especially slippery lubricating properties of the digestive waste products of any critter that poops, but traditionally, that of the goose, as in: "Damn, playa, them Jordans are slick as shit," or "Ryan, come and finish your Capri Sun! And don't run near the pool, it's slippery as goose shit!" As our collective human intelligence continues to erode in conversation, even while the sum total of our statistical knowledge on paper increases at an alarming rate, I know that I am certainly guilty of many such verbal lob shots, so that if I want to express an extreme of really any circumstance, I am prone to use "as shit." *This blacktop is hot as shit. These jalapeño poppers are tasty as shit. Mario Lopez's abs are ripped as shit! And his teeth? Glory be, them pearlies are white as shit.* You get the picture, I imagine, since you are likely perceptive as shit. I believe I commit these errors with some frequency, an indiscretion I would like to correct going forward, perhaps thanks to an historical vigilance installed in me by my mother and her mother telling me not to say "ain't" enough times that it finally stuck. I love words and I want to use them positively, so I'll need to police myself from here on out, as my grandma Eloise is gone, and I don't see my mom frequently enough for her to save me, which is lame as shit.)

As I was saying, James Madison was right intelligent. He graduated from Princeton in only two years' time, supposedly subsisting on four to five hours of sleep a night. The man was a compulsive student, first in college and then in the halls of life. He was commonly described as a nose-to-the-grindstone worker, which is another attribute of his that gets me fired up. He saw the work that needed to be done, so he rolled up his sleeves and he did it. Madison understood inherently that men and women love being divided against them-selves. In the Federalist Papers, he wrote, "So strong is this propensity of mankind to fall into mutual animosities, that where no substantial occasion presents itself, the most frivolous and fanciful distinctions have been sufficient to kindle their unfriendly passions and excite their most violent conflicts." In other words, if things are relatively calm, we the people will come up with any old bullshit to squabble about, because it's in our nature, because deep down, we're dumb as shit. James Madison "got it" because he was sharp in the noggin, or thinkin' bucket, and so he went on to attest: "The regulation of these various and interfering interests forms the principal task of modern legislation, and involves the spirit of party and faction in the neces-sary and ordinary operations of the government." By the way, he was about thirty-seven years old when he penned these notions, which might seem more appropriate coming from a wise old sage, like maybe a colonial Dumbledore. This young warlock of a man, one of Virginia's finest minds, was so invested in his share of the responsibil-ities regarding the drafting of first the Articles of Confederation, then the Constitution, and finally his full authoring of the Bill of Rights, that he risked even life and limb to see them completed in a satisfac-tory manner.

Examine, if you will, the Constitutional Convention. Congress was summoned to Philadelphia to discuss revising the Articles of Confederation. James Madison arrived *eleven days early.* Oh, hang on. Back up, sorry. This was *after* Thomas Jefferson sent him two trunks containing twenty-one books on political histories. Even Thomas Jef-ferson knew which tiny horse to bet on. Madison was preparing for this dustup by reading the political histories of the Greeks, the Swiss, the Dutch, and the Germans. I nodded off just writing that list! He was *boning up* big-time, while the other congressmen were probably hanging out with Jefferson and Sally Hemings, smoking bongs and getting "jiggy" with "it," whereby "jiggy" refers to, I think, penis play, and "it" refers to the female vagina. This was pre-Constitution, remember, so anything goes. Or went. Shit was goin' down like a David Lee Roth video dressed in the wardrobe and furniture from *Amadeus.* Meanwhile, our man was making carnal advances of his own upon his homework in as stiff a fashion as he could muster, utilizing all the myriad mental powers of a brain engorged with blood like an erect John Thomas (bringing that metaphor to completion).

Let's also remind ourselves that George Washington did not want to attend yet another reunion of his highfalutin, loudmouthed, smarty-pants cohorts. Washington was tuckered out from *fathering our nation,* and he just wanted to recline on the porch and get his snack on at Mount Vernon. He was obstinate and likely would have succeeded in avoiding the sausage party had not our Mr. Madison hauled his insubstantial fanny to Washington's side and convinced him that his attendance was imperative to the successful carrying of the day. Spoke Madison to Washington, "It was the opinion of every judicious friend whom I consulted that your name could not be spared." Now, I am not saying that I *am* sitting here ogling some man-on-man Greco-Roman wrestling magazines and singlet/headgear catalogues, but if I *were* enjoying such fare, I may well have Madison to thank for lighting the figurative fire under George so that he was subsequently able to ensure that such freedoms would one day be mine to enjoy in the comfort of my own domicile. Harrumph.

To resume: Madison arrived eleven days early. Did he leap about the room, commanding the attention of the assembly with his winning flourishes and fulminations? Did he sing the truths of American democracy into every ear present? Did he run a deep flag pattern, burning Aaron Burr, who stood futilely holding his own jockstrap while Madison caught a fifty-yard toss from General Washington for a game-winning touchdown, resulting in a flamboyant Madison nut grab and moonwalk across the end zone? He did not. He sat close-mouthed as near as he could manage to the action, and he took notes. And, because the delegates were sworn to secrecy, his notes actually became the invaluable record of the convention.

A note about arriving early: I am of the opinion that, if you are habitually late, it is inconsiderate to others and also just inefficient, but I am not here to discuss that particular imprudence. What I am suggesting, for myself if no other, is that being on time is also frequently not good enough, if I want to do as good a job as possible. My dad taught me to get there early. Case the joint. Examine the lay of the land. Evaluate the facility, find out where to piss, see if there's a drinking fountain. Evaluate the breeze/draft patterns so as to determine the best location from which to stand freely farting and escape detection. What are the pros and cons of the balcony versus the orchestra? I like to experience life, whenever and wherever possible, at a steady pace that some might call laborious. I suppose this makes me much more of the proverbial turtle than the hare, but I firmly believe that slow and steady wins the race. Madison had the perspicacity to roll into Philadelphia with eleven extra days to find his footing, scout the location, canvas the participants, and begin to weigh fairly all the information that was about to be dumped into his lap.

Coupled with punctuality, the other meritorious quality in this set of bookends is follow-through. Again, my dad crops up in the mental "how to live effectively" manual that he and my mother painstakingly installed in my tool kit. When I hear the word *follow-through*, I am immediately reminded of my dad's lessons in shooting a basketball and throwing a baseball and swinging a bat. Follow-through is what produces the backspin on a basketball shot, that stabilizing centrifugal force that allows a greater level of consistency to be realized in one's shooting percentage. The same technique can be applied to any task one undertakes in life, inspired by the idiom "If you're going to do a job, do it right." Wittingly or no, Mr. Madison was certainly an initiate into this school of practice, because his follow-through in regard to the Constitutional Convention was extraordinary to a degree that can be described only as "nothing but net."

His commitment to the ultimate American thesis, our Constitution, was superhuman. He refused to leave the site of the historic proceedings with the single exception of dire visits to the thunder closet, overextending himself financially to the point that he was flat broke by the end of the convention. These straits required him to borrow a hundred dollars just to get himself to New York, where, presumably, there would be an ATM at his disposal. Once the convention disbanded and the document was drawn up, it then required ratification, or considered approval, from the many delegates, who had returned to their disparate home states. Madison proceeded to canvas mainly his home state of Virginia, debating the merits of the fledgling Constitution with his fellow lawmakers, resulting in a successful ratification in the summer of 1788. This taste of victory would prove to be a brief comfort, however, as riding home from a debate at James Monroe's crib that winter, he exposed himself to the elements to the point that he suffered frostbite on the end of his nose. His commitment to the cause of our nation's success left him suitably decorated for life, in the form of a scar on his noble sniffer.

So, great, all these erudite honkies had gotten together and come up with a revolutionary new democratic method by which to govern a country, but the finer points needed intense scrutiny before the system could be deemed "ready for consumption." In letters he exchanged with Thomas Jefferson, Madison was hell-bent that (a) the plan be ratified by the citizenry, (b) the people's representation in Congress be based upon population, and (c) the power be divided between different branches of government; all of which turned out to be quite potent and effective ideas. I believe he also insisted that (d) upon voting, citizens would each receive three "smokeable papers for the rolling of tobacco products *only*," which never really caught on except in the states of California, Washington, Colorado, Oregon, and Alaska. Along with Alexander Hamilton, John Jay, and other, less famous white people, Madison fervently campaigned for the newborn Constitution to be approved. They energetically lobbied, visiting fellow congressmen and constituents in person, but the three also published a series of essays in support of the document's ratification, which came to be known as the Federalist Papers.

Comprised of eighty-five (originally) anonymous essays, the Federalist Papers are considered to be the most influential factor in seeing the Constitution ratified into existence—the most influential, that is, after the three "factors" visible through Hamilton's wide-open "barn door." Madison contributed twenty-nine of these written pieces, which contain some of his most quotable sentiments, such as "Those miscreants who break breeze within a shuttered chamber, particularly if there be no draught of exhauste cleansing the vapours of the vestibule, I finde to be categorized amongst the most scurrilous and contumelious of the brute creatures with which Providence has graced this verdant paradise," or "The clock reads but noon of the day, and yet I am but fatigued near to prostration. I would that our new Constitution might foment a climate of creativity by which our apothecaries may brew me a physicke in a tiny vial for to replenish mine corporeal form with energy for a surpluss of say, four, or even five, hours of time. A five-hour energy draught, if you will."

Much less interesting, but perhaps more poignant to our discussion, is this portion from essay number fifty-one, Madison's most famous quote: "If men were angels, no government would be necessary. If angels were to govern men, neither external nor internal controls on government would be necessary. In framing a government, which is to be administered by men over men, the great difficulty lies in this: you must first enable the government to control the governed; and in the next place, oblige it to control itself." Now, I know what you're thinking: "No shit, James Madison." But let me remind you that nobody had thought this crap up before. For spit balling, this was not a bad piece of work. I mean, sure, it seems that he was rather obsessed with angels, creatures of fiction much the same as faeries and unicorns, but I think he kept it under control enough to focus on the task at hand. Let's just be thankful the Constitution doesn't require any wee folk or thrump-ins to command seats of political office. That is, as far as we know. Who can tell what the bylaws of Freemasonry demand? Not me, you silly goose, for I am not a Freemason. Don't be ridiculous. Ahem.

Thanks largely to these efforts by the Federalist Papers' authors, the Constitution remained alive, but the work had only just begun for James Madison. Remember that the colonies had just won their freedom from the tyranny of the tea-sipping British monarchy, and so the citizens were very nervous about the amount of power that might be afforded to this new federal government, and with good reason. I mean, we were not about to start a country in which we called the trunk of a car "the boot," for fuck's sake. The Bill of Rights came about as a reassurance to the people, to assuage their fears of an overweening central power by asserting their individual rights in writing. James Madison, aka "the Mad Jam," expressed his opinion of this first set of constitutional amendments to be a "nauseous project," but he knew that he had to get it together if he wanted the Constitution to happen. One substantial public concern was that by naming certain explicit rights of citizens, other unlisted, or "crybaby," rights might then be limited.

These great thinkers like the Mad Jam had to take an unimaginable amount of bellyaching onboard from all sides and then hold true to their astonishing foresight. They had the Magna Carta as a starting point, sure, and they knew a lot of cool vocabulary words, I get it, but they had to combine all this knowledge, stir in a large scoop of gumption, and thereby concoct the bubbling loaf of our legal system, in which the people are represented directly in the legislation, and crimes would be prosecuted fairly in the judicial system. (I don't know about you, but when I have to merely take down burrito orders for the eight of us at Offerman Woodshop, I grow befuddled and overwhelmed, and the *last* thing I can think about is making certain that everyone feels fairly represented. "Thomas, they were out of carne asada, so I got you a bag of tortilla chips and some tomatillo salsa. And half a churro. Get off my dick! Whattaya think this is, the Constitutional Convention? You don't like churros? Why don't you move to North Korea?!") Therefore, the thought of equitably laying out a set of rules by which all Americans could be protected fairly equally beggars my feeble thinkin' pan. Not only did the Mad Jam manage to accomplish this unappetizing task in the face of ambivalence and opposition; he did it all while running a campaign against his good pal James Monroe for Virginia's seat in the first House of Representatives. In fact, it is widely held that Monroe would well have ridden his slight electoral edge to victory had it not been for the cold efficacy of Madison's slanderous campaign slogan: "Mo' Monroe, Mo' Problems."

A great deal of Sturm und Drang, not to mention blood, sweat, and phlegm, went into the initial sculpting of our governmental system. One of the most progressive aspects of the documentation detailing our newborn government, indeed possibly that decree's most admirable attribute, is the fact that the framers of the Constitution made it fixable. To greatly simplify this notion: The men who wrote the Constitution included the special feature of *malleability*. If the pronouncements and laws of the American government didn't altogether work for the people, why then, the people could change those laws with the help of their representatives.

Of seventeen proposed amendments to the Constitution, ten were ultimately approved by Congress and the states. These amendments were written precautions on behalf of the citizenry to safeguard individual liberties and place specific indispensable limits on government power.

There has been a lot of talk in this chapter about the "rights" of "the people," and I just want to take a moment to remind us that at this juncture, "the people" referred quite specifically to white people who happened to bear a penis and testicles, which excluded "people" like women and minorities. I'm of the opinion that the crafters of the Constitution were all too aware of the conundrum in which they found themselves. I again refer to the duplicitous task of setting down the "God-given rights" of the individual in an era when a great deal of the economy was largely dependent upon the use of slave labor. I should think that this particular moral pickle played an important part in the motion to make these documents "correctable." I would liken the situation to the modern dilemma regarding our voracious consumption of fossil fuels. By now we as a society have grown painfully aware that we are damaging our land and water and air *irreparably* via the extraction of fossil fuels such as coal, oil, and natural gas, as well as by the generous amounts of resultant waste products with which we pollute the planet, yet we continue to simply shrug, grin, and doggedly drive our monster trucks across the continent, whining to our mommies if we're unable to view the latest Disney fare on a TV screen in the backseat.

We'll discuss more of that later, but the new American United States found themselves in just such a state of denial. It had dawned on the more enlightened members of the early legislation that perhaps these Africans who had been captured and sold like mules, and who were now being employed similarly like beasts of the field, bore an awfully uncanny resemblance to human beings. Really, it began to seem like these creatures from Africa were like human beings in damn near every way except for their darker skin pigmentation. Unfortunately, the notion of including these two-legged "commodities" of the slave-labor system in the greater discussion of human rights was utterly unthinkable, since the larger part of the economy, particularly in the then most populous state, Virginia, was utterly reliant upon this labor force to keep their tobacco, cotton, and other crops profitable.

If Madison had possessed the foresight to suggest that black people be included in this discussion of inalienable rights, he would likely have been taken out back and shot, presumed rabid or dangerously daft. Therefore, since he couldn't begin to address the massively looming issues of civil rights, he did the next best thing. He punted. Correctly predicting that our nation would grow and prosper at an astonishing rate, Madison and his collaborators equipped this new national owner's manual with a correctability, as though to say, "I know there will be some problems that we couldn't get to in this initial Constitution, impressive though it may be, and so among its attributes will be its ability to be *amended* as time and progress require."

The Bill of Rights was an astonishing innovation for its time. The first ten amendments were an extremely effective security blanket that allowed the people to feel like their well-being was on the mind of the administration, which was a great way to get the people to vote for said administration. Some of the amendments are rather drier than others, or outdated at the least, since they had to do with our nation being at war on our *home turf*, an important distinction considering that it's been more than two hundred years since we have had to worry about "one if by land, two if by sea."

So, for example, the Third Amendment, which reads, "No soldier shall, in time of peace be quartered in any house, without the consent of the Owner, nor in time of war, but in a manner to be prescribed by law," doesn't really have any effect on us nor will it for the foreseeable future, barring some cataclysmic reversal of planetary fortunes.

On the other hand, there are some amendments in that original ten that are getting a great deal of attention. Let's roll through a few of these as a slight refresher, shall we? If you're anything like me, it may have been a while since you actually considered the letter of the law as opposed to whatever it is your favorite pundit has been spouting.

The First Amendment: "Congress shall make no law respecting an establishment of religion, or prohibiting the free exercise thereof; or abridging the freedom of speech, or of the press; or the right of the people peaceably to assemble, and to petition the Government for a redress of grievances."

Oh, hello. I believe the first part of this amendment refers to a notion I applaud loudly, the separation of church and state. Practice the religion of your choice, as you're free to do, and keep it out of the public arena. It seems worth remarking upon that this was the very first protection Madison awarded us American citizens. PS: Those of you trying to recruit people to your religion may not be violating the actual written law, but you're certainly pissing all over the laws of common decency. Jesus would hang his beautiful Nubian head in shame.

The second section, the one making mention of "freedom of speech," has been of particular benefit in my life. For example, I am free to pen the sentence "Jesus would hang his beautiful Nubian head in shame" without fear of imprisonment, lynching, or, in the case of the Spanish Inquisition, being subjected to the Judas Chair, the Spanish Donkey, or the Crocodile Shears, all of which I would recommend you do not look up if you care to retain your lunch. These monstrous torture devices (in the name of the greater glory of the Catholic Church, no less) were once all the rage for punishing a blasphemer like myself, but not in America, you hypocritical sons of bitches. Thanks to our Founding Fathers, we can finally speak the truth without fear of chastisement on the part of our government. Generally speaking, that is. There have been periods in our history when subjects like communism, racial integration, Dixie Chicks lyrics, or most recently terrorist activities/Muslim leanings could land you in some literal hot water(boarding). Excepting those indiscretions or lapses in constitutional policy (whoopsie!), we are free to speak or print the truth and also to speak or print utter bullshit, and it's up to the individual listener/reader to decide what he or she will swallow. Only in such a climate can free ideas be aired and exchanged, making the slow evolution of decency in our country possible.

The Second Amendment: "A well regulated Militia, being necessary to the security of a free State, the right of the people to keep and bear Arms, shall not be infringed." Okay. This one has proven to be a regular can of worms. Let's just break it down. I think guns are an awfully nifty piece of engineering, and I have seen a great many examples of beautiful handwork in both the metal and wood surfaces on firearms of all sorts. Further, I support the wild-game hunter much as I support the fisherman (or -woman). Beyond that use, I'm afraid the angry defenders of this amendment lose me.

The preface to the part about "to keep and bear arms" makes reference to "a well-regulated militia" as the prerequisite to the second part. In other words, our civilians, as members of the militia who had been fiercely and proudly defending our country from the British and the French, as well as the indigenous peoples from whom we had just brutally stolen "our" land, should keep their black-powder weapons at the ready, in case we need to form up the militia once again, should we be invaded by such an enemy. Unfortunately for the gun enthusiasts, this amendment is simply rendered moot by two undeniable factors. It was written in a time when we (a) were potentially in danger of a foreign military invasion and (b) were wielding muzzle-loading guns that an expert could fire perhaps five times a minute if he or she was very nimble. In other words, this amendment was penned when the revolver was still several decades away from ready availability, let alone the massacre machine that is the automatic weapon. The rather loud machismo of the NRA (methinks the lady doth protest too much?) on the topic of assault weapons seems like yet another antiquated, fear-based position that is being slowly eroded by a more genteel attitude of decency and compassion. It's worth noting that I don't see a lot of people who aren't white hollering about needing their guns to protect themselves. Which brings me to a theory.

Human beings are not simple. We are, in fact, quite complicated. In recent American history, we have engaged in such contradictions as owning slaves, while declaring all people to have equal rights, while heading to church to pray for peace and tranquility, while dropping bombs on Middle Eastern nations to secure the oil we need to fuel our vehicles in order to drive to church. We're a mess, and we have to count ourselves as part of the whole, because we're all complicit. So when I think about that time that we established our nation and economy while indulging in the unthinkable brutality of slavery, and then we also actively exterminated the Native American tribes across the continent because they stood in the way of our real estate plans, and then we *freed* the slaves and didn't manage to wipe out all the indigenous people, in fact we made them and every other race besides white people our "equals" as citizens, at least on paper, so they could come over to our houses and look us in the eye if they so choose, I can then understand why we're scared. It gives me fear as well to imagine the recompense that might be visited upon us, should the suppressed rage of all the victims of the Manifest Destiny be brought to bear upon our doorsteps. It makes us cry with secret terror that we want our mommies or our guns, or both.

But then here's this other point of view: When unspeakable violence is enacted upon innocents, say, in a school or movie theater, and the survivors and the families of the victims, in the throes of pain and anguish, want to ask, "Why did this happen?," "How did this happen?," and "What can we do to prevent this from happening again?," and one of the areas upon which they (still we) focus their scrutiny is that of the highly efficient weapons of warfare that are casually available to us citizens of the United States, then we frightened gun lovers have the chance to be human and say, "Okay, this is a horrible tragedy. Let's open up a conversation here." Instead, I'm surmising, out of fear, we throw up our defenses and behave in a very confrontational way toward such a conversation, citing the Second Amendment as the ultimate protection of our rights, no matter how ridiculously murderous the firearm, which, unfortunately, makes us look like total dicks.

Clearly, if we could magically remove all the guns from the planet, we as a species would still occasionally want to kill one another. We're animalistic that way, because, despite having Netflix, we're animals. Taking away all the guns is not going to stop murder, just like making us remove our shoes at the airport is not going to stop terrorist acts. We may be animals, but we're exceedingly clever animals, so we'll find a way to do as we please, despite the law. We always have. If that's the case, then should we not perhaps try instead to examine the way we treat one another, so the chances that any of us want to shoot up a school are lessened?

Finally, haven't we all learned from action movies and Westerns that the ultimate hero is the one who needs no gun? True grit, real bravery, is exemplified by an openhanded confrontation, rendering the handshake or the embrace the ultimate method of laying waste to evil. If our foreign policy sees us engaging in nefarious and shameful and often just openly bullying practices to strong-arm other nations into giving us what we want, should we then be surprised when radical extremist factions of those nations fly planes into our buildings or commit other acts of retaliatory violence? And is the most effective method by which we might bring about the cessation of their hatred of us really to go and "kill them right back," an eye for an eye, Hatfield-and-McCoy style? If the bravest protagonist is the one who lays down his or her weapon, then doesn't our desperate clinging to our guns make us cowards?

I fear that if James Madison were to show up today, he would be pretty depressed about what pedantic babies we've become in our handling of his excellent document. The last time we made any sort of amendment whatsoever was 1992, and it was just about what the members of Congress would be paid. We do an awful lot of griping about the flaws in our system, and yet the means by which we can change it are already in our possession. All we have to do is pay attention.

The Orator

4

━━━━━━━◆◆◆━━━━━━━

FREDERICK DOUGLASS

Hey, it's a black guy!

Relatively speaking, by which I mean in the grand scheme of recorded history, the historical period containing American slavery occurred about fifteen minutes ago. When I was an actual book-larnin' student in my teens and twenties, these early years of America's development seemed like they occurred eons ago, perhaps shortly after the dinosaurs made their undignified exit. As I have achieved the more cantankerous age of forty-four, however, and I think back to purchasing my first Kurt Vonnegut book or my first Tom Robbins, nay, my first Duran Duran record thirty years ago, and then I consider the fact that Abraham Lincoln's Emancipation Proclamation of 1863 occurred a mere factor of five times since I was first besotted with the song "Hungry Like the Wolf," I realize just how recently we "modern" Americans actually engaged in such depravity.

When I began to compile the list of possible subjects for my book, the flaws in my own proclivities quickly emerged. For example, my editor, Jill, told me that, although Chicago Cubs legendary second baseman Ryne Sandberg had indeed turned in a most impressive career both at the plate (277 career home runs) and in the infield (nine Gold Gloves; .989 career fielding percentage), his contribution was perhaps too specialized for the "general" audience (by which she means dullards? soccer fans?). Discussing Ryno, she asserted, would be literally too "inside baseball."

However, it almost immediately occurred to me that I would want to talk about some assorted social issues like racism and slavery, gender inequality, homophobia, red-meat rights, and so forth, and so I argued that I could find all these peccadilloes fully represented in a comprehensive history of the Chicago Cubs Major League Baseball team, widely regarded as the greatest team in the history of the sport (after next year's season—just you wait and see). What is probably quite clear to you by now is that Jill did not approve the "Cubbies' Gumption" idea. I would need to extend my gaze beyond the friendly confines of Wrigley Field.

Despite the overall laudatory tone of the first three chapters, I have also hinted at some of the more shameful episodes surrounding our nation's beginnings, and so I thought it would only be fair, yea, and balanced, to examine those darker spots with closer scrutiny. Yes, our Founding Fathers did some amazing head-scratching, hollering, and ultimately heroic document scribbling, but they also engaged fulsomely in, for example, the horrific practice known as slavery. From that purview, then, it is not surprising that I should next be enthralled with Frederick Douglass. So:

In 2005, when Ryne Sandberg was inducted into the National Baseball Hall of Fame, he spoke stirringly about paying the appropriate *respect* to the game of baseball, whether one is belting a home run or laying down a sacrifice bunt. In a final selfless turn, he also campaigned for a similar induction into Cooperstown on behalf of his former Cub teammate the great Andre Dawson, aka "the Hawk." It occurs to me, Jill, that I can metaphorically include Ryne Sandberg's virtues in my book, if I (a white guy) similarly get behind Frederick Douglass (a black guy) for induction into my own personal "Gumption Hall of Fame." If we are agreed, then, upon this apt comparison, let us proceed. Go, Cubs, Go!

I had known the basic outline of Douglass's story, namely, that he was a famous orator and abolitionist who had begun his life as a slave. As is the case for so many topics in the distant safety of my midwestern history class, however, I never really thought about what that journey entailed, from a simply human point of view. I thought, "Okay, he was a slave, which was a total bummer; then he escaped to freedom and it turned out he was smart—smart as shit, in fact—so he did some orator stuff, so then he was not as bummed out." Upon revisiting his story, however, I could not help but gape at the details my soft, privileged ass had not previously digested.

Frederick Douglass was born into slavery on the eastern shore of the Chesapeake Bay in Maryland, never knew his father (who was rumored to have been his master), and was seldom allowed to see his mother, since "it was common custom to part mothers from their children at a very small age." He guesses he was born in 1818 but was never certain of his age because not only were slaves disallowed to learn to read and write, they were also not taught things like the months or years of the calendar.

After his mother died, he was sent to Baltimore to serve at the house of one Hugh Auld. Auld's wife, Sophia, a kind woman, began teaching young Frederick the alphabet, despite the Maryland state law that forbade teaching a slave to read. When her husband found out about these lessons, he was outraged, and she was strongly admonished (not with a whip or anything, but probably some pretty stern talking), because Hugh held, as did the status quo, that literacy would ruin a slave, as "he would become dissatisfied with his condition and desire freedom." This statement sadly infers that the slaves were otherwise "satisfied with their conditions," which means that these white folks must have been either deeply stupid or viciously evil, or, quite possibly, both.

Frederick Douglass possessed a prodigious intellect, which, like an ineludible superpower, began to assert itself once he began to apprehend the world around him. Coming into his strength as a young man, Douglass became aware that the world held opportunities for forbidden learning in unlikely places. Consider this example of gumption: Douglass was sent by Auld to work at Durgin and Bailey's shipyard down at the wharf. As he worked alongside the builders of wooden ships, he began to notice that once they had completed crafting a piece of the ship—a plank, frame, or knee—they would write two letters upon the piece to signify where on the ship the piece fit. If it was for the starboard side, forward, they would mark the piece with an "S.F.," and if the larboard side, rear, or "aft," then upon the plank would be written "L.A.," and so on. By means of assiduous studying, Frederick Douglass was able to surreptitiously master his first four letters.

Since he was unable to continue his education at home, Douglass began to secret away small hunks of bread to exchange for quick lessons with neighborhood white boys of his own age. He collected every stray newspaper and brochure, and his knowledge grew incrementally, one letter and then one word at a time. On the next occasion in which your put-upon kid bitches about a spelling test, please relay this anecdote to him or her.

The Aulds had a son named Thomas who was learning to read and write in school, right out in the open (I guess he must have been a white kid), and this Thomas had practiced his writing skills in several copybooks, which were kept in the house. On Mondays, when he was left alone to mind the house, risking a vicious beating, if not worse, Douglass took to copying Master Thomas's sentences over again in the spaces between the lines, tediously self-training his hand and brain, until he finally succeeded in learning how to write. Okay, so maybe the Founding Fathers were fed up with some overzealous taxation on the part of England. Douglass could literally have been *killed* for merely trying to learn to write his own name. Talk about gumption. This guy makes George Washington look like Little Lord Fauntleroy.

Douglass was then hired out to a shipbuilder named William Gardner on Fell's Point, where he was trained to caulk the seams of a boat's hull, a step in boat construction imperative to ensuring watertightness. Caulking entails the use of a dull, flat, wide, chisel-shaped iron and a specialized mallet to drive gauzy cotton or oakum into the seams between the planks of the hull. Once the seams have been packed tight with the ribbons of organic fibers, they are then covered with pitch. Douglass loved the work, when he wasn't being run ragged all over the wharf and back, running errands for the rest of the crew, comprised of freemen both black and white.

Although he was earning wages, the highest wages paid to a caulker, in fact, he was still required to turn over every penny to Hugh Auld every Saturday night, which rankled all the more intensely, since he felt so tantalizingly near to freedom, being paid for his honest labor.

For so many people the ocean and particularly sailing boats represent a sense of wide-open freedom, but for Douglass, working on the wharves every day, they had the opposite effect. He later wrote this moving recollection of his ill feelings toward the ships whilst gazing upon Chesapeake Bay, "whose broad bosom was ever white with sails from every quarter of the habitable globe": "You are loosed from your moorings, and are free; I am fast in my chains, and am a slave! You move merrily before the gentle gale, and I sadly before the bloody whip! . . . O that I were free!"

Okay, first of all, this language is from the guy who learned to write from ship parts, specifically beginning with *A*, *F*, *L*, and *S*. Extraordinary but true. And this is just an excerpt of a paragraph that goes on ten times longer, a heartrending and elegiac bemoaning of his unthinkable condition. Second of all, when did we stop using "O!" as an exclamation? It's so effective poetically as an evocation of longing or lament. O I would like a delicious cheeseburger. O I wish the people at the airport would not crowd into line like lemmings. O I wish I were half as smart as Frederick Douglass!

Beyond his secret herculean efforts to learn his letters, Douglass was also required at times to call upon muscle of a wholly less figurative sort. As he was assigned tasks requiring more responsibility about the Aulds' property, he also found himself more vulnerable to the overseer charged with establishing the boundaries of those responsibilities. Douglass found himself offering defiance in the face of his oppressors, almost involuntarily at first, earning himself several vicious beatings, until he finally fought his overseer, a Mr. Covey, to a brutal defeat.

> *My long-crushed spirit rose, cowardice departed, bold defiance took its place; and I now resolved that, however long I might remain a slave in form, the day had passed forever when I could be a slave in fact. I did not hesitate to let it be known of me that the white man who expected to succeed in whipping, must also succeed in killing me.*

So, you know, as a kid learning about slavery, I had been able to grasp the bullet points of horror, from the brutal and murderous capture of the African natives to the shackled, forced labor and incredibly inhuman conditions of life working on a plantation. In my reading, I picked up further rapacious details over the years from the writings of Toni Morrison and Alice Walker and *Uncle Tom's Cabin* and *The Adventures of Huckleberry Finn*, and more, and of course I had seen *Roots* and *Gone with the Wind* and *The Color Purple* and *12 Years a Slave* and *Glory* and their ilk. Consuming these narratives obviously made me no expert, but I had viewed and read of many harrowing and viscerally depressing accounts of life in the days of slavery.

What I had not yet encountered, until I read Frederick Douglass (who penned three autobiographies, two of them before the Civil

War!), were the bald circumstances, so succinctly rendered, that a brain and spirit such as those possessed by Douglass were so effectively the worst nightmare of "the White Devil." So typically of the American media, Abraham Lincoln gets all the press when it comes to emancipation buzz. It brings to mind the way we as a (white) people were finally allowed to comprehend the plight of the Lakota Indian tribe only when beautiful Caucasians Kevin Costner and Mary McDonnell went and lived with them in *Dances with Wolves*.

In 1838, having navigated a daring escape from Baltimore by stealing aboard a freight train with the uniform and identification of a free black seaman, traveling by train and then steamboat to Philadelphia and finally New York City, all in fewer than twenty-four hours, Douglass finally succeeded in claiming his rightful place in the Land of the Free. He later wrote of his indescribable feelings upon the occasion, at the tender age of twenty: "Anguish and grief, like darkness and rain, may be depicted; but gladness and joy, like the rainbow, defy the skill of pen or pencil."

Before this book project I did not realize what a singular superman the abolitionist movement had found in Frederick Douglass. Right they were, the proslavery fuck-nuts, to fear that just such a firebrand as he would be powerfully instrumental in helping to bring about the end of slavery. I find it noteworthy that, despite his superior wits, it was his hard work and elbow grease that ultimately earned him the opportunity to utilize his genius for language. Once he had escaped to the free Northern states and settled in New Bedford, Massachusetts, Douglass was still unable to find work as a ship caulker because of prejudice. He was unfazed, exhibiting no apparent bottom to his well of gumption.

Finding my trade of no immediate benefit, I threw off my caulking habil-iments, and prepared myself to do any kind of work I could get to do. Mr. Johnson kindly let me have his wood-horse and saw, and I very soon found myself a plenty of work. There was no work too hard—none too dirty. I was ready to saw wood, shovel coal, carry wood, sweep the chim-ney or roll oil casks,—all of which I did for nearly three years in New Bedford, before I became known to the anti-slavery world.

The takeaway here is that this uneducated, escaped slave did not hesitate to perform any task of physical labor, as he said, "hard and dirty work," in order to continue his rapid climb to the status of a free American who could use words like "habiliments." He grasped, wit-tingly or no, the simple formula for success once he arrived in a (sort of) free country: Make your desired vocation known to those around you, then proceed to exhibit the most impressive work ethic in what-ever occupation is at hand.

Besides earning his keep by means of such labor, Douglass also joined the congregation of the African Methodist Episcopal Zion Church in New York City, a black parish that included such abolition-ist leaders as Harriet Tubman and Sojourner Truth. He quickly became a licensed preacher, as well as a Sunday school superinten-dent and sexton of the church. When examining photographs of Doug-lass, it's easy to understand why the arrival of this fiercely handsome and intensely intelligent young man, who could inspire the flock with his fiery oration and also fix the roof and doors of the church in a pinch, would incite excitement. His appearance and demeanor can be described only as those of a full-on badass.

By age twenty-three he was able to conquer his nervousness about public speaking, and he began addressing antislavery societies and conferences all over the free states. In the eloquence of Frederick Douglass's oratory, the abolitionists had found a perfectly forged, priceless sword that wielded the devastating combination of searing common sense, an inspired talent for language, and a furious commitment to justice, all resting solidly upon the bedrock of his all-too-real history in bondage and brutality.

Frederick Douglass continued to risk life and limb in disseminating his message, as even in free Northern states he often faced violent opposition from proslavery factions. Many white males did not want to relinquish one iota of the unfair powers afforded them by the suppression of the rights of African Americans and women, and they weren't above resorting to intimidation to have their way. In fact, intimidation was often their opening move.

It wasn't long before Douglass recognized the similar oppression being dealt to women of the age and allied their cause to his own. At the 1848 Seneca Falls Convention in upstate New York, Douglass said that he could not accept the right to vote as a black man if women could not also claim that right. He was quite aware that the world could begin to spin in anything approximating a rotation of fairness only if women were allowed to participate in the political arena as well. "In this denial of the right to participate in government, not merely the degradation of woman and the perpetuation of a great injustice happens, but the maiming and repudiation of one-half of the moral and intellectual power of the government of the world."

Douglass's rhetoric carried a very clear message that was powerfully successful in slicing away so much of the bullshit surrounding the issue of slavery. Many filthy antagonists wanted to discuss the abominable practice as a matter of economics and financial health, going so far as to mask their avaricious intentions by suggesting that the "Negro race" was less human than people of other skin colors, a pattern of "justice piloted by wealth" that we'll see come up again in this book. It's amazing, the wool the people in power of any nation will try to pull over the eyes of the citizens if there's a buck to be made. Unfortunately, human nature seems to allow this to occur regularly, out of laziness and ignorance.

As Douglass penned, "If there is no struggle, there is no progress. Those who profess to favor freedom, and yet depreciate agitation, are men who want crops without plowing up the ground. They want rain without thunder and lightning. They want the ocean without the awful roar of its many waters. This struggle may be a moral one; or it may be a physical one; or it may be both moral and physical; but it must be a struggle. Power concedes nothing without a demand. It never did and it never will."

His cause was much more obvious, some 160 years ago, since slavery (as well as women's suffrage) was such a clear and egregious violation of basic human rights, but it remains clear today, even after emancipation and integration and legalized voting, that the scales of justice are still considerably out of whack. Consider this quote concerning the law prohibiting African Americans to marry: "The marriage institution cannot exist among slaves, and one-sixth of the population of democratic America is denied its privileges by the law of the land. What is to be thought of a nation boasting of its liberty, boasting of its humanity, boasting of its Christianity, boasting of its love of justice and purity, and yet having within its own borders three millions of persons denied by law the right of marriage?" This sounds rather familiar to me now in a land where a percentage of the population is being denied their marriage rights in exactly the same way, based upon sexual orientation instead of skin color.

Human beings are lazy. White people, especially males, still hold a disproportionate share of the political and financial clout in our country. If, as Douglass asserts, "power concedes nothing without a demand," then it only stands to reason that these white men will not strive to right every possible wrong, refusing to rest until minorities and women are, say, earning a wage equal to theirs. We're lazy assholes. That's our nature, so I say let's at least cop to it. We haven't remotely righted every wrong; we've merely made things just good enough to stop people bitching as loudly. We eradicated slavery and we gave blacks and women the right to vote, but doing so did not magically remove all the racism or sexism in the states—not by a long shot.

In the June 2014 issue of *The Atlantic*, Ta-Nehisi Coates wrote an incredibly eye-opening essay about the issue of reparations toward the families of former slaves. I call it "eye-opening" because personally, as a relatively comfortable and therefore lazy white guy, I was not immediately aware of the severity of injustices still being practiced upon the black population by white people in power. I'm not suggesting I'm naïve enough to think that racism hasn't continued its rampant destruction in our land, but this article was a much-needed wake-up call to the fact that mass *organized* discrimination is alive and well, just cloaked more effectively in mortgage scams and voter fraud.

"Voter intimidation," by the way, can be open to some pretty horrifying interpretations.

In 1946, Theodore G. Bilbo, an *elected Mississippi senator* and proud member of the Ku Klux Klan, called upon his "constituents" thus, on the radio, no less: "every red-blooded Anglo-Saxon man in Mississippi to resort to any means to keep hundreds of Negroes from the polls in the July second primary. And if you don't know what that means, you are just not up to your persuasive measures."

I was so grateful for Coates's article in a major national journal, because it reminds us that although the initial sins of slavery and genocide are behind us, the mess we made in the commission of such sins is still clinging to our character with all the tenacity of the red, white, and blue—colors, I'll remind you, that most certainly do not run.

This entire subject makes me angry and also embarrassed, because I share a species with sad turds like this Bilbo person. As a human animal, part of me wants to retaliate against such unthinkable stupidity and evil in kind, by punching my ham-fist into someone's face. That Mississippi asswipe is thankfully dead, so maybe I should just go find another "red-blooded Anglo-Saxon man" to attack. "They're all the same, right?"

Then I stop myself and say, okay, hang on. Take a pill. No, those are addictive and bad; that's just what Big Pharma wants me to think. I'll take a breath instead. If Frederick Douglass and millions like him could withstand the animal temptation to take "an eye for an eye" after the plate of shit they were served, then surely I can refrain from punching out an Aryan Whole Foods stock boy. The point is that we are indeed all the same, not delineated by color or sex or any other factor. When Frederick Douglass began to publish his abolitionist newspaper, *The North Star*, in the late 1840s, he got it. The slogan of his paper was: "Right is of no Sex—Truth is of no Color—God is the Father of us all, and we are all Brethren."

Surrounded as I am by openminded individuals with whose politics I generally agree, although they are comprised of many races and every category of sexuality and various religious beliefs, I can easily become inured to the fact that our Manifest Destiny attitude is still dangerously pervasive in many regions of this country. When news items or "patriotic" messaging that suggest our flag is a license to murder, or even just a gung ho, extra-white country music video about "'Murica," it reminds me unpleasantly of the absurd sense of entitlement we Americans seem to feel, "since we butchered our way to the ownership of this land, fair and square"; I often wish I could call upon Frederick Douglass to cut to the heart of the matter for me, as my own clear thinking is clouded by confusion and animosity and shame. Oh. I can:

> *In thinking of America, I sometimes find myself admiring her bright blue sky—her grand old woods—her fertile fields—her beautiful rivers—her mighty lakes, and star-crowned mountains. But my rapture is soon checked, my joy is soon turned to mourning. When I remember that all is cursed with the infernal actions of slaveholding, robbery, and wrong; when I remember that with the waters of her noblest rivers, the tears of my brethren are borne to the ocean, disregarded and forgotten, and that her most fertile fields drink daily of the warm blood of my outraged sisters; I am filled with unutterable loathing.*

PART 2

IDEALISTS

The Bull Moose

5

THEODORE ROOSEVELT

We have had an awfully pleasant look at four early examples of American luminaries, boasting a great wealth of character attributes worthy of emulation. Let us now leap forward with gusto to a fifth, an American for whom I have a healthy sense of rippling admiration. Theodore Roosevelt, our twenty-sixth president, was an avid sportsman, naturalist, writer, explorer, soldier, and historian, known for his lively, masculine personality and fondness for pugilism, in both his backyard and in his politics. His interests were varied and rich, amply served by his voracious appetite for books, adventure, the society of people, wildlife, and the great outdoors. We largely have him to thank for our National Park System, as well as a great deal more preserved wilderness, not to mention the Panama Canal; but before we get to that, let's have a peek at his childhood.

Young Theodore was, for lack of a better term, a wuss. He was stricken with asthma, which left him debilitated, weak, and rather an easy target for the other boys to bully. "Having been a sickly boy, with no natural bodily prowess . . . I was at first quite unable to hold my own when thrown into contact with other boys of rougher antecedents." Ineffectual as he may have been on the playground, his prodigious brain was already enjoying an inspired regimen of reading, a pastime of which he never seemed to tire. A favorite title in his early years was the magazine *Our Young Folks*, which our young Theodore described as containing "interesting [stories] in the first place, and in the next place teaching manliness, decency, and good conduct."

Despite his sickly state, he was as smart as a whip and keen on any topic having to do with nature. After scrutinizing a dead seal at a local market, compulsively measuring the creature's head again and again, Roosevelt was finally awarded the skull, which he employed as the tent-pole attraction in his first amateur museum of natural history at age seven, belying what would become a lifelong obsession with wildlife and its proper exhibition for public consumption. "That seal filled me with every possible feeling of romance and adventure." He was determined to pursue the career path of a naturalist, a notion he eventually gave up, although his instinct to catalogue wildlife would comprise a great deal of his life's writing.

While hiking with his family in the Alps, a still wimpy Theodore happily discovered that the beneficial effects of the exertion were suppressing his asthma and bolstering his timid spirit. His father encouraged him to begin a program of rigorous exercise, including boxing and weight training, and this discipline had a tremendous effect in fortifying Roosevelt's morale. For the first time in his life, but certainly not the last, he understood that with a properly applied dose of gumption, he could accomplish much more than the recently apprehensive version of himself could ever have envisioned. "I felt a great admiration for men who were fearless and who could hold their own in the world, and I had a great desire to be like them."

Theodore quickly came to love boxing, an exercise that not only exponentially improved his physical health, stamina, and coordination but also fortified his self-confidence in physical confrontations. Reveling in his newfound strength, he set about to make of himself an ideal specimen of masculinity, in both body and spirit. He also found that he loved to row a boat, another invaluable labor that served to redouble his love of the fascinating scenery and bracing elements in the out-of-doors. (I can personally attest that admiring nature from a boat, particularly one that is being propelled by one's own muscle, and/or one's own wife, has a nearly magical sense of satiated relish.)

He wrote, "I suppose it sounds archaic, but I cannot help thinking that the people with motor boats miss a great deal. If they would only keep to rowboats and canoes, and use oar or paddle themselves, they would get infinitely more benefit than by having their work done for them by gasoline." Not only will such a strenuous program reinforce a body's muscle and circulation, but it also affords one the advantage of intimacy with all the ineffable pleasures to be found once one steps over the threshold of domestic comfort into the wonderland of woods or prairie. Perhaps within this sentiment lies a clue to enjoying one's life with a Rooseveltian vigor; by metaphorically choosing a path of *more* resistance, a person can provide stimulating challenges to him- or herself on a daily basis.

Roosevelt's encouragement inspires me to get outside and hike, bike, or row rather than remain in the homogenized climate control of the gym. I am also warmed by his sure-footed stance regarding the balance of play versus work in a healthy life: "Play should never be allowed to interfere with work; and a life merely devoted to play is, of all forms of existence, the most dismal. But the joy of life is a very good thing, and while work is the essential in it, play also has its place." In order to successfully execute such a life as Roosevelt's, it's apparently important to "keep one's blood up," maintaining a steady focus on victory, all the while cultivating the horsepower to leap dynamically into action. "It is only on these conditions that he will grow into the kind of American man of whom America can be really proud," he said, but I'm sure he meant to include girls in that pronouncement as well.

Theodore Roosevelt Sr. was a substantial supporter of his son's endeavors, morally and financially, as well as a role model of integrity. As number twenty-six wrote, "He combined strength and courage with gentleness, tenderness, and great unselfishness. He would not tolerate in us children selfishness or cruelty, idleness, cowardice, or untruthfulness," and "I never knew any one who got greater joy out of living than did my father, or any one who more whole-heartedly performed every duty." Theodore Sr. died tragically at forty-six of an intestinal tumor, while his son, nineteen, was attending Harvard. If he could have lived to see the life that Junior accomplished, he would certainly have been comforted by the striking resemblance the younger Roosevelt's ideals bore to his own.

Theodore Roosevelt rode his proactive methodology straight into a political career that started in the 1881 New York State Assembly, when he became the youngest assemblyman on the floor by winning a Republican seat at the age of twenty-three. Charging immediately into the fray by staunchly opposing the rampant corruption he found there led quickly to some heated altercations. As Edmund Morris writes, "'Big John' MacManus, the ex-prizefighter and Tammany lieutenant . . . proposed to toss 'that damned dude' in a blanket, . . . [but] fortunately Roosevelt got advance warning. . . . Marching straight up to MacManus, who towered over him, he hissed, 'I hear you are going to toss me in a blanket. By God! if you try anything like that, I'll kick you, I'll bite you, I'll kick you in the balls, I'll do anything to you— you'd better leave me alone.'"

This event hardly proved to be singular, as the young assemblyman found himself establishing his turf again and again:

> They stopped at a saloon for refreshments, and were confronted by the tall, taunting figure of J. J. Costello, a Tammany member. Some insult . . . caused Roosevelt to flare up. "Teddy knocked him down," Hunt recalled admiringly, "and he got up and he hit him again, and when he got up he hit him again, and he said, 'Now you go over there and wash yourself. When you are in the presence of gentlemen, conduct yourself like a gentleman.'"

Such grit is certainly rare among the politicians I have watched in my life, and I am thrilled by Roosevelt's display of fisticuffs in the defense of decency. Part of my exhilaration is no doubt due to the fact that such a valorous example could simply not occur in our modern litigious society, without the "J. J. Costello" suing the "Roosevelt" for his bloodied nose and bruised public image. I completely agree that we should always strive for decency and politeness, but the animal in me will never fail to enjoy a well-deserved ass whuppin'. That is why I practice the policy of "hug first."

Surviving the jungle of American politics required a particular attitude of a man, which Roosevelt famously described thusly: "He must walk warily and fearlessly, and while he should never brawl if he can avoid it, he must be ready to hit hard if the need arises. Let him remember, by the way, that the unforgivable crime is soft hitting. Do not hit at all if it can be avoided; but *never* hit softly."

In the interest of maintaining his own ability to never hit softly, Roosevelt, now governor of New York, engaged the services of a championship wrestler to swing by the Albany office three or four afternoons a week to wrestle him. This program, agreeable to Roosevelt, did not, however, meet the approval of the comptroller. He refused to honor the bill for the wrestling mat, suggesting that a billiard table might be more appropriate. Roosevelt acquiesced by terminating the wrestler and hiring a professional oarsman instead. The oarsman would also swing by the office, but instead of rowing, they would wrestle each other. By God, our man Roosevelt was going to see himself wrestled! This apparent solution didn't last very long either, however, as on the occasion of only their second grappling session, the oarsman had one of his ribs broken, while Theodore badly bruised two of his own and nearly dislocated his shoulder in the balance. Roosevelt finally but reluctantly relinquished his insistence that wrestling occur at his office.

Later in his administration as president, he decreed that "each [military] officer should prove his ability to walk fifty miles, or ride one hundred, in three days."

Thanks to the stringent upkeep of his body's constitution, Roosevelt was able to withstand slings and arrows of every sort, figuratively but also quite literally: While campaigning in Milwaukee in 1912, he was shot in the chest just as he was about to speak. The bullet passed through a thin steel case for his glasses and a fifty-page copy of his speech folded in half in his inner breast pocket. Like some magnificent Hector, he merely paused, considered the wound, determined that it had not reached his lung and so was not immediately dangerous, then stepped to the podium to say, "Ladies and gentlemen, I don't know whether you fully understand that I have just been shot; but it takes more than that to kill a Bull Moose." Come on. What? Then he spoke for ninety minutes. Blood slowly soaked his shirt a bright scarlet, but he stood and staunchly delivered his oratory. It was later decided that the least dangerous solution was to leave the bullet in the muscle of his chest, and so he carried it there for the rest of his life. Gumption.

Besides wrestling any strapping cuss he could get his hands on, Theodore Roosevelt also continued to see his love of the outdoors made manifest as he grew into middle age. "There are men who love out-of-doors who yet never open a book; and other men who love books but to whom . . . nature is a sealed volume. . . . Nevertheless among those men whom I have known the love of books and the love of the outdoors, in their highest expressions, have usually gone hand in hand." Which means that if you're reading this right now in the woods, or floating down the Sangamon River in your canoe, then you would have been held in high esteem by old number twenty-six.

Roosevelt's love of nature and adventuring led him to the great frontier beyond the Mississippi River, where he enjoyed the exploration of the wilderness almost as much as he loved hunting wild game.

A well-born East Coast Yankee, he found that he flourished in the trappings and environs of the great hunters of the West, as well as the "cowboy life" of the great cattle ranches of his era. He even went so far as to try his hand at ranching in the Dakota Territory, a rugged and unforgiving land that brooked no weakness of body or, as it turned out for a few unlucky thieves, of character.

Whilst working the Elkhorn Ranch along the Little Missouri River in the early spring of 1886, Roosevelt and two companions awoke one morning to find that their boat had been stolen. The ice on the flooded river was just breaking up, rendering it extremely danger-ous to navigate. The ranchers rightly suspected three known local horse thieves, but there was little to be done, as theirs had been the only boat known in the vast wilderness. Roosevelt and his compan-ions, however, were not about to take this setback lying down. In a few days' time they constructed a flat-bottomed skiff in which to give chase to the thieves.

On top of his service as an assistant deputy in Billings County, Theodore Roosevelt also took this criminal action as an attack on his personal pride and safety. In the lawless wilds of the Badlands, where one couldn't call the sheriff or even send him a telegraph, a person needed to depend on himself for protection. As Roosevelt relayed in his book *Ranch Life and the Hunting Trail*, "To submit tamely and meekly to theft, or to any other injury, is to invite almost certain rep-etition of the offense, in a place where self-reliant hardihood and the ability to hold one's own under all circumstances rank as the first of virtues."

Naturally (albeit impossibly), Roosevelt and his merry men caught up with the thieves and captured them with no trouble. Now, normally in this wild land, as I've said, each man got to play judge and jury when it came to doling out punishment for known crimes. The three criminals were known to be wanted for not only cattle-killing but horse-thieving, which was considered the greatest crime one could commit on the frontier, thereby punishable by an immediate hanging. Throw in the boat-stealing (the rowboat was clinker-planked, no less, a hand-hewn craft made with care and skill), and nobody would have blamed Roosevelt for shooting these reprobates on sight.

But that was not the way of our Bull Moose. He boated them laboriously down the river, commenting, "The next eight days were as irksome and monotonous as any I ever spent: there is very little amusement in combining the functions of a sheriff with those of an arctic explorer. The weather kept as cold as ever." Roosevelt then marched them overland through ankle-deep mud for thirty-six hours (!) to the town of Dickinson, "and I was able to give my unwilling companions into the hands of the sheriff. Under the laws of Dakota I received my fees as a deputy sheriff for making the three arrests, and also mileage for the three hundred odd miles gone over—a total of some fifty dollars."

There is little about this anecdote that doesn't beg flat astonishment. I suppose the fact that they were running a cattle ranch in the wintry, Native American–infested wilderness can begin to give us an idea of their mettle to begin with, but by then literally risking their lives, Roosevelt and his two fellow champions amaze me. All done just to see justice served, for as he described the miscreants further, "They belonged to a class that always holds sway during the raw youth of a frontier community, and the putting down of which is the first step towards decent government." The paperwork of decency was well ensconced faraway in the more modern urban centers of government, so maintaining the integrity of the law on the frontier depended wholly upon citizens like Roosevelt and company.

The second of my many favorite details from this story is the fact that these redoubtable cowboys, when faced with a seemingly irredeemable loss, simply gathered the best planks they could find, along with some tools and a modicum of gumption, and built themselves a solution, one of the most venerable objects a human being can create: a wooden boat. Somehow, in my examination of a list of Americans with gumption, boats, particularly those crafted of wood, seem to keep cropping up in a substantial way. I may have to look into that as we proceed.

The final tidbit from this tale (a story so heroic that it would have needed toning down if it were a Jack London fiction) is simply that in the midst of this chase, both when the pursuers would stop each night to camp and then after they had collected their quarry, continuing to camp at night, Roosevelt pulled out the only book he had brought along. "As for me, I had brought with me 'Anna Karénina,' and my surroundings were quite grey enough to harmonize well with Tolstoï." Most any one of us soft, modern Americans would scoff—and loudly, at that—were you to suggest that we trek out even to the mailbox in inclement weather. Theodore Roosevelt not only took it upon himself to achieve this vigorous pursuit worthy of an Indiana Jones movie, but he did so at times putting his feet up by the fire and perusing the Tolstoy novel in his pocket. What a stud.

Among the many tributes to him in present-day North Dakota, including Theodore Roosevelt National Park, perhaps the most appropriately august recognition is to be found at the Pitchfork Steak Fondue, gleefully pointed out to me by that extremely well-traveled woman of letters, Sarah Vowell. Every evenin' 'round suppertime, the cowboy chefs load several raw steaks onto a pitchfork and fondue 'em, cowboy-style. This, of course, means they dip them in a barrel of hot cooking oil. Imagine my shame to have been caught unaware of this repast of glory sizzling in our midst. By the time you are reading this, I fully intend to have severally sampled this barrel-fried beef in the town of Medora, North Dakota, especially after glimpsing this tantalizing morsel in a review on the computer web: "The Fondue is served before the musical." Tickets booked.

On a more sober note, it's hard to deny that Theodore Roosevelt's stance on many hot-button issues would not fly with our modern, progressive society. His outspoken views on the American Indian and women, for example, would be enough to place him in hot water, and I don't intend to defend him. He was an irrepressibly virile man, the sort one might describe as "macho," living in an era when such a personality could be richly celebrated and rewarded, particularly by the white supporters of an imperialistic American worldview.

If one *were* to mount a defense on behalf of his principles, one might argue that his good deeds and acts of valor could be thought to far outstrip his rather archaic, occasional sexism and bellicose approach to foreign relations. The degree to which his misdeeds might overshadow his innocence is a complicated topic, to be sure, but in no arena so much as his love of killing wild animals.

If one examines the young Theodore's fascination with a seal skull at age seven, then observes his penchant for not only claiming wildlife prizes of every stripe for his trophy collection but assiduously cataloguing them and describing their behaviors and habitats with a scientist's eye for detail, only then perhaps can one fathom the lust that besotted the man when presented with the teeming wilderness of the American West.

Roosevelt was absolutely smitten with the romance of traveling into the unbroken frontier, tracking and stalking his prey, and then most of the time successfully shooting that prey for food or display. He killed a great many creatures, a hobby for which he received a lot of criticism, even during his lifetime. As I have stated, I stand in support of hunting and fishing as incredibly satisfying methods by which to put dinner on one's table. If you are a person who disagrees with that stance, I am okay with that; I just won't take you fishing. I feel that these, like all forms of harvest, should be performed responsibly with respect for the ecosystem and future generations, but that doesn't mean you can't have a beer in the boat.

Now, killing critters for a reason that doesn't involve a practical use—that is not my bag. Wasting a large elk because its head will supposedly look good over the fireplace does not appeal to me. But when such a sticky topic comes up, I try to remember that my own position has a lot to do with my time and place. I was brought up catching fish, not shooting bighorn sheep. If I had grown up in Colorado or Wyoming, or really just in a different family in Illinois, then I might well be an avid hunter. This perspective keeps me from feeling I need to judge the hunters, just because it's not what we did at my house. At the same time, I also try not to judge the folks who gripe about the hunters, because that's also not what flies in my house.

A funny thing about Roosevelt is that when he wasn't out killing a large pile of black-tailed deer, he was fighting fervently to preserve our nation's forests and wildlife. The thing I try to remember about a figure like him is that, for all his epic accomplishments and feats of bravery, he was still a human being. This means he was as fallible as any of us. For example, how many of us (rightly) rail against the evils of corporate fast-food fare, only to catch ourselves in the devil's drive-through some late and ravenous night? That happens to me about once or twice a year, and I simply shrug and try to wolf down the briefly delicious, offending pap before it cools off and turns to inedible rubbish. This doesn't make me a supporter of fast food as a lifestyle; it merely exposes me momentarily as a human being who contains just the type of lager, or "weakness," upon which fast-food companies prey. We all have such weaknesses by definition, and understanding this to be true is an important step toward curtailing a lot of the whining we do about things like shooting a deer for venison or using a pair of leather work gloves.

To my way of thinking, Roosevelt knew, or at least he intuited, that the type of unrestricted hunting he so enjoyed had a very definite expiration date. On one hand, he made incredible strides toward the preservation of nature in all her beauty with the legislation he passed and his instituting of our National Parks. On the other, he swooped in and selfishly indulged himself on the flesh-and-blood fruits of that same nature's bounty for his own pleasure. In his defense, when he arrived at the party, there was still plenty of beer, as it were, but knowing well the magnitude of the approaching traffic, he was able to enjoy his sport while at the same time comprehending that such pillage must come to end.

In his book *Hunting Trips of a Ranchman*, Roosevelt takes pains to obsessively detail each of twenty-seven discrete species of quarry, their habits and attributes, and how best to hunt them. At the same time, he also speaks to the responsible thinning of the herds in order to preserve the wildlife from a conservationist's point of view. Thus, he manages to wear both hats even while hunting in his prime, which I feel speaks very well of his character. He did not approve of the killing of animals just for the sake of sport but instead considered hunting just one of the avenues by which he could learn about the nature and topography of a given area. Consider this passage from *The Wilderness Hunter*:

> In hunting, the finding and killing of the game is after all but a part of the whole. The free, self-reliant, adventurous life, with its rugged and stalwart democracy; the wild surroundings, the grand beauty of the scenery, the chance to study the ways and habits of the woodland creatures—all these unite to give to the career of the wilderness hunter its peculiar charm. The chase is among the best of all national pastimes; it cultivates that vigorous manliness for the lack of which in a nation, as in an individual, the possession of no other qualities can possibly atone.

On one famously unproductive 1902 hunting outing in Mississippi, a scout finally snuck ahead and cornered and chained a black bear to a tree so that Roosevelt could claim its life and they could all go home. The scout was disappointed when the big-game hunter refused to senselessly slaughter the shackled beast on the grounds that it would be extremely unsportsmanlike. Newspapers loved the story, and Clifford Berryman immortalized the moment in *The Washington Post* with a humorous cartoon of the scene. A Brooklyn candy-shop owner saw the cartoon and got the idea to sell his stuffed animals under the new moniker "Teddy's Bears," which is how the teddy bear got its name. And that's one to grow on.

Even when Roosevelt wasn't in the woods, he was still avidly fueling his pursuit of the ideal masculinity, for himself and also for America. While serving as William McKinley's assistant secretary of the navy in 1897, he aggressively took over the command of our country's navy, bolstering its readiness for battle. When war was officially declared with Spain, Roosevelt shocked those around him by resigning his (civilian) navy post and enlisting in the army so that he could go to Cuba and fight. He and army colonel Leonard Wood formed the first US Volunteer Cavalry Regiment, which the press immediately christened "the Rough Riders." Roosevelt once again proved his mettle, and then some, when he led the limping regiment uphill into flagrant enemy fire at the Battle of Kettle Hill.

On the day of the big fight I had to ask my men to do a deed that European military writers consider utterly impossible of performance, that is, to attack over open ground unshaken infantry armed with the best modern repeating rifles behind a formidable system of entrenchments. The only way to get them to do it in the way it had to be done was to lead them myself.

Say what you will of the man, but he was as good as his word. When the going got tough, his rough-riding ass got going, so much so that this civilian volunteer was promoted to colonel during the fighting and nominated for a Medal of Honor. Upon his return to the States, he preferred being called "the Colonel," stating that the decisive battle had been "the great day of [his] life."

We should all be infinitely thankful that Theodore Roosevelt was on our side. In his political career, he worried no adversary more doggedly than the corrupt corporate influences that aimed to take advantage of the citizenry: "To dissolve the unholy alliance between corrupt business and corrupt politics, is the first task of the statesmanship of the day." As effective as he may have been, we apparently have not escaped this unholy alliance in our modern society, as Washington lobbyists openly spend *billions* on the purchase of congressional favors. Would that Colonel Roosevelt were present today to whip some sense into all of us.

I'd love to imagine paddling my canoe down, say, the Snake River with Roosevelt (he'd be in the stern, of course) and engaging him in a discourse about the great advances in equality between the genders since his day. That is, if I could get him to shut up about all the great blue herons dipping frogs from the shallow water. Despite his very vocal opinions on the proper indoctrination of boys and men, the colonel was also actually rather instrumental in the advent of women's suffrage on the eve of its success. His Bull Moose Party was the first political party to grant women any recognition in the voting arena, to the extent that Roosevelt's 1912 nomination was seconded at the Bull Moose Convention by none other than Jane Addams herself.

The world was a very different place then, particularly in the way that world powers regarded war, before either of the world wars had occurred.

Roosevelt ruled in a different era, one in which a person could remain popular while also openly advocating for war. "All the great masterful races have been fighting races" is not really going to put you in the White House these days, which is why Ted Nugent has not yet seen a nomination. One could argue that behaving more or less like a "man" succeeded insofar as helping the Allies defeat the fascist Axis powers in World War II, but then the same brute force caused us to throw a couple of punches too many when we obliterated countless numbers of Japanese human beings by dropping atomic bombs on Hiroshima and Nagasaki. I have to wonder what the colonel would have thought of our contemporary warfare that ultimately can be conducted from a distance of thousands of miles with the push of a button. Methinks he would have a hard time finding the honor in it.

That said, I wonder if I could convince Theodore Roosevelt (whom I would never call "Teddy," as it was a nickname he despised) that perhaps what America needs, if we hope to evolve into a more decent people, is a little more of the woman's touch? When our citizens are determined to openly wear pistols on their belts to go shopping at Walmart, that signifies to me a failure on the part of the macho ideal. Ostensibly, the handgun is displayed to let evildoers know, in no uncertain terms, that this is not a person with whom to trifle. It then follows that the wearing of the pistol presumes a situation in which the bearer will need to shoot someone, rendering the brandishing of the weapon a badge of fear, does it not? It occurs to me that if we keep on turning to such "masculine" methodology to solve our conflicts, the only inevitable ending is a bunch of somebody's family lying in a bloody schoolhouse, movie theater, or smoking Japanese city. I guess we just hope it's not our family? I don't like the odds.

As will often happen with me, an interesting train of thought will bring to mind a Tom Waits song, and "Day After Tomorrow" is one of his best ever (cowritten with his bride, Kathleen Brennan).

You can't deny
The other side
Don't wanna die
Any more than we do.

What I'm tryin' to say,
Is don't they pray
To the same God that we do?
Tell me, how does God choose?
Whose prayers does he refuse?

Sure, we and our allies have succeeded (so far) in keeping the specters of fascism and communism from overtaking the globe, but there are some extremists in the Middle East these days who are doing things in a way that's awfully hard to stomach. I think we have to examine how at least some of their hatred is fueled by a nation (us) that has succeeded in remaining the reigning bully on the playground for many, many decades. What do our methods amount to, exactly? Have we taken their lunch money one too many times? One hundred too many times? I can't answer that. I am literally just a handsomely paid wiseass, but I do think it's a question worth asking. Would Theodore Roosevelt, the man who said, "The most practical kind of politics is the politics of decency," approve of our casual "policing" wars? Hard to say, but given his stance on the amount of corporate influence governing the "conflicts," I think no.

All in all, the more I read about Roosevelt, the more human he seems, however inspirational. Whether I agree with all the strong opinions he held, I can certainly refuel my own well of gumption with the example he set in a life packed to the gills with adventure. If I could go back in time and help out with his final bid for president, I would have suggested the campaign slogan "Bull Moose: Balls Deep." I do believe we could have left Mr. Taft crying in his fat soup.

In the final reckoning, I will always be grateful to Colonel Roosevelt for providing us with this instructional sentiment, which grows more poignant with every passing day: "Far and away the best prize that life has to offer is the chance to work hard at work worth doing."

The Naturalist

6

FREDERICK LAW OLMSTED

So far, it's likely that my featured luminaries have been relatively recognizable to you. Although if you're anything like me, many of the details seem to have a hard time sticking, unless you happen to be a student of American history. One reason for this apparent glitch is the seemingly illogical, age-specific pattern of prioritization that our brains employ. Like, for example, the fact that I can still repeat from memory several phone numbers from my youth, not to mention the entirety of the rap song "Jam on It" by Newcleus, but now in my forties, it's all I can do to repeat the finer points of a novel I just finished reading. In the parlance of this computer-style age, it would be nice to be able to "empty the trash" and make room for new files, as delicious as that rap song may be. (*Wikki-wikki-wikki-wikki.*)

Consider Herbert A. Simon, a right sharp scientific thinker, who did his thinking most frequently at Carnegie Mellon, by which I mean this chap was smart as shit. Check out some of his smart-thinks: "In an information-rich world, the wealth of information means a dearth of something else: a scarcity of whatever it is that information consumes. What information consumes is rather obvious: it consumes the attention of its recipients. Hence a wealth of information creates a poverty of attention and a need to allocate that attention efficiently among the overabundance of information sources that might consume it." A wealth of information creates a poverty of attention. Slogan-worthy.

Oh, and by the way, ol' Herbert blew that particularly salient jazz in 1971. Prescient as he may have been, he could have had *no idea* what the phrase "overabundance of information" would come to mean in 2015. I feel that I am in a constant battle with the media channels of the world, which are incessantly trying to penetrate the inner sanctum of my focus, because if I switch on even one channel, be it TV, radio, or Internet, I am immediately exposed to the distracting jingles and tits of advertising and corporate agendas. I can immediately feel my focus begin to erode. This constant, inexorable bamboozle, I believe, is also partially responsible for the paucity of attention that I am able to devote to any given subject.

My copy of *Huckleberry Finn* may weigh more than a Kindle, but if I am reading it under a tree in Minnesota, I am in zero danger of any pop-up ads or other apps appropriating my focus. I am also unable to order any shoes online whilst in the middle of my story, perhaps digesting Huck's perfect rationale for pleasure boating: "Other places do seem so cramped up and smothery, but a raft don't. You feel mighty free and easy and comfortable on a raft." And here's the thing: If I traveled all the way to the woods of Minnesota and I don't already have upon my feet all the shoes I need, then I'm a fool.

I digress. I wanted to crow to you about Frederick Law Olmsted, architect of Manhattan's Central Park, and I was going to presume that you are less familiar with him than with George Washington. Here we go! Please wring the appropriate enthusiasm from these exclamatory sentences!

When I was thirty, Megan and I were visiting New York City, and for the first time I had the opportunity to leisurely stroll through Central Park and really experience the delights of its bridges and glades and ponds and forests. It had existed for years in my imagination, rather as a legend shaped by films and books, like every Woody Allen movie, *Ghostbusters*, and *Hair*. Much like in the difference between any real sunset and the photo in which you tried and failed to capture even half of its grandeur, the experience of the park in real life was frankly astonishing.

As luck would have it, while later pillaging a bookstore near Lincoln Center, I happened upon a new volume from Witold Rybczynski, entitled *A Clearing in the Distance*, which encapsulates the working life of the man known for having designed Central Park, Frederick Law Olmsted. "Good Christ!," I merrily blasphemed. "This is just about all right!" I became enthralled with Olmsted's story, and not just because he wore a fulsome beard and dressed like a bucolic patrician whom one might encounter sipping beer at the Prancing Pony. (Rybczynski's book was so engaging that I embarked upon a run of some of his other excellent works, such as *Home, The Most Beautiful House in the World*, and *One Good Turn: A Natural History of the Screwdriver and the Screw*. These excellent volumes are in the nonfictional vein of some other writers I would recommend, such as Bill Bryson, Elizabeth Royte, John McPhee, and Mark Kurlansky.)

Olmsted's life story was splendidly rich and full of surprising tangents, considering that the singular accomplishment of building Central Park would strike me as plenty to get done in a productive lifetime. Once I decided to write about the man, I was lucky enough to spend a day touring Central Park with some experts: park historian Sara Cedar Miller, senior landscape architect Steve Bopp, and director of preservation planning Marie Warsh, all leading members of the Central Park Conservancy. As we canvassed the park's 843 acres, my three guides were able to point out fascinating bits of history as well as new developments in landscaping, park upkeep, and restoration projects like the Obelisk. I was quite impressed by the passion these three invested in their work; they truly seemed to be in love with the park.

As just one example of the myriad treasures housed in Central Park, the sixty-nine-foot, 220-ton Obelisk, aka Cleopatra's Needle, is the oldest man-made object in Central Park and the oldest outdoor monument in New York City. It dates from 1450 BC and was made erect in the park on January 22, 1881. Yes, like a boner.

A time capsule buried beneath the Obelisk contained an 1870 US census, the Bible, Webster's Dictionary, the complete works of Shakespeare, a guide to Egypt, and a facsimile of the Declaration of Independence; a haul of which I think Wendell Berry (chapter 9) would approve. Also, a small box was placed in the capsule by the man who orchestrated the purchase and transportation of the Obelisk. Obviously a Freemason, he will probably remain the only person in history ever to know its contents. That is, until I unearth the capsule in the climax of my upcoming Nic Cage film *National Treasure 23: Immanentizing the Eschaton*.

I should mention, without further preamble, that Frederick Law Olmsted was actually only one half of the design team working on the park. His estimable partner, Calvert Vaux, really gets the short end of the stick when it comes to being credited for their gorgeous collaboration, a fact made quite clear to me by Sara Cedar Miller. Fans of Vaux are quick to point out, with little humor, that we have him to thank for many of the pastoral masterpieces within the grounds of the park, but his name is rarely mentioned when Central Park comes up in conversation. Given the expertise of my triumvirate hosts, and the meticulous work being performed day in and day out by the conservancy, I was in no position to argue. Let it be known, therefore, that Calvert Vaux, an incredible architect and artist, got the shaft.

Let's get back to Olmsted, whom I was to learn was responsible for so much more beauty on this continent than Central Park. In fact, he (they) created Brooklyn's Prospect Park, which he (they) considered his (their) masterpiece, *during* the construction of Central Park. His park designs were amazing, and they continue to enthrall the public today, but Frederick Law Olmsted's path took some interesting turns before he arrived at those opportunities.

As a boy in the 1820s and '30s, he attended a boarding school in Connecticut that was operated on a model that I think could truly benefit the youth of today: The students would spend the day chopping firewood, hauling firewood, tending the fires, and otherwise maintaining the school buildings and surrounding farm grounds, and only then when the chores were done would they participate in classes in the evening. This sounds to me like the perfect school for churning out great Americans, for besides arithmetic and spelling, the pupils were being taught character and the value of a work ethic. Put it all together, and what do you get? A Frederick Law Olmsted. I think this brand of matriculation must have been especially effective for Olmsted, since he described himself thusly: "I was very active, imaginative, inventive, impulsive, enterprising, trustful and heedless. This made what is generally called a troublesome and mischievous boy."

How's this for gumption? Young Frederick threw his plans to attend Yale out the window when he suffered the effects of sumac poisoning about his eyes, weakening his vision to the point that he decided not to trouble his blighted orbs with collegiate studies. Where does one encounter poison sumac? In the woods, of course. The moral of this story: If you spend enough time in the woods, you won't have to go to college.

He tried his luck working in a silk shop, to no avail. He despised the twelve-hour days, six days a week, but the shop was near the harbor, where he caught the bug to be up in the crow's nest, giving the sailor's life a try. At an apprentice sailor's paltry wage of five dollars a month, he could not have been more miserable sailing to China, thanks to seasickness, hunger, and thirst. Life on the high seas quickly lost its allure, and he determined to take a swing at a vocation decidedly more earthbound.

With his father's help, he acquired a farm, first in Connecticut, then at a second spot on Staten Island, where he became obsessed with scientific agriculture, curiously exploring new avenues of horticulture and animal husbandry. A new breed of journal aimed at these new "scientific" farmers who could read (unlike traditional farmers) were like a nineteenth-century Internet chat room for inventive agrarians. Poring over the periodicals, constantly attempting new crops, sustained by new and experimental fertilizers and methods, Olmsted began to write letters to these magazines, like *The Cultivator* and *The Horticulturist*, literally digging into his newfound vocation as a commercial farmer. He experimented with seaweed as a fertilizer. When New York City's market saw an overabundance of peaches, he switched to pears. He wrote to a friend, "For the matter of happiness, there is no body of men that are half as well satisfied with their business as our farmers."

While he was cheerfully embroiled in his farming efforts, an obscure Scottish novel came through Olmsted's lively rotation of titles: *Sartor Resartus*. The story concerned a German philosopher with a dissolute youth (which resonated with Olmsted) who was unable to achieve a sense of blind religious faith (ditto). According to biographer Justin Martin, the philosopher's ultimate conclusion was something like "All is chaos, and one's only option is to construct meaning as best as possible, through work. And not just any kind of work, but rather work that has helping others as its stated goal." This philosophy struck a chord with Olmsted, one that would eventually lead him to find his true calling as the father of American landscape architecture.

Despite his valiant efforts, Olmsted's farm could not be made to satisfactorily bear fruit, as it were, so he ultimately gave it up. His ever-supportive father then sent him on a walking tour of England at the tender age of twenty-eight. Young Frederick was constantly reading and keeping notes of his life's endeavors, and this British ramble proved no exception. He kept a detailed journal of British farming innovations, as well as the beauty of the countryside and some lovely parks, Birkenhead Park in particular. He noted, "What artist, so noble . . . with far-reaching conception of beauty and designing power, sketches the outline, writes the colors, and directs the shadows of a picture so great that Nature shall be employed upon it for generations, before the work he has arranged for her shall realize his intentions." Enjoying his parks, I have often had precisely the same admiration for the artistic foresight of Olmsted himself, albeit with somewhat less eloquence: "Man, he sure thought this up dope. This park is slick as shit."

By the time he was thirty he had published *Walks and Talks of an American Farmer in England*, adding "author" to the growing list of trades of which he was a jack. Although it was considered a rather slapdash work, the book contained enough observations to fill some seven hundred pages, signifying an appetite for language and an apparently tireless writing hand. This penchant for hard work, along with his interest in the slave economy, led to an interview with *The New York Times*. The *Times* wanted him to tour the Southern American states for some months and report on the true state of slavery, a hot issue of the day that sparked a great deal of opinion in the North, but opinion backed up by little tangible knowledge of the actual state of affairs in the slave economy—knowledge that Olmsted was hired to glean.

If, at first, Olmsted's qualifications seemed lacking for such an assignment, the perceptiveness of his selection by the *Times* soon shone through. He had been a farmer, and he had written a detailed report of English farming and her countryside whilst carefully touring the country. This new assignment wanted to be a very similar feature article, with the addition of a particular focus on slavery. Olmsted took to it like a tabloid to celebrity cellulite and managed to interview several slave owners who had also experienced running farms in the North. This farmer-to-farmer discourse allowed our intrepid reporter to deftly run the numbers involved in the efficiency of farm productivity with and without the use of slavery. His findings were quite elucidating, showing conclusively that a slave accomplished about half the work a Staten Island hired hand could achieve.

In a manner of speaking, Olmsted's report clearly proved that, in addition to its obviously onerous qualities on the level of human rights, slavery also just didn't make sense economically. As a farming system it contained myriad inefficiencies in both labor and production. This unique criticism, based solely upon his empirical observation, made an influential splash among the members of the abolitionist movement, whose appeals were more emotional and purely sympathetic. Olmsted scientifically proved that, because of the dehumanizing nature of the work a slave was required to perform, there was very little initiative for that oppressed person to make use of any gumption, and without gumption, the halfhearted labors cost the slave owners money.

As these observations were gradually published, the Southern plantation owners naturally came to be aware of the negative appraisals therein, making the southern climate decidedly less friendly for Olmsted. It took a lot of grit to continue reporting on what had become a very moral issue to him, but it paid off handsomely. His dispatches were widely praised in the United States and overseas, where he had made fans of great thinkers like Charles Dickens, Charles Darwin, and Karl Marx, among others. When he eventually published the collected pieces in his book *A Journey in the Seaboard Slave States*, he won accolades from the press, like this from the *New York Post*: "This remarkable book . . . is certainly the most minute, dispassionate, and evidently accurate description of the persons, places, and social institutions of the southern portion of our confederacy, that we have yet seen." Pretty good for a Staten Island pear farmer.

Okay, let's take a moment to update our Olmsted vocational scorecard. After the brief stint at the silk shop, he made varying degrees of headway as a sailor, a farmer, a journalist, and an author. He'd published two books. At this juncture, he was thirty-five years of age. With such an array of experience under his belt, it should come as no surprise what happened next: Sipping tea at a seaside inn in Morris Cove, New Haven, Connecticut, he struck up a conversation with Charles Eliot, who happened to be a board member on a new project in New York City that had as its objective the creation of a sizable public green space on Manhattan Island. Eliot let slip to our boy that the board would be requiring a superintendent.

Despite very little experience to qualify him on paper, as you may have guessed, Olmsted got the job. A little exposition: In 1857, Manhattan was still mostly farmland and pasture above Midtown, peppered by impoverished shantytowns, peopled by immigrants and newly freed slaves; wee stinky hamlets with monikers like Dutch Hill, Dublin Corners, and Seneca Village. At the time of Olmsted's hiring, the land also housed noxious businesses like tanneries and

match manufacturers, as well as two plants for processing animal car-
casses into charcoal filters and glue. Not exactly the ideal spot to place
a carousel and an ice-skating pond.

The foresight of the city planners, and, ultimately, the park's designers, in comprehending the fact that before long the urban sprawl
would cover the entirety of the island, was most impressive. At a time
when the actual city covered only the forefoot of Manhattan's stocking, these farseeing planners had the clarity to name the new space
"Central Park." The terrain looked nothing like it does today; it had
very swampy areas, with fewer large trees and more scrub brush.

Olmsted oversaw seven hundred employees, who had their hands
full draining swamps and removing stones in preparation for the
park's imminent construction. Lending an air of suspense to the proceedings was an open contest to win the commission to design this
enormous new park. The park's main engineer was a rather uncouth
and colorful character bearing an excellent name for an antagonist:
Colonel Egbert Ludovicus Viele (pronounced *Vee*-lay). His lack of
decorum preceded him, as he was commonly known to employ foul
language in the presence of ladies. Most enjoyably, Viele was fixated
upon the occult, particularly the conjuring powers of eldritch sym-
bols. I'm not saying this guy was not a Freemason.

Viele entered himself in the park's design competition and
undoubtedly gave himself a leg up with his intimate knowledge of the
intended land features and their existing topography. Meanwhile,
Olmsted's crew plugged away, shoulders to the wheel at the treacherous chore of clearing the grounds for the impending face lift. One portion of the crew was struck down with an outbreak of malaria, while

another fell severely and mysteriously ill, with fevers and terrible itching. Apparently they had set a patch of poison ivy vines ablaze in their clearing efforts, the resultant smoke of which will afflict the body just as virulently as direct contact, except the vapors can be even worse when inhaled. I shouldn't have been surprised to learn that some of Olmsted's crew were students about to be exiled to college, thus taking a page out of their superintendent's escape book.

The park's commissioners laid down a very specific set of rules and requirements for the design entries, including a tower, a grand hall, playgrounds, and a formal garden, as well as four roads crossing the park, and a parade ground of twenty to forty acres in expanse. On top of these requirements, the winning plans would also need to be executable within the dictated budget of 1.5 million dollars.

Enter Calvert Vaux. (I recommend this title by Francis R. Kowsky for more on this underappreciated but fantastic artist: *Country, Park & City: The Architecture and Life of Calvert Vaux.*) Vaux had worked with some of the brass involved in the park commission and had not only previously met Olmsted, but he also had read and admired his writing. Calvert Vaux was a talented architect from London whom one would think possessed all the necessary chops to execute a winning design on his own, but he knew better. It was rumored that the topographical map created by the odious Colonel Viele was highly inaccurate—a great disadvantage to those hopeful entrants designing features for that particular area of land and its specific peccadilloes.

Vaux (the French would say *Voh*, but everyone I met pronounced it *Vawx*) cunningly sought out Olmsted, the superintendent of the park, who would likely have an even greater working knowledge of the lay of the land than Viele. Little could he have known that our Mr. Olmsted was a ready-made, ideal partner for just such a design project, well schooled as he was in all varieties of planting and particularly obsessed with trees, of which they would need thousands. Beyond his acumen as a farmer and landscaper, Olmsted possessed two further qualities that proved to dovetail perfectly with the talents of Vaux: common sense and gumption.

The duo relied on their clear foresight to understand that the winning park design should, above all, maintain its integrity for generations to come. As Olmsted wrote, "Only twenty years ago, Union Square was 'out of town'; twenty years hence, the town will have enclosed the Central Park. Let us consider, therefore, what will at that time be satisfactory, for it is then that the design will have to be really judged." Another important factor to recommend their design entry was simply their sense of taste. Thus, they chose to flout the hodgepodge of requirements set forth by the board, which paid off in a design that was all of a piece, putting the other more eclectic designs to shame.

In the final decision of the competition board lies a very satisfying lesson. Olmsted and Vaux continued to fine-tune their design until the final day, fussing at such length that the contest office had closed by the time they arrived with their submission. They were able to hand it off to a janitor and hope for the best. Despite their tardiness, despite their disdain for the prescribed requirements of the competition, among thirty-three submissions, theirs was the clear winner, by a tally of seven first-place votes out of eleven commissioners. The lesson that I would like to draw from this sequence is as follows: If you don't like the rules as they apply to your art, then break the rules.

This won't always work out in your favor, as it also requires a degree of perspicacity on the part of the adjudicators; but if they are able, as Olmsted's and Vaux's were, to look at the broken rules and say, "Oh, this is better. Why did we make that dumb rule?," then taste and good design can win the day.

Before proceeding, I must make mention of another humorous and sad entry in the competition, a certain "envelope #2," which contained only a single, anonymous drawing of a pyramid. It was roundly held that this curious offering could only have been proffered by Colonel Viele, who was later laid to rest in a pyramidal mausoleum of his own design, at West Point, no less. Now, I am *definitely* not saying he was not a Freemason.

I can't help but think that the winning twosome found the path to victory through a great talent for design in nature, sure, but also their insistence that this park be used for the good of all, in as humanitarian a way as possible. "It is one great purpose of the park," Olmsted pronounced, "to supply the hundreds of thousands of tired workers, who have no opportunity to spend their summers in the country, a specimen of God's handiwork that shall be to them, inexpensively, what a month or two in the White Mountains or the Adirondacks is, at great cost, to those in easier circumstances."

Touring Central Park with my esteemed guides lent a great first-person quality to experiencing the intended effects of the designers' intentions. Before we even entered, Sara pointed out that each of the park's eighteen different entry gates has its own special name, as designed by Olmsted and Vaux, carved into the stone wall next to its specified opening—openings, I should point out, for which wealthy

New Yorkers requested grand, ornate gates like those found in the urban parks of London and Paris. Olmsted and Vaux instead opted for low sandstone open gateways to symbolize an accessible city refuge, open to all comers, rich and poor alike.

The gate names themselves have a charming sense of working-class history and creativity: Artisans', Artists', Engineers', Farmers', Hunters', Mariners', Merchants', Scholars', and Woodmen's. Also observing the disparate gender and age strata of the day, there were gates marked Boys', Girls', and Women's, as well as one marked Children's. Apparently nineteenth-century anthropologists had not yet unearthed the mystery of what sorts of creatures comprised "children" (namely, "boys" and "girls").

The Women's Gate, located at Seventy-Second Street and Central Park West, is very convenient for reaching Strawberry Fields, but it must be a bummer, particularly for women across the park's expanse on the Upper East Side, to have to walk all the way around the park to access their gate. Perhaps someday women will find a loophole by tricking men into hiring them as miners or scholars, so that they may more easily enter the park from numerous other points.

On a more poetic note, there were also gates assigned to more figurative groups—All Saints', Pioneers', Warriors', and my favorite for the enigmatic image it evokes: Strangers' Gate. Located at 106th Street and Central Park West, the Strangers' Gate opens immediately onto a wide slate staircase that leads one upward into a shadowy pass between stone bluffs beneath the romantic canopy of hornbeam and black cherry trees, as though by ascending the steps, you are stepping into a fairy tale. Clearly designed as the preferred entrance should

Aragorn, or Strider, if you prefer, ever step out from the pages of Tolkien and into the park from Central Park West, which, o ho, also happens to be known a few blocks to the north as Frederick Douglass Boulevard. Watch me tie this entire son of a bitch together.

My guides from the Central Park Conservancy fervently explained the methods by which the park had been entirely man-made, much the same as Disneyland, except it had been built with stone and soil and trees and shrubs. In excavation, it reportedly required more gunpowder than the Battle of Gettysburg. Olmsted and Vaux wanted the public to begin to experience the park immediately upon entering, again, just like a Disney park. (I suppose I should be thankful that I can enter Central Park without being accosted by a person dressed as a giant mouse.) To achieve their desired effect, the landscape artists ordered a great deal of modification in the elevation of the pathways. Using hills, valleys, walkways, and bridges instead of paints and clay, the duo created what Sara Cedar Miller insists was "the greatest work of American art of the nineteenth century," an estimation I am disinclined to dispute. In fact, Olmsted and Vaux openly stated that their goal was to fabricate a three-dimensional version of a painting like those of the Hudson River School, with the then innovative new style of presenting scenes of nature with romantic realism. Another defining quality of those with gumption often seems to entail getting the trappings of "progress" out of the way and letting nature do the talking.

One of the philosophical bents aligning Olmsted and Vaux on the same artistic path was a penchant for serving all classes of people with their park. Like any successful collaboration, they each had their specialties within a shared overall aesthetic. For example, Vaux designed the park's structures, like the storybook Dairy, originally intended to serve as a refuge where children could enjoy a fresh glass of milk, "warm from the cow." The safe practice of pasteurizing milk had not yet come into use, and New York City was lousy with nefarious purveyors of "dirty" milk that had been thinned out and cut with fillers to stretch out the seller's supply. The Dairy provided a type of official milk dispensary where your little nipper could freely slake his or her thirst in the nurturing bosom of Central Park.

Olmsted, on the other hand, specialized in sculpting what he referred to as "passages of scenery," meaning the meadows and glades that showed off his extraordinary gifts. He developed a signature hourglass shape to these features, making the open area narrow in the middle, then flaring out at each end to create a sense of narrative. As Justin Martin surmised, "Someone standing in such a meadow . . . would be naturally drawn toward the narrow middle. It presented an allure and a mystery. What was on the other side? After walking through the passage, there was a release, like walking through a tunnel into a stadium."

Another of my favorite plebian victories scored by the designers was in the egalitarian nature of the pathways themselves. August Belmont, of horse racing fame, was one of the park's commissioners, and he insisted that the finest sections of the park should be serviced by carriage roads and bridle paths, so that the wealthy would be favored in viewing the scenes. Olmsted and Vaux nipped that idea in the bud by ensuring that all the most pleasant vistas and grottoes were accessible only by pedestrians, so that citizens from every class could use the park with equal opportunity.

Despite their primary focus on beautifully choreographed, "natural" scenery, some buildings and bridges were required. Olmsted insisted on simplicity, but Vaux was able to have his way with a few exceptions, most notably the Bethesda Fountain, which remains an absolute masterpiece to this day. I was taken aback when my guides pointed out to me the beautifully intricate stone carvings in the structure all around the fountain and pavilion, telling the allegorical story of the four seasons of the year in accord with the seasons of a human life. The reason for my shame was that I had visited the fountain many times without fully noticing these gorgeous and painstaking details. It was a valuable lesson in letting one's vision fully relax from the information of the busy world when enjoying the park and the works of Olmsted and Vaux. It hearkens back to the quote that began this chapter, that a surplus of information creates a paucity of attention for features like the fountain. Perhaps my former myopia just means that I'm more of an Olmsted man. Trees and a waterfall for me, thank you very much.

During the twelve years of construction that the park required, a little skirmish known as the Civil War broke out. In those days, the reason a park would feature a parade ground was not for public parades, like the one Macy's throws every Thanksgiving. Parades of that stripe require streets. No, the parade ground in a park was designed as a large open field in which military divisions could assemble and drill, both for practicality's sake and for public display.

Olmsted despised the thought of his open meadow being used as a utility of wartime, for, as he asserted, the park was designed to serve as a refuge from such unpleasantness. He and Vaux wanted the worries of the world to be left behind when a person strolled into their park. Imagine, then, his delight when he and the park administrators elected to populate the parade ground with a large flock of sheep. The sheep proved to be too much of an inconvenience for the soldiers but caught on immediately with the public and became a permanent fixture for many years, so that since that time the parade ground has been known much more pastorally as the Sheep Meadow. A stone building was constructed on the west end of the meadow in which the sheep would slumber at night. This building eventually became a pub and restaurant that is still open today called Tavern on the Green.

To see their combined vision realized, Olmsted and Vaux slogged through countless battles with the park commissioners and the corrupt politicians of Tammany Hall, not to mention each other. At one point Olmsted grew so aggravated that he fled the city, indeed, he fled the Eastern Seaboard altogether to oversee a gold mine in California, and then took part in an early commission to convince the government that Yosemite should be preserved indefinitely by federal funds.

Rubbing elbows with our old pal Theodore Roosevelt in their mutual epiphany that the government should be urged to preserve the most spectacular instances of wilderness in the West, Olmsted became one of our first outspoken environmentalists. His Yosemite address of 1865 was instrumental in getting that particular ball rolling, stating, "The establishment by the government of great public grounds for the free enjoyment of the people . . . is thus justified and enforced as a political duty."

He eventually had to be coaxed back to New York by Vaux, who dangled the carrot of a new park commission, this time in Brooklyn. Newly inspired by his travels in the West, Olmsted envisioned a small ravine and waterfall in what became known as Prospect Park, to mirror the epic splendor of Yosemite. Once again, the team had to completely fabricate the sense of a partially wooded, hilly terrain that would seem as if it has always been there. One specific display of gumption on the part of John Culyer, a lieutenant of Olmsted's through many chapters, was his invention of a tree-moving machine that had the ability to grasp the tree trunk near its base and pull up on it, like one pulls a weed. Apparently, enough of a root ball would be retained to allow the trees to survive being moved to new locations. This allowed some of the more magnificent old growth to persevere, a most worthy cause indeed.

By that time, Olmsted and Vaux were able to exert enough influence to build this park closer to Olmsted's "crafted wilderness" ideal, although it must be noted that Vaux, for all his love of Victorian buildings, made this his personal credo: "Nature first, second, and third—architecture after a while." In Prospect Park they together achieved a masterpiece considered by many to be the pinnacle of their careers. Today, as then, both of their New York City parks boast picturesque bodies of water upon which one can inexpensively row a boat in the middle of a bustling metropolis, preferably with a loved one nestled in the stern (referring to the aft region of the boat, not the beloved's anatomy). That fact alone makes them a most charismatic destination in my book. Is that redundant?

One note of contention, however, that forever rankled Vaux was that Olmsted had been awarded the title of architect in chief at Central Park. I suppose his ire stands to reason, since Vaux was officially the architect of the pair while Olmsted had no formal training in that field whatsoever. Although this was representative of the rancor that colored much of their time together, they still shared a mutual artistic passion anchored in a deep bond of loyalty and respect. All well and good, as long as they weren't required to see each other for more than a few minutes at a time. Even so, Olmsted always humbly recalled that their partnership was Vaux's idea to begin with. "Without him," Olmsted remarked, "I should have been a farmer."

On the domestic front, Olmsted had rather fallen into a marriage with his brother's widow, Mary, after the untimely death of his brother, John. With the widow, Olmsted also inherited a pair of sons in his nephews Owen and John. Apparently, he felt that the stringent guidelines under which he demanded his parks be shaped were also appropriate for the formation of a young man.

In an endless upbraiding (a form for which he was famous—his resignation letter to the Central Park Commission logged in at forty-one pages), Olmsted admonished the headmaster of Owen's boarding school with incessant instruction, detailing all the skills he thought imperative in a young man's matriculation, including: "To saddle & bridle a horse. . . . To ride, drive, pack, clean, feed, bleed & physic a horse. . . . To rescue drowning persons. . . . To ford a river. To kill animals without cruelty; to preserve meat. . . . To make slight repairs in & run a steam engine safely. . . . To preserve clothing from moths." While Colonel Roosevelt (as well as one Ron Swanson) might have heartily approved of these directives, it's hard to imagine a school conducting some of this curriculum without losing a few of the runts, but perhaps that's just exactly where the source of Ron and Theodore's rugged preference would lie.

Despite Olmsted's attempts, his other stepson/nephew (and employee), John, also turned out to be a bit of a ne'er-do-well, as evidenced by a couple of poignant (and typically interminable) letters to the lad. On his way to tour Europe, John probably had just enough time on the ship crossing the Atlantic Ocean to read the instructions sent along by his stepfather, Uncle Frederick; writing that was "to be read over and committed substantively to memory while at sea, re-read in London and again in Paris." Olmsted veritably deluged him with guidance, rife with lists of parks, castles, cathedrals, and estates that John should digest, as well as scores of acquaintances of Olmsted's by whom John might meet with some advantage in knowing.

Above all, his stepfather urged him: "Everywhere examine closely and accurately all small architectural objects adapted to park-work." Seems pretty straightforward, right? I wouldn't think he needed to go into further detail. Wrong: "—pavilions, lodges, entrances, chalets, refreshment stalls, bridges, conservatories, plant-stands, fountains, drinking fountains, lamps, flagstaffs, seats, railings, parapets, copings, etc." As though John would see a chalet and not realize it would be included under the heading "architectural objects"? All this, and Olmsted still had to add "etc." to the end of the list? Isn't that Latin abbreviation usually employed so that one might *curtail* a long list? It turned out that our sweet Frederick had some control issues.

In 1874, Olmsted received a commission to design a park for the Canadian city of Montreal. In 2014, I met Daniel Chartier, who served the resultant Mont Royal Park as the chief landscape architect, early one morning at a coffee shop at the base of the city's small, central "mountain," where he whipped out an 11" × 17" book the thickness of a Chicago Yellow Pages (ask your parents).

I had been steered in his direction by Central Park's Sara Cedar Miller, and it turned out that she could not have turned me on to a more ideal Olmsted *freak*. Mr. Chartier, a trustee of the National Association for Olmsted Parks (NAOP), was an absolute treasure trove of Olmstedian lore and philosophy. He walked me through the massive book he had compiled on the history and ongoing development of the Montreal park, and I was nothing short of delighted by his enthusiasm. After so much reading of the dusty history of these historical figures, it was so refreshing to feel the heart of Frederick Law Olmsted beating with a robust rhythm in a living person.

Daniel, quite excited that this strange bewhiskered American wanted to know anything at all about the man who had inspired his own life's work, began to fulminate, in very enjoyably broken English (my French is for *merde*), about Olmsted's legacy. "A park is for more than air and exercise, it is *poetry*!" he insisted. "Olmsted understood the charm of natural scenery, the genius loci. Please make sure that is in your book." Done, sir. This phrase, meaning "genius of place," combined with Mr. Chartier's passion, brought Olmsted home for me in a way that I hadn't previously considered. It also happens to be the title of another one of my excellent sources for this chapter: *Genius of Place: The Life of Frederick Law Olmsted*, by Justin Martin.

Much the same as my wife, an exquisitely talented interior designer (and goddamn bombshell), can look at a room and conjure— with a few pieces of art, a rug, a love seat, and a couple of throw pillows—a work of such aesthetic genius as to astonish a clod like myself, Olmsted was able to look at a raw park site and envision just particularly the way it should be shaped; the specific story that could be told there in such a way as to bring the utmost pleasure to the visitor. As Mr. Chartier pointed out to me, Olmsted had an elemental knack for the richness of his work's narrative: He comprehended on an almost animal level the value in a lovely open space viewed through the trees; a glade, or a clearing in the distance. When we as a species lived in the woods, open space brought with it a sense of freedom and safety, because there could be no lion or tiger hiding in that open space. Stands to reason.

Daniel continued to regale me with the tastiest of exposition as we began to hike up the mountain. His fervor as we passed beneath a beautiful canopy of old and new growth confirmed a suspicion that I had long harbored: One could land a lot worse employment than to work in Parks and Recreation. As we meandered upon the main road for a spell and then cut straight up the hill on a rugged, rambling path, he pointed out the places that Olmsted's vision had been realized as well as places it had been shortchanged. "A park is a work of art!," Daniel proclaimed as I looked around me with a reverence that made it hard to disagree.

"The long-term protection of a work of nature and art like the park of Mont Royal requires sustained dedication on the part of those responsible for its stewardship. . . . There needs to be a constant process of education at work by which each new generation of citizens comes to learn about the value of Mont Royal and the design that Frederick Law Olmsted created," wrote Dr. Charles Beveridge, who is considered the greatest expert on Olmsted and his work. After enjoying the generosity of Sara Cedar Miller, Marie Warsh, Steve Bopp, and Daniel Chartier, and seeing the good work they have done and continue to do, I couldn't agree more.

The Diplomat

7

ELEANOR ROOSEVELT

Hey, it's a woman!

There are a great many Americans who deserve to be heralded for their gumption-riddled careers; patriots and trailblazers of one ilk or another, for whom I had not room in this book. Many of those excluded are women, beginning with Pocahontas and Sacagawea, Abigail Adams, Martha Washington, Dolley Madison, Betsy Ross, Lucretia Mott, Jane Addams, Harriet Beecher Stowe, and surprisingly, Davy Crockett, "King of the Wild Frontier," who reportedly (according to Sam Houston) had a "fetching holster." Look it up.

Here is an original thought that I just had, and you can feel free to quote me: History is written by the side that didn't lose. That means that most of the history of Western civilization maintains a focus commensurate with the patriarchal domination of society, including a particular emphasis on the achievements of military and sports figures. Reading our histories, one can begin to wonder if there were even any women about, excepting the amount of coverage Ms. Crockett received for her heroic contributions at the Alamo.

Judging by my own sturdy family in Illinois, or even the household of two that I share with Megan Mullally, the scarcity of recorded female influence upon the history of our population until the last century or so is a lot of bullshit. The women running the nation of my life, mainly my mother, her late mother, my aunts, my wife, and many of my stage managers, directors, writers, teachers, castmates, and woodworking peers, just for starters, have been powerful and gentle and beautiful and strong and *vital*. The long misrepresentation of what used to be known as "the weaker sex" is an egregiously offensive load of malarkey perpetrated by chickenshit men (like me) who were afraid their own contributions would be somehow diminished if they admitted to collaborating with ladies. We'll tuck into that topic more substantially, but I wanted to mention it up front as we dive into the first lady of gumption.

Eleanor Roosevelt was born in 1884 to a family of swells who were extremely well-off financially, meaning she didn't necessarily have to pull herself up by the straps of her lady boots, at least at first glance. However, although she and her family could afford the niceties of life, she experienced a poverty of another color, because she considered herself an ugly duckling in an era when physical beauty was somewhat relied upon to determine a young lady's eligibility. In addition, she lost both of her parents and a brother by the time she was nine, adding depression to her already blossoming insecurity.

She was thereafter raised in the household of her maternal grandmother, where she recalled her grandfather forcing the children to walk from the house to the road and back several times a day, with a stick across their backs in the crook of their elbows to improve their carriage. He was "a severe judge of what they read and wrote and how they expressed themselves. . . . The result was strength of character, . . . a certain rigidity in conforming to a conventional pattern."

Eleanor saw the positive effects of this training as well as the downside of strict conformity, and she found her escape in reading (*another* voracious reader) anything she could lay her hands upon, which proved to be tricky. Apparently, when she came upon subject matter that was beyond her knowledge and she asked the adults about it, the book would suddenly disappear. (Note to parents: There is no better way to make your child crave a forbidden item than hiding it away from them.) She would spend days hunting down the concealed books, which I imagine would be considered pretty tame by now. For example, she remembers it occurring with Dickens's *Bleak House*. Good God, what I wouldn't give to get my nieces to take a break from the Bieber chat rooms (or One Direction, or whomever the cute-boy pablum of the moment might be) and read some Dickens!

Her grandfather Hall enjoyed the advantage of wealth that had been amassed by the hardworking previous generations of the family, so he did not feel the need to work himself. Eleanor wrote of the great lesson she observed when the family grew lazy in laboring to maintain their good fortune, and then watched that surplus slip through their fingers over the course of a couple of subsequent generations. Interestingly, she saw her relatives buckle down and reacquaint themselves with the ability to work hard for their bread, just as their forbears had once done. "It always amuses me when any one group of people takes it for granted that, because they have been privileged for a generation or two, they are set apart in any way from the man or woman who is working in order to keep the wolf from the door. It is only luck and a little temporary veneer and before long the wheels may turn and one and all must fall back on whatever basic qualities they have."

This sentiment seems terribly poignant to me today, what with the vast gulf that continues to grow between the wealthiest class of Americans and those who are "working in order to keep the wolf from the door." When those who grotesquely profit from our corporations continue to grow financially fat by selling unhealthy products to the masses, or by overcharging us for pharmaceuticals, or by outsourcing so many millions of jobs that could be performed by staunch American hands, they seem to be forgetting that we are all in this together, and eventually they, or their children, will be made to rue all those flavors of corn-based snacks.

The niece of Theodore Roosevelt must have begun to sense some of his doughty nature in her own genes, discovering her individual mettle through trips to the fields or the woods, where she would completely forget the passage of time by escaping into her reading. By the time she was fourteen, she had begun to sense that one could perhaps succeed without being considered the greatest beauty, as she then wrote in an essay: "No matter how plain a woman may be, if truth and loyalty are stamped upon her face, all will be attracted to her." It sounds like Dickens can do a body some good.

Her confidence grew a great deal further when she was sent to Allenswood Academy, a private finishing school near London. Her instructor, Marie Souvestre, was a noted feminist thinker who encouraged her pupils to learn foreign languages and think for themselves. Souvestre taught that one should experience other cultures as deeply as possible, by enjoying their food, art, and local customs, but most important by understanding and speaking their native tongues, "because of the enjoyment you missed in a country when you were both deaf and dumb." These lessons would prove extremely instrumental in Eleanor's future as a diplomat with the vision to see all nations as one collective of people rather than as opposing teams in the grand arena of world politics.

Although her confidence was bolstered by her teenage schooling, Eleanor was still very much a vestal virgin when it came to canoodling. Remember, this was at a time when using a person's first name was considered the equivalent of a French kiss today. One did not allow a man to kiss one before becoming engaged to that man, at the risk of being considered an absolute slattern. Despite her high-minded clumsiness, Eleanor wrote, "I felt the urge to be a part of the stream of life, and so in the autumn of 1903, when Franklin Roosevelt, my fifth cousin once removed, asked me to marry him, though I was only nineteen, it seemed entirely natural and I never even thought that we were both young and inexperienced."

Eleanor and Franklin proceeded to move into a town house connected by only a sliding door to the residence of Franklin's mother, Sara, whom, it should be noted, was outspoken in her opposition to their union. Although the young couple produced six children, Eleanor did not feel well suited to motherhood and was overshadowed by her mother-in-law in the child-rearing department. This arrangement, in which Sara openly commandeered control of both households, was miserable for Eleanor, and most likely her husband, Franklin, as well, but nobody possessed the gumption at that point to stand up to the overweening matriarch.

Despite the apparently fecund marriage bed that produced those six kids, Eleanor sadly disliked having sex, stating to her daughter,

Anna, that it was merely "an ordeal to be borne," which makes me very glum. It's tough enough these days, what with the kids casually "hooking up," for two lovers to be honest and trusting enough to engage in sexy times that will satisfy both of their appetites and leave no feelings of inadequacy or vexation. Imagining the awkwardness of engaging in stiffly mannered copulation a hundred years ago, when it was considered indiscreet to even sign a letter with any other sentiment than "very sincerely yours," makes me shudder with discomfort.

Despite her best intentions, Eleanor was somewhat out to sea when it came to child rearing. When I was young, growing up in the cornfields of rural Minooka, Illinois, our parents had the luxury of letting us run wild out-of-doors. My dad's whistle was so loud that we could hear him call us for dinnertime even down at the creek near our house. Playing innocently in the sun, we had no idea how modern our lifestyle would have seemed to young Eleanor, who "had a curious arrangement out one of [her] back windows for airing the children, a kind of box with wire on the sides and top. . . . I knew fresh air was necessary, but I learned later that the sun is more important than the air, and I had [it] on the shady side of the house!"

She slowly but surely learned to cook, eventually regaining some sense of control from her mother-in-law. When her husband, Franklin, was stricken with polio and lost the use of his legs, Eleanor finally won an extended battle with Franklin's mother by convincing him to stay in politics and therefore remain vital and active, for his own sake as well as that of the nation. While vacationing in Fairhaven, Massachusetts, with the children, she realized that her young boys no longer had a mentor in the realms of adventure and sport, like swimming, fishing, and camping, and although she was not a swimmer herself, the onus was upon her to literally swim or else sink into the role of insufficient parent. Eleanor faced the music and wrote, "I would have to become a good deal more companionable and more of an all-around person than I had ever been before."

Once she got a taste of succulent independence, Eleanor Roosevelt began to comprehend how her life could be much more satisfying. She began to remain "unavailable" to her older relatives and in-laws, upon whom she had theretofore depended for advice in every aspect of life. As she put it, "Had I never done this, perhaps I might have been saved some difficult experiences, but I have never regretted even my mistakes." As tragic and life-altering as FDR's paralysis must have been, I can't help but also see it as the catalyst that made an American hero of this previously timid housewife.

Eleanor also noted that "Franklin's illness proved a blessing in disguise, for it gave him strength and courage he had not had before. He had to think out the fundamentals of living and learn the greatest of all lessons—infinite patience and never-ending persistence." I believe that's two lessons there, Mrs. Roosevelt, but I'll let it slide . . . this time.

As the governor of New York and then the president of our nation, Franklin Delano Roosevelt could not have provided his wife with a better role model for sagacity in leadership. She often noted the way in which he, being no expert in any particular field, would calmly hear all sides of a given problem before issuing his considered judgment. She also observed the success he enjoyed in canvassing his electorate so thoroughly that even the remotest farmers felt his attentions.

Every president, especially in modern times, is going to have his or her (fingers crossed) high points and then also those other kinds of points in which they, oh, I don't know, assume office despite receiving fewer votes than Al Gore. FDR must have been doing something right, since he was the only president to be elected into office *four times.*

Invigorated by cheating death-by-polio, Roosevelt instituted a set of programs that he called the New Deal, designed to bring relief to a very depressed United States. His various policies were very effective in bringing about relief, recovery, and reform, at least until the politicians mired his decency once again in, well, politics. His was a great legacy, one you can read about in even more depth than my three recent, deeply researched, resplendent sentences. He was such a badass that he has been portrayed onscreen by Jon Voight, Bill Murray, Kenneth Branagh, Jason Robards, and, of course, Alan Cumming in *Reefer Madness.*

Eleanor also took note as Franklin developed a talent for gleaning a great deal of information through simple observation during his campaign trips. "From him I learned how to observe from train windows; . . . the crops, how people dressed, how many cars and in what condition, and even the washing on the clothesline." She continued to report that her husband was "impressed by the evidence of our wastefulness, our lack of conservation, our soil erosion." This was 1932, mind you. I can't imagine what the Roosevelts might think of the sad, cold, monocultural state of our agriculture today.

This habit of cropland scrutiny was perpetuated by Eleanor for the remainder of her career as a diplomat and humanitarian. In all her travels, she paid special attention to a nation's farming habits and how they affected the health of that country's population, both bodily and economically. Her husband's example, combined with her own burgeoning interest in people from every walk of life, culminated in her manifestation as a true activist for world peace and tranquility.

Although she was always quick to denigrate her own gifts, there was no denying that Eleanor, once she had escaped her mother-in-law's nest, was busting her ass. During her husband's tenure, Mrs. Roosevelt wrote a syndicated newspaper column, "My Day," no less than six days a week, even while touring the South Pacific, even when she had to stay up all night to get her column turned in. She typed out this prolific diary-style feature from 1935 until 1962, missing only six days upon the passing of FDR.

Meanwhile, she was commanding a veritable beehive of social activity. A year's worth of guests at the White House in 1939 tallied 4,729 who came to a meal (thirteen a day), 9,211 who came to tea (twenty-five a day), and 1.3 million (and change) who came through to tour the staterooms. I'm hoping she didn't also have to provide that teeming horde with cheese and crackers. I know she didn't personally feed all those guests, but just imagine having that many strangers in your dining room year in and year out. You'd better have a substantial supply of gumption ready to hand. She often cited her exceptional work ethic as a great source of comfort in her life. "At least, I have never known what it was to be bored or to have time hang heavily on my hands."

During the second term of FDR's presidency, Eleanor began to work with the American Youth Congress, hoping to learn from them how to improve the lives of the younger generation, particularly those from less fortunate backgrounds. Unfortunately, she recounted learning much more about the unscrupulous methods employed by the aspiring communists in the group. Apparently, these young strategists were getting an early start in politics, as they would demur to debate certain subjects, causing delays until the other members would tire out and go home. Once enough of the opposition had left, the communists would hold and carry the vote. Mrs. Roosevelt found these shenanigans very annoying at the time, but their lessons would come to serve her well when she eventually had to deal with the exact same tactics on the floor of the United Nations.

With her personable and down-to-earth daily column, Eleanor Roosevelt gave women of the day a sense of empowerment when they were able to learn the First Lady's opinion on any number of subjects. She became an instrumental voice in the struggle to right the imbalance felt by both women and minorities in our country. While touring England, she was inspired by women performing every manner of job that one was accustomed to see being performed by men: "I saw girls learning how to service every kind of truck and motor car and to drive every type of vehicle; I even saw girls in gun crews. . . . I visited factories in which women did every kind of work."

Eleanor was moved by the myriad women, from all walks of life, working side by side for the greater good of their mother England, just as the men were fighting as one for the same cause. Her reason for pointing this up was that the British Isles were considered to be very class-conscious, but here in wartime those distinctions fell away and the citizenry "became welded together by the war into a closely knit community." From her purview, she saw a new set of group values emerge.

This is a nice observation on her part, one that I can certainly understand and get behind: a sense of collective nationalism, brought on by the mutual jeopardy of having guns and bombs aimed at one's entire country. The thing is, it makes me wonder what has become of our own population's ability to stick together. We seem to be beyond a time when another military power can hold us at gunpoint with sheer brute force, and so have we complacently lost interest in what all the other Americans are up to, since we're not "at war"?

It would seem that we still are looking down the barrel of destruction; it's just not perhaps as bluntly presented as a German tank. Water shortages, the exhaustion of fossil fuels, not to mention the subsequent pollution and global warming, the neglect of our own agricultural communities, the insatiable appetites of our mining companies . . . all these seem fully lethal as well. Maybe they won't kill us as succinctly as the Blitz, but we have come to know that they *will* kill us, and I'm afraid it will be in a much more permanent way than the carnage of a gun battle. Cities can be rebuilt with much greater ease than ecosystems.

Like many rational human beings, Eleanor Roosevelt had an instinctive abhorrence of war, and yet she didn't hesitate to get all up in its grill. This was back before it was all long distance, war by remote control. Eleanor joined the Red Cross and took to visiting the soldiers in field hospitals who were wounded in both body and psyche. Exhausted from walking miles of corridors and witnessing every color of injury and trauma, she wrote emotionally, "But that was nothing in comparison with the horrible consciousness of waste and feeling of resentment that burned within me as I wondered why men could not sit down around a table and settle their differences before an infinite number of the youth of many nations had to suffer."

Her answer may reside hidden right within her question—in the noun *men*. Human beings are complex. We're complicated as shit. But I can't help but think that planting a few Eleanor Roosevelts in seats of power might help the scales of justice (held by a lady, after all) tip back toward "not killing people." Women can be assholes too, surely. I realize that war is more than just the men and their Freudian passion for shooting at one another with their penises. It is also about the *billions* of dollars being funneled into their pocketbooks. Women have those accessories as well.

Once FDR had to dance the jig of equivocation that is the American presidency (meaning he had to play both sides of the fence enough to keep his majority), Eleanor began to make waves, what with her commonsense acceptance of all people, regardless of race, political affiliation, or genital inventory.

To put things in perspective, there was a bill sponsored by a couple of Democratic senators from Colorado and New York, called the Costigan-Wagner Bill, that was simply trying to cut down on the number of lynchings taking place in the South. This was 1934. Edwin Hubble, with his swell telescope, showed in a photograph as many galaxies as the Milky Way has visible stars. George S. Kaufman and Moss Hart's *Merrily We Roll Along* opened on Broadway. Katharine Hepburn won an Oscar for *Morning Glory* at the age of twenty-seven, and some uppity Yankee senators thought there should be fewer mob-driven murders of black fellows; the sort wherein they were hanged with a rope by the neck until they were dead.

Now, get this—FDR wouldn't back the bill! He was afraid of losing the southern congressional delegations when he needed their votes to support his legislation! *That's how fucked-up it is to be president.* You can seem as decent a chap as FDR, and yet you can't get behind the suggestion that we make lynching illegal. Eleanor lobbied *for* the bill, so white Southerners didn't like her. Black people, on the other hand, did like her. Go figure.

After the Japanese attack on Pearl Harbor, bogeyman-fear politics saw Franklin sign his Executive Order 9066, a directive born of hysteria that ended up imprisoning Japanese Americans in internment camps; about 120,000 Americans of Japanese descent were incarcerated for two to three years. That was in the 1940s, gang. Eleanor was very opposed to this racist, cowardly act on the part of our nation, for which she was again widely ostracized.

Her famous uncle, whom you might recall from chapter 5, was a Roosevelt with a decidedly less savory attitude toward national violence. I obviously revere much of what he had to offer, but I cannot get behind his opinion that a great country was one that picked fights. Methinks that Uncle Theodore could have used a strong dose of his niece's prudence when it came to dealing with his fellow earthlings.

I'm referring to the lady who penned this: "Nothing we learn in this world is ever wasted and I have come to the conclusion that practically nothing we do ever stands by itself. If it is good, it will serve some good purpose in the future. If it is evil, it may haunt us and handicap our efforts in unimagined ways."

This American champion took some common sense, a healthy dollop of elbow grease, and some natural compassion and set for us a shining example of how we can begin to "settle our differences around a table" instead of looking into the business end of a gun. She worked and worked until her working parts quit on her. I hate to think where we would be today without all the good she did for each and every one of us.

The Maverick

8

TOM LAUGHLIN

Tom Laughlin. May he rest in peace.

You may recognize him better in the slight guise of his heroic alter ego, Billy Jack. If not, please gently toss this book aside, hie ye to your nearest video store (if you're reading this in the 1980s), or I guess whichever Netflix or Amazon channel is providing you with feature-length film treats these days, and watch *Billy Jack*, a movie that may be little known now but was at the time (1971) both a cultural revolution and the highest-grossing independent film of all time, a record it still holds. You'll likely want to devour it at least thrice, so please notify anyone who might be relying upon you to deliver their medication or perhaps pick them up from school, Scouts, or 4-H, if they're especially lucky.

My own obsession began twenty-five years ago. I was in college at the University of Illinois at Urbana-Champaign in 1989, when I first met Darren Critz. Although he was enrolled in the class behind mine, he was a couple of years my senior, having bounced between majors for a minute before landing upon theater, with a focus in directing. His appearance upon our first meeting bears reporting: He was extremely buff, with a wild, shoulder-length mane of black curls festooned with little plastic star beads framing handsome hawkish features, neck entwined in an intimidatingly thick rope of Mardi Gras beads that would have made the My Little Pony hidden inside Mr. T green with envy. He shaved his body hair with clippers, which made the extreme definition of his musculature stand out in all the real estate visible under his flannel shirt with the sleeves and collar cut off. His legs were equally exposed in tattered cut-off jeans before they disappeared into a pair of old-fashioned cowboy boots that Darren had spray painted gold. He was, in short, a self-made psychedelic superhero.

Darren was one of the initial pillars of the Defiant Theatre, the Chicago company comprised of my most invaluable college friends, who inculcated in me the sense of counterculture that would come to define my artistic life. Among the moments of whimsy in which Darren draped me were some powerfully enjoyable sessions of hallucinating and giggling (in the haremlike cave of an apartment he shared with Bobby Goliath Taich, another estimable tea-head) and, of course, a reverential screening of *Billy Jack*.

One of the most popular features in any visit to Darren's place was the tactile art experience known as "Grandma's 'gina." Although you can sadly never know the wonder of this sexual petting, let me walk you through it vicariously as best I can. Generally, before one was ready to comprehend this delight born of Darren's fecund, puckish imagination, one wanted to "put on a buzz" of some sort. Fortunately, the living room that served as the gallery for this masterpiece also housed his roommate's eight-foot bong, which rendered just such a mood elevation handily achievable.

Once suitably baked, the initiate would next sit in the cushioned chair beneath which the "objet d'art" resided. At this point, a fellow stoner, or "docent," would retrieve the large glass bowl filled with a mass of bread dough into which an upsettingly realistic rendition of a woman's genitalia had been shaped. The bowl would be placed in the lap of the participant, who would then, with eyes closed, feel the crusty orifice with his or her fingers. Sometimes a few drops of water would be sprinkled upon it before fondling, upping the verisimilitude. Ladies and gentlemen, I give you Grandma's 'gina.

During my colorful years in Chicago theater, I was inspired by a great many women and men, eccentric iconoclasts who marched quite charismatically to the beat of their own strange drums, but Darren was one of the first to show me how a person could fly a flag that was extremely freakish and still command the respect of professionals in the world of theater. Thanks to his inspiration, I was able to make a great many fashion choices of my own that my dad would describe only as "squirrelly," but they nonetheless allowed me to feel like I was announcing to the world that the particular brand of entertainment I had to proffer was redolent of substance and mirth.

Whether or not it was his intention, Darren made of me a lifelong *Billy Jack* adherent. When I arrived in LA in the late nineties, my newly discovered best friend, Pat Roberts, was also a fan, and together we couldn't get enough of the film. The Internet showed up, and I found Tom Laughlin's website and learned of the politics and philosophy he had been espousing all along. I then set out to learn everything I could about him.

A midwestern boy who played football at both Wisconsin and

Marquette, Tom Laughlin was bitten by the theater bug after taking in a production of *A Streetcar Named Desire*. He met the love of his life, Delores Taylor, while attending the University of South Dakota with her. The pair ended up in Los Angeles, where Tom began to work steadily, landing his first leading role in Robert Altman's *The Delinquents*. This followed his on-screen debut on the television program *Climax!*, which was also known as *Climax Mystery Theater* and was not remotely as prurient as its title. Apologies.

He worked on other films as an actor and a director, leading to the first appearance of his character Billy Jack in the 1967 film *Born Losers*, directed by, as well as starring, Laughlin. Considered a box office hit, *Born Losers* paved the way for the (sort-of) sequel, *Billy Jack*. Which brings us to the meat of the matter.

Much like our former president and star of chapter 5, Theodore Roosevelt, *Billy Jack* makes some statements, both overtly and indirectly, that can be confusing to an audience. First of all, it must be stated that the title character is, in the modern parlance, awesome. Billy Jack is a half-breed Navajo Indian, a recent veteran of the Vietnam War (ex–Green Beret), as well as a master of hapkido, a Korean martial art. When he intuits an impending fight, he slips off his boots and socks. Billy Jack also possesses a supernatural ability to sense danger and wrongdoing, a sort of "Spidey sense." To top it off, he lives in a cave, but his clothes are always clean, and he might show up on a horse, on a motorcycle, or in his Jeep, wearing a full suit of denim and his iconic "rez" hat. So badass.

His heart, the film instructs us, is very much in the right place, as he is a disciple of peace and love, living under the tutelage of the local tribe's shaman, or medicine man, on the reservation. His apparent romantic partner, Jean Roberts (played by his real-life wife, Delores Taylor), runs the Freedom School outside of town, with an openly "hippie" agenda, promoting nonviolence and an open-minded approach to living: "No drugs, everyone had to carry his own load, and everyone had to get turned on by creating something, anything, whether it be weaving a blanket, making a film, or doing a painting."

When the evil, racist, white townspeople threaten violence, Jean and the kids at the school enjoy the Robin Hood–flavored protection of Billy Jack, who is fully onboard with their pacifist teachings, but as he says in the film, "Jean and the kids at the school tell me that I'm supposed to control my violent temper. . . . I try. I really try. Though when I see [this] . . . I just go berserk!" At this point, Billy Jack beats the piss out of the white townie bullies with some devastating hapkido moves. This turns out to be more of the rule than the exception. Since Billy Jack can't control the rage he feels as the result of society's injustices, the film ends up a very violent paean to nonviolence.

I've witnessed a good deal of criticism focused on the inconsistencies in *Billy Jack*, which I have no interest in debating. All I know is that millions of people, including your author, have found themselves profoundly moved by the film's core message, that the evils of society are pervasive enough to drive a person to fight, even though he knows he shouldn't. Things are bad, and something must be done to foment a change. Billy Jack the man, warts and all, shoulders this burden for all of us, which is why, at the end of the film as he's hauled away in a police car and hundreds of citizens lining the road raise a single fist in solidarity with him, I raise my fist as well.

I'll be the first to claim an ignorance in my ability to coldly analyze the film's foibles, because I'm too busy being moved by the hero's plight. Perhaps this is because, regardless of any missteps on the part of Tom Laughlin, he was at least doing some-goddamn-thing about it. His Billy Jack delivers the truth with such a measured pace and undeniable sincerity, I don't give a shit if the story is confusing. This man versus his fellow man, and this man versus himself, happens to be some material I can sink my teeth into, and so it's not that I *forgive* the other parts of the film so much as I just don't notice them.

When I first saw the film, I was about 98 percent naïveté, newly arrived "out in the world" from the small, conservative town I'd grown up in. For the first time, I was living smack-dab among the people on the receiving end of racism and sexism and homophobia. Here was a fellow in a film willing to kick the rich, white bad guy right upside his face when the bad guy (and his thugs, because the bad guy was a chickenshit) had him cornered. It doesn't take a lot of arithmetic to comprehend why I would have found that pretty goddamn swell, regardless of Leonard Maltin's admonitions.

An attribute in Billy Jack, I think, that might have also held true for Tom Laughlin was a stubborn adherence to his own solitary path, including a distrust of authority and "the establishment," which ultimately is thought to have undermined his career. When Warner Bros. released *Billy Jack*, Laughlin was extremely underwhelmed with their strategy, and, sure enough, the film foundered out of the gate. He sued the studio to reclaim the film, which he then rereleased on his own.

In a stroke of brilliance, fueled by his unwavering conviction, Tom Laughlin single-handedly forged the technique of releasing a film nationwide all at once, a "wide release," bolstered by TV advertisements planted during local news broadcasts. Such a move had not been previously dared. This gutsy gambit, combined with a thirst for social change in America's younger generation, turned Laughlin's film into a box office juggernaut, making it, as mentioned, the highest-grossing independent film of all time (after adjusting for inflation). He must have been doing something right.

Here's the thing, or at least here's *a* thing: People have vastly differing tastes. People also have vastly disparate levels of discernment. If you look at the numbers, you would have to assume that the McDonald's factory beef burger sandwich is the most delicious sandwich. In truth, it's pretty easy to understand that in fact, it's simply the easiest choice for a lot of consumers. If there was a fast-food joint selling a Reuben sandwich for the price of a Big Mac, we might see some different stats. I used to judge people for their lazy choices, which, in effect, was me merely judging myself for having the capacity to treat my body so poorly as to eat the burger sandwich of laziness. I believe we all have the capacity for such mediocrity, which is why those motherfuckers are making so much money off us.

So I have learned to refrain from judging my fellow humans in their choices, or at least do my best to refrain. I've certainly improved considerably, but I'm sure there will always be room for more bettering, since I am, after all, human. As was Tom Laughlin.

I like the way Roger Ebert put it in the *Chicago Sun-Times*: "Laughlin and Taylor surface so rarely because their movies are personal ventures, financed in unorthodox ways and employing the kind of communal chance-taking that Hollywood finds terrifying. The chances they take sometimes create flaws in their films, but flaws that suggest they were trying to do too much, never too little."

There's not much better praise for a person in my book than that his or her heart was in the right place and the utmost of gumption was employed. No matter what anybody says to me about the films of Tom Laughlin, I will never cease to raise my fist as "One Tin Soldier" (the film's theme song, by Coven) kicks into the chorus.

Tom Laughlin would have occupied a place in this book no matter what. But an amazing set of opportunities gave me a personal connection to Tom and his family that makes this chapter even dearer to me. It began in March of 2013, when I had the extreme pleasure of appearing (vocally) as a guest on *The Treatment*, the venerable NPR show about the film business, hosted by über-cinéaste Elvis Mitchell. Elvis nearly made me mist up with gratitude at the simple attention he had paid to much of my acting work in films that are usually much too obscure to be noticed by professional film buffs. Among the details he had gleaned was an awareness of my devotion to *Billy Jack*. When we had finished the interview and were saying our brotherly "so longs," he mentioned that he was responsible for programming screenings at the Los Angeles County Museum of Art, and would I like to host a screening of *Billy Jack*? Suffice it to say I answered with enthusiasm.

I had never seen *Billy Jack* projected on a big screen, and so I was rather beside myself with excitement. Shortly before the screening, we received word backstage that Tom Laughlin's son, Frank, would be in attendance, as well as actress Julie Webb, who played the troubled teenager Barbara in the film.

Suddenly things took a strange shift for me, as it hadn't remotely occurred to me that Laughlin's family might be around, let alone any of the actors from the film, despite the fact that I had actually worked with one for a day in the Patrick Swayze/Melanie Griffith romp *Forever Lulu*. It was shooting at the storied Hollywood watering hole Boardner's, where I was as pleased as punch to be squaring off with another of my life's heroes, Mr. Swayze. In between takes of the role I assayed, "Man at Boardner's," I was chatting with another of the bar patrons, a cute, rather elfin fellow who, in the course of things, mentioned that his name was Beans Morocco. Well, if you were as sweaty for *Billy Jack* as myself, you would have immediately recognized that name from the credits, in his hilarious work with Howard Hesseman and the improv players from the film's Freedom School. Comprised mainly of San Francisco–based troupe the Committee, the group hilariously commandeers a couple of sequences of the film with improvised comedy scenes. Beans Morocco plays the cute, rather elfin fellow with the hat.

He seemed somewhat surprised at being spotted from his work in *Billy Jack*, which was nothing short of sacrilege to me. I at least got Patrick Swayze to agree with me that *Billy Jack* was worthy of a young man's adulation. (You best believe that there was also a great deal of *Road House* worship happening, not to mention *Red Dawn* and *Point Break*. The first AD was not onboard, however, when every time he would call, "Roll cameras!," I would answer with, "Wolverines!")

At the LACMA screening with Elvis Mitchell, however, I was nothing short of flabbergasted that these vestiges of real life were invading my own personal *Billy Jack* fantasy. I was still so provincial in my comprehension of show business that I was utterly gut-punched when I met Frank Laughlin after the screening, with his lovely daughter, Jessica, and he mentioned that his mom and dad, Delores and Tom, would have loved to attend, if they'd only known about it! Frank and I struck up a friendship, and he and Jessica came to see Megan and me in our stage production of *Annapurna*, a great two-hander by Sharr White. We were loosely planning an occasion for me to meet his dad between all the traveling I'd been doing for work, when Tom unexpectedly fell ill and passed away. I was devastated to have missed my opportunity to shake the hand of the man who had brought me so much inspiration, but at the same time I was very touched when his kids invited me to the funeral.

Pat Roberts and I drove up to Malibu together, as we had so many times before, heading to the beach or to deliver furniture in my old '59 Ford flatbed truck. This time the atmosphere in the car was weighted with a strange combination of excitement and somber reverence. We arrived at Our Lady of Malibu Catholic Church and found parking. It was immediately strange, as we walked up and into the church, and a few people began to recognize me from *Parks and Recreation* as I greeted Frank and his two sisters, Teresa and Christina. I was rather embarrassed at their generosity in allowing me, a relative stranger, to attend this private event in the midst of their grief.

Pat and I sat in the very back of the congregation, to the extreme house right. My mind was roiling to keep up even as my heart was vacillating with conflicting emotions. One, I was titillated to be at the funeral of my hero. Pat agreed. Two, I was ashamed of my titillation, which felt somehow cheap in the face of the reality of our surroundings. Pat agreed. Three, the ceremony began with Tom's widow, Delores, being helped into a front pew. Suffering from the onset of Alzheimer's, she was still beautiful, with the stately air of a woman who had accomplished a great deal while saying little.

The priest kicked things off with a reverential welcome, and I was aghast as it slowly dawned on me that there was to be no flaming pyre? No sacrificial bighorn sheep or grizzly bear? "There won't be any trumpets blowin' come the judgment day"? What the fuck?! Didn't these people know whom it was we were burying today?

At this point, I caught myself, extremely mortified at the power of my selfishness. Of course these people knew. "These people" belonged to Tom Laughlin, and he belonged to them. I was the egotistical asshole who had been graciously allowed by these people to attend this solemn occasion with my asshole friend. Pat agreed. Like true modern Americans, we wanted this man's funeral to be somehow about us and our (superficial) experience of him. Fortunately, we caught ourselves in time to arrest our descent to the nadir of good taste toward which we were plummeting.

I know how a Catholic Mass goes, having grown up reciting it. I find it pretty mundane, so I continued to be displeased that Tom Laughlin was going to be sent off to glory with a mere Catholic service. Then his granddaughters, Jessica, Ellery, and Lily, ascended the pulpit to deliver the readings from the gospels, and things began to calm down a bit in my asshole alarm centers. Here were beautiful young ladies, timorously delivering ancient poetry in ceremonial honor of their deceased patriarch. This was more like it.

Jessica eased us into the doctrine with a combination Bible verse/popular rock song by the Byrds, which got some black-stocking'd toes tapping and girdled hips swaying (mine). She chanted, "A time to be born and a time to die, a time to plant and a time to uproot, a time to kill and a time to heal, a time to tear down and a time to build, a time to weep and a time to laugh, a time to mourn and a time to dance, a time to scatter stones and a time to gather them, a time to embrace and a time to refrain from embracing," etcetera. You know how it goes. It holds up. The Byrds knew what they were about.

Ellery said things like, "In my Father's house are many mansions: if it were not so, I would have told you. I go to prepare a place for you. And if I go and prepare a place for you, I will come again, and receive you unto myself; that where I am, there ye may be also. And whither I go ye know, and the way ye know." Now, this I could also wrap my head around. This succinctly chosen passage from the Book of John is an example of when the Bible works best for me, that is, when it can be easily applied metaphorically to our real, tangible lives. The older I get and the more I pay attention, life's messages seem to reiterate: We're all the same. We're all in this together. Interestingly, sitting there in church, I thought of Tom Laughlin's impact on my life, which made me think of John Lennon, who penned, "I am he as you are he as you are me and we are all together."

Lily picked up the scriptural baton with "Do not be surprised, my brothers and sisters, if the world hates you. We know that we have passed from death to life, because we love each other. Anyone who does not love remains in death. Anyone who hates a brother or sister is a murderer, and you know that no murderer has eternal life residing in him. This is how we know what love is: Jesus Christ laid down his life for us. And we ought to lay down our lives for our brothers and sisters." The beat. It goes on.

Like any such function—baptisms, weddings, a few particularly memorable key parties—this funeral had my mind swimming with existential questions, as well as an examination of my own personal scorecard: How was I doing as a husband, a son, a sibling, a friend, an uncle, and so forth? I quickly switched from being disappointed at the lack of fireworks in Our Lady of Malibu to being moved by the sincerity of the service and the privilege of being invited to sit in remembrance and celebration of an astonishing man.

That's when the bagpipes fired up. The player, in full dress, launched into a few selections that brought wetness to even the most insensitive eyes in the house. "Abide with Me," "The Minstrel Boy," "The Wearing of the Green," and, finally, "Danny Boy." I had wanted pageantry in this observance. Now, this was something like. Once the family made their recessional, Pat and I drifted outside to discuss the rich experience and what assholes we were. The congregation was invited next door to the multipurpose room, where a more informal celebration was about to go down.

I spoke briefly with each of the three children, Frank, Teresa, and Chrissy, and they convinced me to stay, despite my embarrassment at feeling like an outsider. I'm so glad I did, because act two of the afternoon contained much more of the flavor I had been hoping for.

Frank started things off by thanking us all for being there and then using the word *fuck*, which immediately let us know that misbehavior was welcome. He went on to liken his childhood (favorably) to "being raised by wolves." With the comforting demeanor of a good father, as well as the oldest child, Frank thanked all the appropriate people for putting together this event and went on to share some anecdotes about his folks.

The most indelible story I heard later from Frank was about the way Tom and Delores reclaimed *Billy Jack* from Richard Zanuck Jr., who was running 20th Century Fox at the time. As Frank tells it, Zanuck was deeply involved in CREEP, or the Committee to Re-Elect the President, Richard Nixon. There is a line in *Billy Jack*, delivered by Teresa, no less, comparing Nixon's actions to those of Hitler, which of course could not remain in a film coming from Zanuck's studio.

Since Tom had (approval of) "final cut" on the film, Zanuck had to secretly plot to cut the offensive dialogue. Unfortunately for his machinations, a secretary in his office notified Tom and Delores that this was happening. The Laughlin duo neatly ran over to the sound studio where the film was being mixed and kidnapped the many reels of sound tape, which they then held for ransom. Zanuck had the film reels but Tom had the sound, without which the film was merely an unreleasable silent film art project.

Zanuck was notified by Tom that he needed to let Tom buy back the film, which only served to make Zanuck laugh. Tom told him that for every day he refused to sell the film back to Tom, Tom would erase a reel of sound. Presumably Zanuck laughed again, until Tom sent over a reel of blank magstripe. Zanuck absolutely flipped out and sent the reel down to the lab to be analyzed, only to receive confirmation that it had in fact been wiped.

The plan worked, and Zanuck allowed Tom to orchestrate the following sale by Warner Bros. Frank spoke with a grudging respect for his dad's methods. Although things didn't always go his way, you had to hand it to Tom Laughlin for sticking up for the things he felt were right.

Teresa spoke next, emotionally, laughing about the way her father used to challenge studio executives to beat her in tennis or arm wrestling to settle lawsuits and contractual disputes.

Side story, if you'll permit me—in 2014 I had the pleasure of screening *Billy Jack* a second time in New York City at the IFC Center down on Sixth Avenue, and Teresa was able to attend with me. She is the only one of the three kids who plays a prominent role in the film (Frank doubled his dad in motorcycle shots, Christina had just been born months earlier), playing one of the brighter, more outspoken kids at the Freedom School.

I had probably seen the film ten times before the Internet Movie Database (IMDb) made it possible to discern that she was actually the daughter of Tom and Delores. Pat Roberts and I had an LP of songs from the film, upon which Teresa had a couple of tunes, and so we were very big fans of her music as well. When we discovered that she was also the daughter of the filmmakers, well, she achieved a status in our household previously reserved only for the likes of Meat Loaf or Dusty Springfield.

Watching the film then, next to Teresa, who was embarrassed about "this art thing" she had done with her parents, was very humanizing.

Seeing the film through her eyes gave me such a different perspective, which made me appreciate her entire family with a profound, new understanding. That they made these films together only served to redouble my respect for the Laughlin-Taylors, using the tools at their disposal, karate chops included, to communicate a message of love to the world.

But back to Malibu in that December of 2013. Chrissy spoke last, and although she's the baby in the family, she was by no means the least. She told us that her dad always said that everybody has a voice, that everyone has a message of their own; they just needed to find that message and share it with the world. Tom was crazy for books. He read voraciously and encouraged his kids (and everyone around them) to do the same.

At this point, some items were passed around the room: a bowl of paper strips and a box of envelopes, of which we were all encouraged to partake. Chrissy explained that the strips of paper were her dad's favorite quotes, torn from their books. He would always make the kids stop whatever they were doing and pay attention to whichever given quote had caught his fancy, and those quotes, with their attendant meanings, stuck with the kids. She wanted his quotes distributed so that her dad could have one last shot at disbursing the wisdom that had guided him.

The envelopes were self-addressed, stamped letter-size envelopes, all set to be mailed back to Chrissy. She asked us to use them if and when we had accomplished a dream, if we would then write down the accomplishment and send it to her. She said they were a way to give each of us a reminder that life is short, that inspiration is precious, and that living life fully and unafraid is probably the only thing that matters. Tom accomplished some amazing things in his life when he charged forward, bravely, with purpose. If that could inspire others, including herself, what a gift it would be. If folks wrote back, and the family could keep those envelopes for his grandkids, and their grandkids beyond, what a poignant legacy it could be. She finished up with an Oliver Wendell Holmes quote that she found as a bookmark in the prayer book of Tom's father, as she was sorting out his things: "It is faith in something, and enthusiasm for something, that makes a life worth looking at."

I found each of the siblings' offerings to be very moving, each in its own regard. The creativity of Christina's disseminated quotes and her empty, prestamped envelopes I found particularly moving, as though her dad's spirit was truly moving through her and into us. I have had a very lucky year since attending Tom's funeral, but nothing has felt appropriate to write to her about until now, finishing this chapter. I believe I'll write to her about it; this chapter in this book, with which I hope, among other objectives, to engender mirth and spread the message of love among all my brothers and all my sisters. That seems an awfully sincere thing to say without a joke at the end, but I am going to let it fly.

The Farmer

9

WENDELL BERRY

Good gracious. For me, the fact that you are now reading a chapter on Wendell Berry is quite momentous. If you are (about to be) new to Mr. Berry's work, let me tell you right to your face that you are in for a treat. Not a treat like ice cream or some other confection. A much more substantial treat, perhaps constructed cleverly of leather or hickory or copper, like you just won a barn, and someone is going to help you build it, and then that person is going to tell you how one might prosper from the use of a barn in your life. You can't know going in that it's not the barn itself but rather the building of it and its cumulative use that are the real prizes. That kind of treat.

Those of you who already know him (which, it's been said, is to love him) will understand just from where I'm shooting in this effort. Chances are that many of you readers are still with me here because you have perhaps enjoyed the show *Parks and Recreation*, or for a much smaller group, my woodworking portfolio, and I have managed to seduce you sufficiently with descriptions of George Washington's teeth and the ship-caulking prowess of Frederick Douglass to get you this far into this particular tome. Now, as long as anyone is listening, I will holler about Wendell Berry. If you are inspired by nothing else in this, my sophomoric effort, for Pete's sake, please read his works, and then pass them on. His well of common sense is deep enough to slake all our thirst, with considered sips of perspicacity that are cool, crisp, and ever so refreshing to the palate.

Because I am such a student and adherent of Wendell Berry's writing, this chapter, and hopefully this entire book, will contain much less hyperbole than I would sophomorically like to apply to it. Wendell, if you have so run out of useful things to do as to be reading this, I must warn you to prepare yourself to endure some compliments, but, out of the respect for economy that I am very slowly learning from your own work, I will do my best to refrain from over-egging the pudding.

Wendell Berry is the greatest writer ever to have sharpened a pencil. Dang it. That was not a good start. But you are stuck with me, such as I am, so let's just press on with best intentions.

In 1995 I was working as an understudy and a makeup artist on the Steppenwolf Theatre production of *Buried Child*, Sam Shepard's masterpiece of a play, with a late, great character actor named Leo Burmester in the role of Bradley. Leo had grown up in Kentucky and was an absolute sweetheart, as well as a substantial talent. Because of our similarly rural upbringings, and I suppose a shared proclivity for playing beefy/sensitive types who might be as comfortable wielding a darning needle as a broadsword, Leo took a shine to me. Upon the show's closing, he gave me my first Wendell Berry, a book of collected stories entitled *Fidelity*.

I am tearing up a little as I write this, for a few reasons: (1) with gratitude that Leo saw in me a budding initiate who would possibly flower in the sunlight of Berry's words; (2) with remorse that Leo passed away in 2007, before I had the chance to tell him what a profound impact his gift had exacted upon my life; and (3) with relish for the impact itself, which simply moves me to tears. Which is why I'm doing my level best to pass along the gift of that influence to you, the reader, whom both Leo and I would have undoubtedly described as "better looking than us."

I read the stories in *Fidelity* and was simply gobsmacked at, sure, their beauty and humor and emotional specificity, okay, but what really made me sit down abruptly upon my fanny was that I recognized my own family and my own town in these tales. The small community of families, made up of characters of every stripe, simultaneously called to mind the inhabitants of my own youth and delighted me with new players as well, ones I had not yet discerned in my travels.

These first five stories ran the gamut from stomach-churning drama to staunch familial loyalty to easy raillery between friends and neighbors. The simplicity with which the journey in "Making It Home" resolves itself never fails to fill me with a warm flood of emotion. But it was the story "Fidelity" of which I was most enamored. It concerns a young farmer's decision to "kidnap" his dying father from a Louisville hospital, so that he may expire in the presence of love, with dignity.

I wrote to Mr. Berry to request his permission for the right to adapt this story to stage or screen, I cared not which. His charming reply gently explained his disinterest in countenancing any such adaptation of his work. Because the whole of his body of fiction (ten novels, five collections of short stories to date) exists in the same setting and is peopled by the same genealogies across some hundred years or so, he considered it (he still does) a work in progress. Now that I've read the entire canon through more than once, and some of it more than thrice, this makes perfect sense. Anybody else's take on a portion of that work, he feels, would have an unwelcome alien effect on the whole of the town mural, as it were. I was disappointed, but the good news was I still had many years' worth of his writing to consume.

He also suggested that I write my own story and take this opportunity to deliver the themes I preferred in his work within my own vehicle. I explained that of course this had occurred to me, and perhaps it would even one day come to pass, but my calling has proven to be much more that of story*teller* than story *writer*. Besides, no one can write like him. He writes with the economy of the farmer, which I know he'll understand I mean as a high compliment. The farmer quietly derives his or her pride from an ability to produce the most bountiful yield with the minimum of extravagance. There is nothing superfluous on the ideal farm; there is no need for applied adornment, because, on a farm, like a Shaker chair, the beauty lies within the structure, in the care of the farm itself. Mr. Berry has described the Shaker style thus: "humble, impersonal, and perfect artistry, which refused the modern divorce of utility and beauty." Through their respective health, the buildings, the land, the animals, and the garden all tell the tale of the farmer's attention, and it is beautiful to see. So read the sentences of Wendell Berry. I can't imagine I'm the first to float the metaphor that his paragraphs have all the neatness of a well-planted field, ideas bursting through the topsoil, yearning toward the sunlight of our gaze, with nary a weed in sight.

In this day and age, the reading of books has possibly a greater number of easy distractions than ever before, in the ever-present availability of the Internet, not to mention our ability to actually watch films and television shows upon the small-screened devices we carry in our pockets. I especially love to read writers of serial fiction, like J. R. R. Tolkien, Laura Ingalls Wilder, or Patrick O'Brian, who continue to flesh out the world and characters in their stories over a series of books, allowing me to binge upon their work for several episodes, repeatedly forestalling the heartache that invariably descends (if the writing is good) at the end of the final page. I was to discover that the stories and novels of Mr. Berry's Port William membership fall most satisfyingly into that category.

Wendell Berry was what you might call a right smart young whippersnapper, growing up on his family's farm between Louisville and Cincinnati before leaving home to matriculate as a man of letters, first at the University of Kentucky, and then at Stanford as a Stegner Fellow, which means he was one of an incandescent group of young, revolutionary thinkers collected by Wallace Stegner; impregnable minds to whom he could teach his principles of writing. Ken Kesey, Edward Abbey, Tillie Olsen, Ernest Gaines, Robert Stone, and Larry McMurtry rounded out this astonishing, unlikely pool of talent, comprised of writers who produced a disproportionate amount of groundbreaking and incendiary work in their careers.

Following up his stint in Alameda, Mr. Berry, newly paired with a fetching young bride named Tanya, traveled to France and Italy on a 1961 Guggenheim Fellowship, where they farmed and kept house together while he continued his studies. After two years they moved back to America, settling in New York City, where, teaching at New York University, Mr. Berry was poised to become one of our nation's brightest literary talents after the publication of his first novel, *Nathan Coulter.* Everything looked as bright as one might hope, future-wise, but there was just one problem: Wendell was homesick.

It was at this juncture that Wendell and Tanya made the decision that would come to shape the rest of their lives together. In 1965 they moved their family back to Kentucky, to the farm upon which Mr. Berry had grown up. He was still fully invested in his vocation of writing; it was just that he wanted to write about the people and the land that he knew most intimately, and those subjects just simply happened to reside on the banks of the Kentucky River in Henry County. On the farm, he cultivated his tobacco crop, even as he planted words in the furrowed minds of his hungry readers, seeds of love that would take root all around the world and bear an ever-increasing yield.

I exchanged a few more letters with Mr. Berry over the years, hoping to gently convince him to let me adapt one of his stories, and then eventually I just wanted to go and work with him on his farm. Ever the gentleman, he prudently kept me at arm's length while never hurting my feelings. I continued to read everything he had written, completing his body of fiction and moving on to his essays and finally his poetry. Meanwhile, I had moved to Los Angeles from Chicago, only to discover firsthand how superficial and materialistic so much of the television and film industry were. I suppose I had known this to be the case, but I naïvely thought that I would remain somehow above the filth of commerce that so permeates the very atmosphere in that town.

By saturating myself in his words and identifying with his characters, I was able to maintain a sense of my origins, the hardworking and loving family I had left in Illinois in order to pursue my goal. Even before I got to the plain-speak of his essays, I was powerfully moved by the common sense running through his fiction. The grace and reverence with which he described hard work, the people who performed it, and the resultant satisfaction they derived from it, struck a chord within me that rang robust and true.

My own father and mother had given me these same lessons, and given them well, but the power of Wendell Berry's art reinforced them, bringing them to the forefront of my psyche. Girded by his narrative, I ceased chasing many of the minor paste-brass rings that Hollywood dangles and instead renewed my focus upon my tools, and the people in my own fellowship, to build myself a foundation upon their love.

I want to point out that this is much easier to describe now, with the clarity of twenty years' distance. At the time, I was just following my gut instinct as best I could, navigating through a haze of bourbon, striving to strike gold with the confusing balance of carpenter, actor, country lad, and clown. What I do know is that through all the distracting chatter of popular culture and sour-mash medication, I kept steadily reading these stories for the guidance with which they were laced.

For the past fifteen years, if you've had a conversation with me that ran on longer than seven sentences, then you've been told about my favorite writer, Wendell Berry, who is "this amazing Kentucky agrarian who never quit farming with horses." Thanks to my bottomless yammering, a saintly friend in Austin named Holly Sabiston—if you know her, (a) you're lucky, and (b) please buy her a cupcake—put me in touch with a pithy young filmmaker and mother of five boys (!) named Laura Dunn, who just happened to be making a documentary film about Wendell Berry.

Through Laura's generosity, and the reported approbation of Mr. Berry's granddaughters for my television show, I was put in touch with Wendell and Tanya's daughter, Mary Berry. I wish that I had saved the initial voice mail Mary left me, but, with apologies to her, I will attempt to paraphrase: "Hello, Nick. This is Mary Berry. I have to say I don't really know who you are, but my girls seem to think you hung the moon, and Laura Dunn is also vouching for you, so give me a call and we'll see if we can get you in to meet Daddy."

I'll spare you the girlish delight that flooded my beefy corps from that moment, through a most illuminating October afternoon visit, and right up until this very typing. It continues yet. Suffice it to say that Wendell and Tanya were as quietly generous with their time and their thoughts as granddaughters Emily Berry and Tanya Smith were with their giggles.

I'll only mention that the Berrys' son, Den, came through at one point (having just rehung the barn doors, naturally), and he was interested to meet me without any real awareness of my work as a song-and-dance man—he knew me from an article I had contributed to *Fine Woodworking* magazine about a shop-made router sled for flattening large slabs of wood. He had constructed and employed the jig to great effect on a book-matched ash slab for an handsome coffee table. I mention this episode because I gratefully feel that my woodworking may have legitimized me far beyond any other qualifications in the eyes of the Berrys. Just a hunch.

By the way, Laura Dunn's documentary is called *Forty Panes*, and I came on as a coproducer, which is a fancy way of saying I did a bunch of cheerleading and a bit of fund-raising. It's a very moving film about my favorite subject, upon which she did one hell of a nice job while managing five boys with her husband, Jef.

Wendell and Tanya and I spoke at length about one of his themes that drives me with constancy, that of "good work." One aspect of this topic that I often regurgitate is his dislike for a society that celebrates the notion of "Thank God it's Friday!" Taking this position, people are necessarily saying that they despise five of every seven days of their lives. He said he first noticed it when he was teaching college, that people would answer the question "How are you doing?" with "Well, pretty good, for a Monday." This exposed a joylessness that filled Mr. Berry with concern. "It's a great harbinger of what's to come. If you don't like the classes about what you're going to do, you're not going to like going to do it."

"More importantly," he said, "the collegiate system and the importance that's placed upon it has demeaned and is doing away with the trades." This is a topic of his that has always gotten me fired up. When I was in high school in the eighties, only the underachievers and burnouts were relegated to the area vocational school. It was considered a substantial demotion in life, brought on only by poor grades or attitude. "John, I don't think you have what it takes to get through trigonometry. How about we make a welder out of you?"

I was going to be headed to college because I was not planning to work in a field so low as mechanics or clothing fabrication or (forfend!) woodworking. I even worked at a couple of trades, namely, house framing and blacktopping, in order to earn money for my college education. Only later as a penniless actor would I recall the robust wages I earned at those "low" jobs, while all around me friends with degrees in everything from business to political science were earning the minimum wage as depressed baristas.

A main focus of this indecency, in Mr. Berry's view, is what this attitude has done to the small farmer. A particularly insidious American dream is being whispered into the ears of our young people as soon as they can hear a television set, that things will be better for them someplace else. It also feeds our conditioning as consumers, that we'll be happier if we can just get that new car, home, swimming pool, or wife. I was lucky to grow up in a household where that message was refuted, despite our youthful desires to honor it. The reason his writing struck me so profoundly and stays with me, unflagging, is because it's precisely what my admirable, wholesome parents taught me, just in an extremely well-written package.

Mr. Berry also had some welcome things to say about limitations. He mentioned an Amish neighbor who lived by an excellent rule: He refuses to harness a beast after supper. This regulates how much acreage he is able to farm and thereby puts a comfortable limit on himself and his family and his animals. In direct contrast to this, we were driving a couple of towns over and we had to clear well off the road while a veritable parade of John Deere combines, tractors, and wagons paraded past, looking sincerely like something out of a frightening science fiction film. These machines were the size of buildings. Wendell shook his head and said, "That's just no way to farm."

I know just what he's getting at, and yet I think we both feel for these "small" farmers who have fallen victim to a system by which they can never seem to get out in front of the corporate interests; those who sell them their seed, dominate the market, and approve them for million-dollar loans that they'll never be able to pay off. We continued driving up a lane through the woods to a venerable, solitary wooden structure. He said, "I thought you might like to see this." He thought right.

In his old barn, we guessed at the probable history of the used timbers, based upon the mortises, or "joint-holes," located in peculiar places. Wendell had a solid theory that the structural upright posts had once housed a pulley wheel, based upon the remaining joinery. In the main bay of the barn sat some disused antique tobacco equipment, including a little two-horse riding cultivator. It was a steel V with the bottom of the V pointing forward, like a skein of geese. Beneath the frame were small trowel-shaped plowing shoes, which had adjustable fixtures for angle and depth and such, with a seat on the point of the V for the driver. He said it was a McCormick-Deering, "and you'd do eight rows. There's about a thousand ways you could adjust these things to get the furrows turned just right. They would do what the old people called 'pretty work.' They'd say, 'That's pretty work.'"

I was quite taken with that. These days, who among us can say with any regularity, "That's pretty work"? The fact that most of what we do in modern America doesn't fall into that category is precisely what he's driving at in his writing. You know who does get to say it? The kids who went to vocational school. The welder, the seamstress, the cobbler, the potter. Those who work with their hands. Those who work in jobs in the only category that is so devalued that most schools in the country have fully cut their shop and home economics programs. Creating a deficiency even more elemental, our kids are no longer being taught to write in cursive. This seems so shortsighted and flatly idiotic to those of us not in love with our pocket televisions. We are being trained into a complete homogeny, and we're all just going along with it. Tanya asked me especially to point up the folly in the exclusion of this most basic life skill.

This general state of affairs was getting me down until I began touring the country as a humorist and talking about the imperative value of pursuits like knitting and boatbuilding, and I began to meet young people everywhere who were curious and excited about working with their hands. I am also encouraged by the growing locavore movement, in which small, local farm operations are being sustained by the increasing awareness of the importance of locally sourced agriculture.

At Wendell Berry's table, I said as much, that I considered myself a bit of a Michael Pollan optimist, a word choice for which I was immediately taken to task. "The programs of optimism and pessimism are cop-outs because you're taking the responsibility off of yourself to keep trying." Soundly admonished, I could only nod in agreement with his truth. He meant that in either case, you were excusing yourself from responsibility in a given situation, as in: "Well, I think everything will turn out well, so let's go watch TV," or "Nothing is possibly going to turn out well, so let's go watch TV." He also told a story about a recent community victory of which they'd been a part at the courthouse, fighting an unsavory land developer. "Usually you go in there not expecting to win, but sometimes you get a little surprise. Now, if you're an optimist, you never get a little surprise."

He said that instead of subscribing to optimism, he understands that he's *hopeful* because he knows the right work to do and he's going to do it. He went on: "I want to deal with people who are at work because they see the real reasons to be at work. That's what I call hope if they can keep going. But I keep telling young people if you get into this with the idea that you're going to win, you're not going to last. The reason to get into it is because it's right, and because it's interesting work to do, and because you're enjoying it. If you're not having any fun you better quit right now."

And his opinions aren't always popular, either. Wendell Berry is hard-core. In 1987, *Harper's Magazine* published an essay of his entitled "Why I Am Not Going to Buy a Computer." In it, Mr. Berry neatly lists the very sensible and practical reasons that he prefers to write with a pencil or pen, and then have his work typed and edited by his wife, Tanya. *Harper's* then printed a handful of letters in response to the essay, in which the writers snidely criticized Mr. Berry's position on a few counts, including some very mean comments about his "use" of Tanya. Allowing Berry to then respond to his detractors provided one of the most entertaining, and again, fairly presented, comprehensive literary drubbings I have seen. It was so enjoyable that Mike Schur, my dear friend and creator of *Parks and Recreation*, was inspired to write his lengthy senior term paper about Wendell Berry and the argument back in 1993.

In fact, knowing this about Mike, I might even go so far as to theorize that some vestiges of Wendell Berry remained with him in so meaningful enough a way as to contribute to the overall stance of my taciturn character, Ron Swanson. Consider this statement from Berry's computer essay: "A number of people, by now, have told me that I could greatly improve things by buying a computer. My answer is that I am not going to do it. I have several reasons, and they are good ones." If that's not Swansonian dialogue, then I don't know what I'm about, son.

We were talking about good work. The method of unheated debate by which Mr. Berry makes complete jackasses out of Bradley C. Johnson and James Rhoads and Nathaniel S. Borenstein is unyielding. Their insulting comments prompted Wendell Berry to call them "audacious and irresponsible gossips," which is merely his opening salvo. He then lays them out, one by one, standing firmly on the moral high ground because he speaks factually. The man does his homework and then brings simple facts to bear objectively upon his topic. It's quite clear that he's pissed, but it's amazing how he trounces their sneering opinions without ever once having to pay deference to his emotions. This is a type of good work.

In 1993 Wendell Berry published an essay entitled "Christianity and the Survival of Creation" in which he begins by stating that a pulpit "is always a forcible reminder to [him] that [he is] an essayist, and in many ways a dissenter." I find that this proclamation brings me comfort, because he's telling us that his own opinions are drawn from a well-considered personal assessment of the accepted wisdom. I am comforted that a person with the horse sense of Wendell Berry is keeping an eye on things and reporting back to us that many aspects of modern society are in serious need of rethinking. That essay, for example, is a terribly satisfying dressing-down of contemporary "big" Christianity, specifically in its tacit support of the industrial economy, which translates to a failure in honoring as God's holy creation every last bit of the natural world, even the "biting and dangerous beasts."

The sound comeuppance with which he slaps ecologically ignorant Christians about the face would also make Rocky Balboa quiver in his fancy tall boxing shoes. One of the main reasons that I am so passionate about Wendell Berry's writing is because I very strongly agree with a great many of his stances, but he is able to couch them so damn much better than I ever could. Besides his smarts and his talent and his particular combination of timing and terroir and perspective, I also believe that his thoughts are so well articulated, thanks to his understanding of pace. He has written in more than one place of the severe disadvantages brought about by our accelerated modern living.

Time was; a body either walked to town or rode at the speed of a horse. At that pace, one would have the opportunity to soak in the details all around, with all the senses coming into play. You could see past your neighbors' house into the garden and discern that they were still having worm trouble with their tomatoes. That time has long since passed, and now we travel at the speed of the automobile, hermetically sealed off from the smells and the sounds of the neighborhood, zipping along too quickly to take in much beyond the mailboxes. I am postulating that, by willfully keeping his boat pulled over in the slack water of progress, Mr. Berry has also given himself the gift of time to think things through properly and completely, in a way that the vast majority of us would find incomprehensible. The advantage he has culled by figuratively "refusing to harness a beast after supper"? That is a type of good work.

We were talking about good work. In the Christianity essay, he also tells us, "If we understand that no artist—no maker—can work except by reworking the works of Creation, then we see that by our work, by the way we practice our arts, we reveal what we think of the works of God. . . . These questions cannot be answered by thinking, but only by doing."

In his excellent book *Why We Make Things and Why It Matters*, Peter Korn makes a similarly philosophical argument for handcrafting items such as furniture. "Prior to the Industrial Revolution, virtually every object had been produced 'by hand.' Subsequent to it, making things by hand became a potentially subversive act—something one did in opposition to prevailing societal norms." Korn's thoughtful book makes a persuasive case for the ways in which we choose to make items with our hands: "The [handmade] desk is at odds with our society's rampant consumerism. It speaks of durability at a time when most goods are disposable." Then: "Furniture, after all, is more than an object of contemplation; it is a prescription for the life to be lived around it." That is certainly a type of good work.

Mr. Berry's essay "Life Is a Miracle" is rife with assertions culminating in a wary defense of the mysteries of art and of life itself. A favorite passage goes like this: "Good artists are people who can stick things together so that they stay stuck. They know how to gather things into formal arrangements that are intelligible, memorable, and lasting. Good forms confer good health upon the things that they gather together. Farms, families, and communities are forms of art just as are poems, paintings, and symphonies. None of these things would exist if we did not make them. We can make them either well or poorly; this choice is another thing we make."

However, despite the beauty of his words, his life, and his career, I believe that he would want me to urge you to refrain from running out and trying to start a farm of your own. As he put it, "For God's sake, people who know *how* to farm are failing." I used to get down on myself because the schedules in my household aren't conducive to raising even a garden, let alone a crop of more significance. We work on the road for many months out of the year, and so I could pay someone to tend my garden, but that would feel a bit too "gentleman farmer" to me. What I have realized, however, is that there is no need to be so literal with my pursuit of a Berry-infused lifestyle. I must simply look around for the patch of fecund ground that will accept my turnips (a euphemism) and grow the produce of affection where I may.

Thus, I realized that my woodshop is my garden. It is there that I am a member of a fellowship; our dusty gang of studious woodworkers work together and separately to achieve a robust harvest year in and year out. Even there I am more than half absentee, but I remain in correspondence as though they were my lifeline, because they are. Answering a question about glue choice or spline placement from afar can feed me for days. I actively pursue a continuous fidelity with my woodworkers because together we make a life of craft, in which we take raw wood and transform it into beautiful and useful implements. Chairs, ukuleles, baseball bats, canoes. I feel like what gets done at Offerman Woodshop can be considered a type of good work. I also plant my flowers in my writing and in my work as an actor, and I love to see those efforts blossom. Although, I must confess that I will always nurture a fantasy of setting up shop on a little farm one day and raising the finest bacon in the county, with a healthy crop of garlic, just like my dad's.

Mr. Berry has written a great many poems, some of which call us to action with lines like "Be joyful though you have considered all the facts," and some of which call to mind the beauty of a riverbank with its attendant leaves and birds and insects and sky and breeze, but the one I will share with you is not of that stripe. It is Wendell Berry telling the magnificent truth as only he can:

A WARNING TO MY READERS

Do not think me gentle

because I speak in praise

of gentleness, or elegant

because I honor the grace

that keeps this world. I am

a man crude as any,

gross of speech, intolerant,

stubborn, angry, full

of fits and furies. That I

may have spoken well

at times, is not natural.

A wonder is what it is.

He is eloquent, he is beautiful, and he is funny as shit. I have left out so much. There is a cornucopia of beauty and joy and mirth and tragedy and romance and charm and nature and humanity to be found in his writing. There is a bumper crop of common sense. Perhaps his greatest talent is to be found in his proclivity for telling it like it is.

As our conversation waned around the Berrys' kitchen table, Mr. Berry said, "Well, you wanna see my barn? I'll show you my barn."

I replied, "Boy, I won't turn down that invitation. But then get me out of your hair. I don't want to overstay my welcome."

He said, "All right. Well, when we get back in, you can leave."

Then we giggled.

The Legislator

10

BARNEY FRANK

I love you. You love me. We're a happy family." Would that these words were describing the slogan of our nation's population. Despite my infrequent indulgence in television, not to mention my adult age, these are the words that come to mind when I hear the name Barney, as they are the theme song from a children's television show that was so ubiquitous in the 1990s that it jumps to the fore of any associations. I also think of Barney Fife and Barney Rubble, two characters who brought me a great deal of enjoyment in my younger years, with their supporting sidekick hijinks on *The Andy Griffith Show* and *The Flintstones*, respectively.

As my adult attention, however, has been drawn (slightly) away from cartoons and ever increasingly toward the real world in which we live, a new Barney has emerged to capture my notice with his actions of a decidedly more protagonist nature. Barney Frank, an American Democrat from Massachusetts's fourth district who served in the US House of Representatives for thirty-two years (1981–2013), is considered to be our country's most prominent gay politician. As a reputation, "most famous gay politician" could be seen as a substantial bit of gossipy click-bait; really quite an attention grabber, but the charismatic thing about this redoubtable fellow is that his accomplishments speak much more loudly than his sexual orientation.

His record shows that he has been a legislator in the truest sense of the word. From the moment he arrived on the political scene in Boston in the early 1970s, he has been advocating for those positions he deemed in need of his attentions, not to mention his bulldog-like tenacity and his well-sharpened wit. Although he remained closeted about his own sexuality until 1987, Mr. Frank introduced Massachusetts's first two gay rights bills in 1973.

In May of 1980, Barney Frank won his first congressional election, gaining the seat abandoned by Father Robert Drinan when Pope John Paul II issued an order for all priests to step down from political office. Said Barney Frank, "The irony was pretty clear. I think I said at the time that apparently [papal] infallibility doesn't extend to picking members of Congress. And I've since asked people who know something about me to name the unlikeliest person in the whole world who would have wanted to make me a congressman, and very few of them get it."

Although he was still years away from coming out publicly, Mr. Frank was asked by a local LGBT rights organization if he would support a bill for gay rights, to which he said yes. Little did he suspect that he would be the solitary signee, and so he became, in one fell swoop, the instant leader of the movement for gay rights in Massachusetts and then the nation. Thank you, Holy Father.

Since then, he has remained one of the nation's leading proponents of LGBT rights. In case you are not familiar with that initialism, it stands for "Lesbian, Gay, Bisexual, and Transgender."

Please allow me to begin this particular conversation with a warning; not to you, but to myself: I would like to caution myself against becoming too emotional in my writing about discrimination against homosexuals. Something I discussed with Mr. Frank was the increasing ineffectuality of impassioned partisanship, or more simply put: shouting. In past writing, I have expressed some opinions in an emotional fashion that, while honest, I now feel to be less than the ideal volume at which to communicate if I wish the reader to remain fully open to my ideas. I have been warned. To you, dear reader, I would issue only an entreaty: Regardless of your politics, your religion, or your shoe size, please consider these following thoughts with an open mind.

Let's take a moment to examine the trait of homosexuality. I think "trait" is acceptable? A condition born of nature, like hair color or height? There's a lot of well-earned prickliness around the terminology of gay culture, since it has become such a hotly contested topic. For example, "sexual preference" is a serious no-no, since one of the ignorant claims made by the ignorant is that homosexuality is a choice rather than a natural-born state of being. It is this misconception that causes Christian organizations to suggest that homosexuals should be able to "pray the gay away," as though it was as impermanent and superficial a condition as dandruff or a sunburn, or at worst an addiction or sickness, like alcoholism. In truth, they might just as well encourage their congregants to pray away their blood types or perhaps their eye color. The cruelty of this attempted brainwashing, especially in children, is yet another factor of this conversation that makes my blood boil. Again, these groups of vicious people who profess to follow the teachings of Christ, who embarrass themselves in the arena of mercy by afflicting their followers with guilt and denial rather than embracing them, are shameful and abhorrent.

"Gay-free" churches may be the biggest asswipes under the banner of heaven (oops, there I go), but at least they are not engaging in the far more brutal discriminations that have plagued homosexuals throughout history.

It's no wonder that Barney Frank remained in the closet as he rose to prominence in his career. The America in which he lived instructed him to do just that if he hoped to advance without being unfairly persecuted because of the flavor of person he desired to kiss. For Hollywood actors and actresses, politicians, and, to some extent, professional athletes—all performers of different stripes who depend upon the approbation, adulation, or at least approval of the masses to retain any semblance of job security—the specter of open homosexuality and its concomitant disapproval presents far too great a risk.

As Mr. Frank said to me of discriminatory behavior, "I think that there are some people who genuinely don't realize that it's offensive. There are some who are just bigots who want to offend, but . . . there are some people who have been brought up this way, and they have not fully thought about the fact that it's very, very insulting." Here's the thing, team: No matter what you have been raised to believe about anyone with a sexual orientation other than heterosexual, the simple fact is that being gay is as inbred to the human being as is his or her back hair.

The only folks who seem to disagree with that statement are some sects of Christianity, who are basing their opinions upon a few Bible verses that reference sodomy. Islam also considers homosexuality a crime against Allah, but I feel like the vitriol toward same-sex marriage in this country is rather monopolized by self-professed Christians. I'm unaware of a prominent Amercian politician who is Muslim making anywhere near as much illogical noise as the likes of outspoken Republican and Tea Party politicians Ted Cruz, Sarah Palin, Rick Perry, Michele Bachmann, and Tom DeLay, who said in a 2014 interview, "I think we got off the track when we allowed our government to become a secular government. When we stopped realizing that God created this nation, that he wrote the Constitution, that it's based on biblical principles."

Now, you see, if I hadn't given myself that careful warning earlier, it's language like what Mr. DeLay said right there that would cause me to become very emotional. Even now, I can feel my knickers threatening to get themselves into a twist, but instead, I will endeavor to emulate that great practitioner of common sense, Wendell Berry. In his essay "Caught in the Middle," he describes the way in which all creatures can be considered of a kind, or kin; all members of one family, as we surely are. He tells us, "Much happiness, much joy, can come to us from our membership in a kindness so comprehensive and original. It is a shame, as I know from long acquaintance with myself, to be divided from it by the autoerotic pleasure of despising other members."

This is a very important human truth to recognize: It feels good to despise those who are different from us. It is precisely this aspect of human nature that I am trying to arrest in myself so that I may look past our differences in such policies to focus upon what it is we all *share* as Americans. Sentiments like that of Mr. DeLay, and those in agreement with his ilk when it comes to opposing same-sex marriage in our country, are flatly dehumanizing to any citizens who wish to live within a marriage and who happen to be other than heterosexual.

The sad thing is, at their core, religious writings like the Bible are founded upon beautiful wisdom and guidance for how we might live in kindness, but when such verses are appropriated by humans like DeLay to support more petty and hateful means, the original intent is not only lost, it's completely desecrated.

Mr. Frank said this to me, of religious texts: "It's very lovely what they're talking about. Sadly, an awful lot of people think [they're] a great stick to hit other people with and use as a weapon rather than a way to embrace people." He makes my point, and Mr. Berry's point, beautifully. Aren't Christians supposed to embrace people? "Love thy neighbor as thyself"? I have never witnessed as much vitriol and seething hatred in public politicking as that issuing forth from these particular Christians in regard to such issues with their "neighbors."

When Mr. DeLay, a prominent former congressperson from Texas, made that statement, he urinated on both the Bible and the Constitution. Our nation is the greatest nation on earth for exactly the opposite reason of his speech. The Constitution *protects* us from such a silly idea, so that wherever you come down on the subject of the Bible or any other religion, you will be treated with an equal amount of fairness as the next citizen. His statement is patently anti-American, as well as patently unholy. The last time I checked, the Bible was not concerned with limiting its benevolence with respect to the borders of *any* nation, including ours. This sort of absurd rhetoric strikes me as having strong similarities to the communist paranoia of McCarthyism, and the hysteria of the Salem witch trials. His stance would be laughable, if it weren't for the fact that people like him are being elected to political offices of the highest importance, where they can encourage the perseverance of discrimination.

Back to the good guy. Besides his triumphs in equal rights and financial reform (from 2007 to 2011, he also served as chairman to the House Committee on Financial Services, where he was instrumental in cosponsoring the Dodd-Frank Act of 2010), Barney Frank has also been a great champion of civil rights throughout his sixteen terms in Congress. His ability to garner deals that cross party lines has been admirable, considering the virulent bipartisanship ruling our current White House. He said that the members of Congress can be openly duplicitous depending upon when the timing of any proposed initiative relates to the timing of their primaries.

> *I had one moderate Republican; I asked him to support us on the question of protecting transgendered people against discrimination, and he said to me, "Well, if it comes up after my primary, I can probably vote with you, but if it comes up before that, I have to vote against you."*

This sense of being seen by one's constituents as strictly Democrat or Republican is an issue that has really begun to stick in my own craw. As Barney Frank tells it, "Twenty years ago, people had a common set of facts that they read. . . . They got their information generally from newspapers and broadcasts. Now the activists, left and right, live in parallel universes, which are both separate, and echo chambers for each."

This juxtaposition has occurred to me in recent years, as I have begun to feel like our politics are yet another area in which we are being trained to blindly consume the messaging that we're being fed, either by the "liberal" channels of Jon Stewart and Stephen Colbert, MSNBC and *The Huffington Post,* or conversely by the Fox News/Rush Limbaugh side of any debate. Regardless of our red- or blue-team membership, we all rather lazily follow along with what we are told to hate about the policies of the opposing side. This leaves no middle ground, which, it seems to me, is where most of life actually resides.

Because of the black-or-white commodification of our votes, candidates are no longer allowed to say, "Hey, let's stop and examine this issue" from any perspective but the far left or right. I am a great fan of the humorous news programs like John Oliver's and Colbert's, but Barney Frank makes a good point when he notices that their messaging is almost exclusively negative. Funny, yes; poignant, yes; true, yes; but is it helping us toward any progress?

There is a difference in kindness, certainly, a most substantial difference, between your John Oliver and your Sean Hannity or Rush Limbaugh: The difference is that Oliver has it. When Oliver gets loud, he does so to condemn a person's or organization's *actions*. Also, his is a comedy show, including self-deprecation, lending the silly presentation a softening quality from the get-go, which I think makes a big distinction from the right wingers who are flatly mean and vicious without humor. They are so severe about "saving our country" that their rants remind one of nothing so much as an angry child throwing a tantrum, which is often hilarious to the grown-ups around them, although we must contain our mirth lest we exacerbate their tiny tempests. Bill O'Reilly proves with ever-increasing desperation that when you take yourself that seriously, you are perceived as a joke.

But, no matter. The delivery systems of each "side" may differ in taste and decorum by a wide gulf, but their net results are similarly low when it comes to fostering progress. When we tune in to either flavor of entertainment, are any of us lending any brain power to solving these problems? Or are we a righteous, chuckling choir, pumping each our respective fists at the drubbing our "entertainer" has just delivered that asshole across the aisle? If we, all of us, just continue to call one another assholes, then what good is that doing anybody? Will we ever recognize and subsequently tire of the futility of this exercise?

As Mr. Frank points out, we used to cull our information from more unbiased sources so that we might then engage in our own conversations—millions of tiny debates on any given topic across the nation, the smallness of which allowed for the influence of local conditions. Citizens in Phoenix are going to have one opinion about Monsanto's development of GMOs, for example, while the farmers in Nebraska will have some very different things to say on the topic. Urban dwellers will invariably exhibit different needs than suburbanites whose concerns will vary from those of small, rural towns. All these disparate opinions, combined and weighed to strike a balance somewhere in the middle of our two starkly polarized parties, were once a great strength in our nation's politics, a strength that we have evidently all but lost.

On both sides of the congressional aisle, this creates a stark divisibility in which it can be hard for our legislators to find compromise. Barney Frank said, "For some politicians, one of the hardest things to do is to differ with some of the people you agree with on *most* issues on any *one* issue. And people need to learn that that's not a betrayal, because . . . if you want to agree with Stewart eighty percent of the time and Limbaugh twenty percent, people get very angry. There's no tolerance for that kind of disagreement within the faction."

He then stated that he thought we should adopt a second national anthem, at least in regard to politics: "It's all about the base."

I said, "It's all about the bass?"

He replied, "You know, 'It's all about the bass—no treble'?"

I said, "Ah, yes."

"The political song is: 'It's all about the base—no moderates.'"

Thus did this Democratic firebrand, thirty years my senior, make a clear and effective point whilst simultaneously schooling me in popular culture. I'll confess that I was rather nervous to interview him after listening to and reading several other interviews in which he nimbly demonstrated his ability to vigorously dismantle any agenda and quickly clarify the heart of any matter at hand. Part of the reason I'm typing this here book in the first place is because I have become aware of my blithe ignorance when it comes to politics and my place in them. However, once he made his "all about the bass" joke, I knew that he would be gentle with your humble pilgrim of an author.

In a 2012 issue of *New York* magazine, he said, "You know, it's the primaries: People who want to be moderate lose. And when we try to compromise, what you find is not people simply objecting to the specific terms of the compromise but the activists object even to your trying to compromise, because they say, 'Look, everybody I know agrees with us, so why are you giving in?'"

Mr. Frank feels that this extreme bipartisanship began to take root in the 1980s. The Republicans were desperate to find a pot in which to piss when Newt Gingrich took it upon himself to demonize the opposition, as a new and unscrupulous political tactic. This was followed by the right-wing takeover of the Republican party, which was followed by this red/blue bifurcation that occurred in modern communications.

The modern brand of campaigning, then, utilizing low techniques like slander and attack ads, completely distracts voters from anything resembling a productive conversation, encouraging us instead to violently back our own team, whether it's for or against the fashionable issue of the season, like gun control, immigration, health care, abortion, or same-sex marriage.

Condemnation by category is the lowest form of hatred, for it is cold-hearted and abstract, lacking the heat and even the courage of a personal hatred. Categorical condemnation is the hatred of the mob, which makes cowards brave.

This quote from Wendell Berry's essay "Caught in the Middle" seems like it could apply equally as well to this brand of political hate-mongering, as to the continuing discrimination against homosexuals in our country.

This "hatred of the mob," of which Wendell Berry writes, I think is what has begun to rankle me when it comes time to vote. With the exception of the exaggerated optimism that surrounded the first campaign of President Obama, which had less to do with tangible issues,

I think, than with his generally appealing to a Democratic idealism, when's the last time I voted for the candidate who impressed me with proactive results as opposed to the one who seemed the lesser of two evils?

Even the language behind the campaigns is a problem. The terms that surround issues of homosexuality, like "tolerance" or "defense of marriage," have done nothing to assuage my feeling that this long-running prejudice is nothing short of criminal. That any person's sexual orientation should require "tolerating" is a flagrant example of discrimination. I could sadly name a few altar boys who might have something much more tangible to say about "tolerating" the sexual orientation of their superiors in the sacristy of the church. As for the "Defense of Marriage Act," Barney Frank told me, "I asked on the floor of the House how does [a same-sex union] threaten your marriage? Anyone who's married stand up and tell me how it threatens your marriage. So one Republican got up and said, 'Well, it doesn't threaten my marriage, it threatens the institution of marriage.' I said that sounds like an argument that should be made by someone in an institution." This is splendid. As my *Parks and Rec* costar Retta would say, "Barney Frank got jokes."

The Christians who are so offended by homosexuality point to the references in the Bible wherein gay love is described as a perversion, but Mr. Berry fairly points out in "Caught in the Middle" that he can see no reason why perversion should be reserved as an indiscretion particular only to the homosexuals. It goes without saying that the condemnation of the perfectly normal lifestyle of homosexuals as a "perversion" is egregious. It again smacks of the elitism of the Manifest Destiny mentality that allows a veil of false righteousness to cloak the true brutality of a people's actions from their own self-reckoning. Vicious behavior is justified by ideas like "God's plan for the white people," or in this case, the straight people.

Further, there are plenty of legitimate perversions being enacted by straight people every day with as much gusto as anyone, rendering their complaint rather toothless, or at least powerfully hypocritical. Wendell Berry also hilariously points out that anything going on in the gay bedroom is going on in straight bedrooms as well, with interest. He asks, "Would conservative Christians like a small government bureau to inspect, approve, and certify their sexual behavior? Would they like a colorful tattoo, verifying government approval, on the rumps of lawfully copulating persons?"

I asked Mr. Frank if the climate of "tolerance"—you know what, I'm going to say equality; no, decency—if the climate of decency had changed in the halls of Congress since he voluntarily came out in 1987. He said, "To use a cliché—it's like night and day. Well, I think dawn and noon would probably be better." When he came out, he explained, his friends tried to talk him out of it, because it was assumed that his credibility and approval rating would drop through the floor. In recent years, he has seen that his homosexuality and his marriage to his husband in particular have helped him in the polls more than, say, getting the financial reform bill passed.

Like many of the indiscretions we white folks have inflicted upon groups of "others" over the centuries, discrimination against gays has some very colorful chapters historically: colors like black and blue and crimson red, primarily. Skipping past the early English punishments for "sodomy," like burning alive and hanging, let's zero in on what has been going on in modern-day America. "Sodomy" (I am putting it in quotes, because I am confused by the term. Does it refer merely to sex acts between a gay couple? Seems like a rather prurient topic for the law to concern itself with. The lady doth protest too much?), while no longer considered a capital crime, does remain an offense for which one can be imprisoned in twelve states of our nation (as of April 2014).

Okay. Let's just hang on here and remind ourselves that what we're talking about, specifically, is an act of physical love between two consenting people. In the vernacular of Mr. Berry, then, apparently twelve state governments still deign to identify *unlawfully* copulating persons.

In the year 1610, Virginia adopted Great Britain's "sodomy" laws, which basically made the act of copulation between men punishable by death. In 1777 Thomas Jefferson raised eyebrows when he proposed that the penalty for sodomy be reduced from death to castration. (I can almost hear the haters demeaning Jefferson: ". . . classic Hollywood liberal.") Of course this proposal was deemed as too lenient and so was never enacted.

America's armed forces have also been a hotbed of discrimination and controversy throughout our history. Initially, soldiers could be discharged only if witnessed in flagrante delicto, mano a mano, but after World War II, simply admitting to homosexuality became grounds enough for dismissal. The army began asking soldiers for their sexual orientation, yet another shameful example of the government sticking its nose where it didn't belong. In '53, Eisenhower, the president of the United States, *banned* gays from employment in the federal government! By executive order! And this wasn't repealed until 1975! Oh, hello, we have arrived at Barney Frank.

Now we have a little clearer idea of the guts Mr. Frank exhibited in taking up this cause for equality, even years before he himself came out. Despite the very real prejudice that existed then, and is still prevalent (although thankfully somewhat diminished) today, he didn't bat an eyelash in his pursuit of legislation that will serve us all in our continuing quest for decency. Simply, he has put up with a lot of shit in thirty-two years in the House, and he has risen above it.

Look, this job certainly didn't make any sense in terms of maximizing my income or minimizing my stress or maximizing the comfort of my life. I think it's a wonderful job to have, because I'm able to work to make fundamental changes in society and improve the quality of people's lives and eliminate and diminish unfairness at various times. If I wasn't able to do what I thought was important public policy, it would be a stupid job to have.

Mr. Frank and Mr. Berry and I all seem to agree that we humans are complicated and messy animals in many ways. It's our nature. Despite that nature, in order to fulfill our Founding Fathers' vision of a nation where no persons suffer unfair prejudice, we must find ourselves an uncomfortable place in the middle of issues. If we all can consider gay people, including lesbian and transgender folks, simply "folks," only then can we move forward with addressing all the *actual* tasks we have in front of us. More hugs, less punches.

The Artist

11

YOKO ONO

Oh, Yoko.

If any of you hear her name and think, "Oh, you mean the no-good so-and-so who broke up the Beatles?," well, let's get that cleared up right off the bat. There happen to be some incredibly satisfying accounts of the Beatles' history in book form (my favorite recently was *The Beatles: The Biography*, by Bob Spitz) that should serve to satisfyingly untangle any misapprehensions we fans might have been under in regard to the forces that actually did bring about the end of the greatest rock band in history. But before that information was available to me (or rather, I to it), as a rather simple rube pretty fresh off the sweet-corn truck from Illinois, I was certainly subscribing to that particular inaccuracy about Yoko. My beautiful bride set me straight, yet another reason they call me "the Lucky Bastard."

In 2002 Megan announced to me that we would be attending an art opening at the Shoshana Wayne Gallery in Santa Monica, California, and that the opening was for Yoko Ono. I squinted slightly and blinked a couple of times as I determined that, no, this was not some sort of uproarious ruse. "What kind of *art*?" I believe I asked. "You don't like her, do you? You know . . . the Beatles?"

Then it was Megan's turn to gauge my sincerity. She blinked thrice while inhaling, then sighed and, evincing forcible restraint, set down her spatula. She quietly said, "Her art is amazing." Then added, with defeat, "You don't know about her art?"

I hadn't known one bit. Considering all the ways in which I am still profoundly ignorant today after reading a hell of a lot of books, you can only imagine the breadth of my innocence thirteen years ago. Megan has been the most tolerant of teachers, understanding inherently that, in my case, the fruits of the tree of knowledge must be plucked, chewed, and digested but one at a time, if she wants me to keep them down. Fortunately, that night was the perfect time for some fruit.

We went to the opening early, because if you're famous, like Megan had become after four seasons of *Will & Grace* at that point, you can get into the gallery before the public for a preview, which also means you can get dibs on purchasing pieces of art, should you be so inclined, before they get scooped up. Megan is a keen art collector, so she was known to the gallerist, who in turn mentioned her to Yoko.

Well, it turns out that Yoko was a very big fan of *Will & Grace*, and so when we arrived at the preview, she was there to greet us with her son, Sean. If I was incredibly excited to meet Yoko and Sean Ono Lennon, an *amazing* musician in his own right (and a right sweetheart), then Megan was on the roof. Hell, she was over the moon. We all made pals, and Megan and I toured the collection, which included some Cloud Pieces, as well as a series of photographs of a window in her apartment at the Dakota building on Central Park.

But this was far from Yoko's first gallery showing, by forty or more years' distance. What Megan had explained to me before we arrived was that Yoko Ono had already been an iconoclastic and groundbreaking conceptual artist when she and John Lennon met in 1966. She had mounted a show in a swell-sounding pad called the Indica Gallery in London, to which John arrived (for a preview, natch), on the invitation of the gallery director, John Dunbar. Apparently, Yoko was not a fan of popular music, as she had not heard of John Lennon, but Dunbar explained that he was a rich chap who might like her work and hence buy something.

As he toured the work, Lennon noticed an apple for sale for two hundred pounds. "I thought it was fantastic," he said. "I got the humor in her work immediately. . . . There was a fresh apple on a stand—and it was *two hundred* quid to watch the apple decompose." First of all, two hundred quid in 1966 pounds was equal to about three thousand pounds in today's purse.

Second, the idea of reducing the artist's participation in the experience to the mere curating of a scenario in which the patron was paying to watch nature work one of her many miracles—in this case, rot—was indeed hilarious, but also visionary. It recalls Michael Pollan's description to me of the Chez Panisse dessert of pear and fig that could not be improved upon (see chapter 12), but in the case of Yoko's apple, one was meant to "enjoy" the fruit with eyes and nose and, of course, imagination and humor.

Now, this was getting good. The more I heard about this early brand of Yoko's mischief, the more I liked it. In the early sixties, according to Alexandra Munroe of the Guggenheim, "[Yoko] was the first artist, in 1964, to put language on the wall of the gallery and invite the viewer to complete the work. She was the first to cede authorial authority in this way, making her work interactive and experimental." (I'm a tad puzzled by Ms. Munroe's authorial redundancy, but as an aspiring student, I will let it stand, in the name of accuracy, however much it may make my cheeks blush a reddish red.)

Another piece from 1964 that is considered by some her most courageous work was called *Cut Piece*. In a more theatrical setting, it was wholly interactive; almost more performance art than a conceptual piece, in which Yoko sat, silent and unmoving, while the audience was invited to approach her and snip away at her clothing with a sizable pair of scissors. Again, for the early sixties, this was shocking material to comprehend. There's a filmed piece of it on YouTube. If you examine it, try to imagine the vulnerability and submissiveness of this tiny, young, beautiful Asian woman, allowing herself to be so subjugated in front of an audience. One young white man in particular becomes rather rapacious with his cutting, as though to say, "Well, I'll show you how this is done." The way that makes me feel: That is the artistry of the piece. Yoko has long been a master of using her skills in disparate media to leave her magic roiling, not on the wall or the stereo, but within the brain and heart of the receiver.

Megan and I recently saw the excellent documentary *Marina Abramović: The Artist Is Present* (highly recommended), in which Ms. Abramović is described as "the grandmother of performance art." Megan exclaimed, and said, "Make sure you put it in your chapter that Yoko was doing *Cut Piece* a decade before Marina even started!" Perhaps, then, Yoko could be considered the great-grandmother of the medium.

The omission seemed too obvious to be accidental, but perhaps it occurred partially due to the world's inability to put a label on the many varied disciplines of Yoko's art. While Abramović is specifically a "performance artist," Yoko Ono defies any one moniker. According to the Guggenheim's Munroe, "What makes her so slippery is that she is so wide-ranging. She is a musician and a poet, a peace activist and a performance artist, a maker of objects and a conceptual artist— and married to John Lennon."

Speaking of John, let's get back to their first meeting. There was one more item in that Indica Gallery show, the description of which incited me to immediate Yoko discipleship, and it happens to have been the artwork that hooked John Lennon as well, so let's let him describe it: "There was another piece that really decided me for-or-against the artist: a ladder which led to a painting which hung on the ceiling. It looked like a black canvas with a chain with a spyglass hanging on the end of it. I climbed the ladder, you look through the spyglass and in tiny little letters it says 'Yes.' So it was positive. I felt relieved. It's a great relief when you get up the ladder and you look through the spyglass and it doesn't say 'No' or 'Fuck you' or something. It said 'Yes.'"

When I heard about that historic moment from 1966 London thirty-seven years later? Christ, *I* fell in love with her. To me, this anecdote sums up what I most admire about Yoko: her positivity. The spirit of everything she has created, and continues to create, is swaddled in an unmitigated message of, quite simply, love. In the name of love, she perpetually challenges us to reexamine the dogmatic thinking of our time, to expand our emotional capabilities beyond the mediocre level of decency to which we've acquiesced.

Quite possibly the greatest artistic couple in the past century had met and begun to recognize the magic between them. John would never be the same, certainly, but in fairness, how could we ever blame Yoko for John's subsequent maturation? When anybody falls under the sway of true love, what use can there be in blaming the beloved? If you're an ardent fan of John, Paul, George, and Ringo, then the supposition that Yoko could have caused the Beatles' breakup, even indirectly, doesn't actually make much sense. Particularly in the case of John, who was nothing if not an intensely discriminating individualist. That one of his life choices was to be with Yoko at that point was certain, but *their* relationship's blossoming had considerably less to do with the Beatles' disbanding than John's own relationship with his mates.

John said, "That was it. The old gang of mine was over the moment I met her. I didn't consciously know it at the time, but that's what was going on. . . . That was the end of the boys, but it so happened that the boys were well-known and weren't just the local guys at the bar." To accuse him of the pithless character that would have been required to in any way let "Yoko break up the band," as though he had no free will to divorce himself from them of his own accord, is seriously demeaning to the man we reportedly admire so. Those of us who have chosen domesticity (a wise choice) have all been there. You sacrifice the pub, as it were, for the household.

The most explanatory but seldom mentioned fact is that the Beatles were simply done. They had created a gorgeous collection of music together, a prolific body of work that altered the landscape of music and, arguably, Western culture, more expansively than anything since the printing press. The creative flame of the collective had burned terrifically bright and then, having consumed its fuel, gone dark. How can we complain at the duration of the candle's life when what remained was the best bunch of records ever cut by four cute white boys?

As significant as the Beatles were, it turned out that John had even bigger fish to fry. With all their work as "passive activists," John and Yoko cleverly began using their fame as just another medium in which to practice creativity. Their campaign "War Is Over! If You Want It" was born of their antiviolent contribution to the national protests against the Vietnam War. Aware that their wedding would bring with it a tsunami of press attention, the couple took the opportunity to shift the focus to their experimental protest efforts in the name of peace.

In 1969, as the conflict raged in Vietnam, Yoko and John staged two "bed-ins" from their hotel rooms in Amsterdam and Montreal. The "bed-in" (a humorous take on the more traditional sit-in, in which protestors camp out at a location until they are either arrested or evicted, or, conversely, their demands are met) simply involved the press entering the couple's hotel room, where they conducted all-day press conferences on exploring new methods of cultivating world peace. John later said of these, "It's part of our policy not to be taken seriously. Our opposition, whoever they may be, in all manifest forms, don't know how to handle humour. And we are humorous."

I can't help but cite the similarity to these lines from Wendell Berry's "Manifesto: The Mad Farmer Liberation Front":

As soon as the generals and the politicos
can predict the motions of your mind,
lose it. Leave it as a sign
to mark the false trail, the way
you didn't go. Be like the fox
who makes more tracks than necessary,
some in the wrong direction.

Yoko and John's ideas were indeed simultaneously funny and inspiring. They introduced a new methodology called "Bagism," which entailed a person covering his or her entire body in a cloth bag, so that they would be perceived by others without regard to appearance, race, sexuality, hair length, age, habiliments, etcetera. The use of the bag would free the public from the influence of stereotyping and its resultant prejudices. Pretty hilarious but also true.

Another gesture from this period in 1969 that I find very touching was when Yoko and John sent a gift of acorns to the heads of state from fifty countries, asking them to plant the acorns as a symbol of peace. The couple had such an excellent attitude about addressing the political entities that engaged our nations in "warfare" then, as does Yoko still to this day, although I have to put "warfare" in quotes, since we have relegated the inaugural American foreign policy of "justified fair fighting" to the distant past. (Now we are fed the softening line that we're engaged in "policing actions," as though that makes the victims on both sides any less dead.)

In a substantial way, John and Yoko were the forerunners of today's best source for open-minded news: the comedy news program. Let's face it—the state of our nation's decency is an absolutely shameful mess. It's become perfectly clear that our democracy is being run, not by the people it supposedly represents, but by the corporations who control the vast majority of those people, as well as the vast majority of the nation's wealth.

Meanwhile, as we discussed in chapter 10, those of us who don't necessarily agree with the McDonald's ads telling us that they "love to see us smile" have come to depend upon the comedy of Jon Stewart and Stephen Colbert and John Oliver, and others of their redoubtable ilk, to deliver our "news"; polarized medicine prescribed with a spoonful of ribald sugar, in a fashion that is approximately 87 percent more truthful than that of the straight news channels. As John Lennon (and Yoko) deduced, "Now I understand what you have to do: Put your political message across with a little honey."

The billionaire Koch brothers recently announced their projection to spend 889 million dollars on the campaigns of their candidates for the 2016 presidential elections. Has it come to this? The corporate interests are now so cavalier that they can publicly, *preemptively* announce the magnitude of their influence on our supposedly "democratic elections"? Jon Stewart, on *The Daily Show*, suggested that we should just give up the ruse and elect the money itself as president. As hilarious as that joke is, it's even sadder in the amount of truth it contains.

John and Yoko set an admirable precedent in the humor they brought to the proceedings surrounding the public treatment of the Vietnam "conflict." Their "War Is Over! If You Want It" serves as a constant reminder to us that we don't have to be a part of this nefarious system. To this day, you can visit the movement's website and print up posters and download computer wallpapers of the slogan in more than a hundred languages. Yoko has also recently given her blessing to a feminist movement that has appropriated the phrase for a campaign to further support women's reproductive rights in particular called the "War on Women Is Over! If You Want It."

So, given my appreciation for her art and her message, I became absolutely hooked on Yoko. A most beautiful spirit, she won me over with the empathetic envelope pushing she has practiced as a vocation for the past fifty-five or sixty years. Megan and I had such a lovely time meeting her and Sean, and we have been most gratified when our lives have brought us back into her orbit, which eventually, as fate would have it, brought us to the threshold of the Dakota.

Also known as the apartment building in which *Rosemary's Baby* is set, the Dakota is where John and Yoko lived together when he was tragically gunned down by Mark David Chapman on the night of December 8, 1980. Rereading the events of that night has been emotionally harrowing, but one fact stood out to lighten the burden: Several witnesses at Roosevelt Hospital, where Lennon had been rushed after the shooting, reported that at the moment Lennon's death was pronounced, the Beatles' "All My Loving" coincidentally came floating over the hospital's sound system: a small flower blooming in the carnage of the battlefield.

Here my ignorance cropped up once again. We were invited to have dinner with Yoko, and only upon our arrival at the Dakota doorway where John Lennon had been shot did I realize the enormity of the fact that Yoko never left. After fourteen or fifteen years together as a prolific artistic couple in a marriage that pursued mirth in the service of humanity perhaps more than any conjoined man and woman in the modern era, Yoko had lost her other half. And she didn't just lose him but witnessed him torn from her in a most unspeakably violent manner.

Now, here is the thing about Yoko that blows my mind. She suffered the murder of her husband and, more, her partner in their life's work: to promote the ideals set forth in his song "Imagine," easily the most profoundly beautiful piece of song writing in history. That Yoko, after grieving, simply picked up her figurative picket sign and stayed staunchly true to the course that she and John had been sailing strikes me as supremely heroic. She did not flag nor fumble. She has carried on, utilizing the tools and resources at her disposal to continue the life's work that she and John began together.

Many wonderful songs have been written encouraging us to be nice to our fellow people, but "Imagine" stands alone in its social penetration and relevance. "I hope someday you'll join us. And the world will be as one." John wrote the song, but it held the message they both shared. Just the simple phrase "Imagine Peace," another slogan that has served as a sort of figurehead for so many of Yoko's efforts, is such an effective message of positive thinking, when held up against the less effectual ilk of "No Nukes" or "Make Love, Not War." The suggestive nature of the command "Imagine" allows the recipient to

quietly choose to follow the directive or not, of his or her own voli-
tion, in the privacy of the mind; a contest that is more likely to see a
gradual and passive victory when compared to the number of people
swayed by something more like, "Stop that!"

Yoko and John, when he was with us, always managed to make
sense. Their activism has always had a charismatic quality of brattiness to it, but at the same time, they had done their homework. They
weren't just getting attention; they were *drawing* our attention to
whichever simple message upon which they wanted us to focus.

When Nixon was scared of John in the early seventies, frightened
that his popularity might actually create an antiwar groundswell that
would see tricky Dick lose the upcoming 1972 election, he denied
John a green card and insisted he be deported. Among the many
methods John and Yoko employed to combat this treachery was their
invention of a new country, one from which they were simply the
visiting ambassadors. The country's name, according to Yoko? "Nutopia. We announced the founding of a new country called Nutopia at
a press conference. The flag was the white flag of surrender, and there
is a photo of John and I waving the white flag."

In the thirty-five years since John's assassination, Yoko has not
wavered in her mission to communicate a message of love and peace
to the entire planet, utilizing a variety of creative channels. The Guggenheim's Munroe said, "The sheer breadth of her output has taxed
curatorial and critical skills. [Her] originality cannot be underesti-
mated, even though it has often been unrecognized."

Around the time that John first met Yoko, she had conceived of a project that she called a "light house." This was a hypothetical structure that would be ephemerally constructed of only beams of light emanating from prisms. John got wind of this idea and asked her over to his place for some luncheon (perhaps a bagism lunch?). He asked Yoko if she would consider a commission to build her "light house" in his garden.

"Oh, that was conceptual," Yoko answered him. "I don't know how to do it."

For all these many years, Yoko Ono has been weaving webs of whimsy and compassion in front of our eyes, leaving the eventual outcome up to us and our willingness to see the gossamer wisps that trail her limbs as they arc through life. We are free to see, or at least imagine them. On the day we met Yoko, we bought a framed piece of eggshell paper upon which was written in her delicate hand:

KITE PIECE

Enlarge your photographs.

Make many kites with them and fly.

When the sky is filled with them, ask people to shoot.

You may make balloons instead of kites.

We also purchased one of the shuttered-window pieces. The series could be arranged so that the shuttered window slowly opened, revealing the sky and Central Park out her bedroom window at the Dakota, or the order could slowly bring the shutters together, representing the end or birth of day, or season, or life. The interpretation of the chiaroscuro was, and is, as with all Ono creations, up to the individual viewer.

In 2007, possibly Yoko's greatest masterpiece was unveiled in Reykjavik, Iceland. According to its press release, *Imagine Peace Tower* is "a tower of light which emanates wisdom, healing and joy. It communicates to the whole world that peace & love is what connects all lives on Earth." This outdoor work of art, conceived by Yoko, was first illuminated upon the sixty-seventh anniversary of John Lennon's birth. Every year it is fired up on John's birthday, October 9, and it remains visible until the anniversary of his death on December 8. The tower of light projects upward out of a wishing well, upon which are inscribed the words *"Imagine Peace"* in twenty-four different languages. She finally managed to create John's "light house" for him.

About to turn eighty-two at the time of this writing, Yoko, I believe, may be kicking more ass today than ever before. She played the Glastonbury Festival last year with the Plastic Ono Band. She recently collaborated with Lady Gaga and Wayne Coyne of the Flaming Lips. She and her son, Sean, seem to be everywhere on the planet at once, raising money in benefit concerts for, among others, Japanese earthquake and tsunami victims, groups that are fighting the environmental abomination of fracking in the United States, and typhoon victims in the Philippines. She is hauling *and* whupping ass like a rock-and-roll ninja lady, dispensing wisdom freely like a sexy Asian Gandalf. She doesn't expect it, but she certainly deserves our reverence.

John Lennon called her "the world's most famous unknown artist. Everyone knows her name, but no one knows what she actually does"—a pretty astute observation from her life's partner, then and now. Asked in an interview with Daniel Rothbart what "is [her] most important legacy?," Yoko replied, "They're going to make it up anyway and I hope they're a little bit kinder to me than now. But I don't believe in the legacy so much. If my work is going to give people inspiration, encouragement, and joy after I pass away, then that's beautiful, and I'm thankful. If it does that's fine and if it doesn't I can't complain, that's fine too."

Oh, Yoko. I know we're all human beings, and so, by definition, we can't always be as mellow as that particular piece of erudition, but I am delighted that you sent it into the world for us to absorb in the hope that we'll see our way to imagining a little more peace.

Let us relish this benediction from Yoko Ono with a final flourish of the heart:

"A dream you dream alone is only a dream. A dream you dream together is reality."

The Sleuth

12

MICHAEL POLLAN

One of my favorite qualities in this delicious life is serendipity. The interconnectedness of the myriad facets of the world never ceases to delight me. All it takes is a bus driver in Tuscaloosa to put on Tom Waits's "Lucky Day" or I discover that David Trachtenberg, the top-drawer film editor of both *Casa de Mi Padre* and *Me and Earl and the Dying Girl* (two films I'm in), is best friends since childhood with American hero Tom Magill, who was the A-camera operator and then director of photography for seven seasons of *Parks and Recreation*, a television program upon which I was also an actor. The world grows ever smaller, but I can't help suspect there is some magic in play as well.

One unexpected hub has turned out to be Michael Pollan. I earlier mentioned the swell author Witold Rybczynski, whose Olmsted book got me off and running on a few more of his titles, neatly followed, thanks to Amazon, by Michael Pollan's *A Place of My Own*. Now, I would strongly encourage you to read all his books, and to do so in order if you can. They work wonderfully on their own in any order, but I really appreciate the train of thought traveling through his body of work. Olmsted got me to Rybczynski, who got me to Pollan. There will be more to come.

A Place of My Own is Michael's recounting of the planning and construction of a one-room writing studio in the woods behind his house in Connecticut. If you know me at all, you know I'm sold on just that log line right there; no pun intended. Like Rybczynski and Bryson and some of my other favorite writers, Mr. Pollan delves into the anthropology of why we funny Homo sapiens build things, and then describes the ups and downs of trying his own hand at such an undertaking (he puts it, his own two "unhandy hands").

Well, I was smitten. Michael Pollan has a very friendly yet intelligent and deeply researched style that renders any topic quite gripping. For example, if you were to try to pitch me a book about any writer building a cabin, I might rather just build the cabin. However, in those "unhandy" hands, the subject matter takes on a charm and a glow that lends a great deal of charisma to the given topic.

After *A Place of My Own*, Pollan's focus turned to different aspects of food writing, and he penned important popular tomes such as *The Botany of Desire*, *The Omnivore's Dilemma*, *In Defense of Food*, and *Cooked*, among others. He doesn't just drily write about food or a cabin or flowers; he tells us what it is about these subjects that makes them so irresistible to humans. In *The Botany of Desire*, he explores the relationship between humans and plants, specifically the apple, the tulip, the potato, and marijuana, unveiling the ways in which these four plants have made themselves desirable to humans, and therefore have become indispensable to us. It's a fascinating look at the interconnected evolution of the plant and animal kingdoms. His work in

general explores the manner in which things like cooking and cultivating and nature are invariably intertwined with our human lives,
quite often for the better.

But back to serendipity. It turns out Michael Pollan was an executive editor of *Harper's Magazine,* the very one behind the Wendell Berry
typewriter essay/letter campaign hilarity. I only just learned this when
I sat down to lunch with him at one of his favorite restaurants, Berkeley's superb Chez Panisse (famously delicious farm-to-table grub). I had
known that Pollan was a fan of Wendell Berry's when Mr. Berry published a collection of older essays centered around his illuminating
instructive phrase "Eating is an agricultural act." Michael Pollan wrote
the introduction to this collection, which caused me to think, "Oh,
swell. These two writers whom I love have become buddies." I suppose
that was true, in the sense that Michael's work had brought him into a
more direct correspondence with Wendell, as though he had been promoted to a rank something closer to General Berry in the army of
agrarian thinkers. Perhaps "Colonel Pollan."

We met upstairs, which is the more casual half of the restaurant,
as evidenced by Mr. Pollan's short pants. We shook hands and he hit
me with the blinding display of teeth that caused Wendell Berry, a
few weeks later, upon hearing that I had interviewed Michael, to ask
with an impish look in his eye, "He still grinnin'?" Mr. Pollan handed
me an inscribed copy of *A Place of My Own,* asking if I had heard of it.
He was surprised to hear it had been my first Pollan text, as he
explained that it was his slowest seller. So, ladies and gentlemen, do
please purchase that one first. Full-price hardback is the way to go,
and you know, books also make great gifts.

Within minutes of sitting down, I mentioned George Saunders as one of my subjects, whose incredible *Tenth of December* I had just read on the plane, and Michael was very excited because he had also just read it and had some very astute things to say about Saunders's incisive ability to satirize our society in a terrifying way, while simultaneously making us laugh until our guts hurt. More on him in chapter 18.

Michael ordered the soup and the eggplant entrée, and I got the garden lettuces and the pork. The food was exquisite, but incredibly clean and honestly presented. Mr. Pollan's pal Alice Waters, star chef and author, and proprietor of Chez Panisse, has been advocating for forty years her philosophy that cooking should be based on the finest and freshest ingredients that are produced locally and sustainably. It shows. Michael pointed out that diners sometimes complain about the relative simplicity of the dishes, because of all the plaudits the restaurant has received, and I replied, "That's America. If somebody says it's 'good,' then it must be big and fancy. This just looks like pork!" (Note to chefs: Please stop with the salmon mousse.)

Obviously, Wendell Berry dominated the early conversation. In his introduction to *Bringing It to the Table*, Michael adroitly points out that a lot of the great "new" ideas in his own writing were questions that had been posited by Wendell Berry a couple of decades earlier; it's just that not enough people were listening. What initially inspired Pollan was actually some Berry gardening wisdom, and of course the *Harper's* typewriter broadside, but upon later rereading, he was agog at the number of notions in his own work that had been previously framed in some way by Wendell Berry and Berry's own predecessors, such as Sir Albert Howard, the British botanist and organic food pioneer who died in 1947.

Fortunately for us, seeing his feelings and thoughts echoed by earlier thinkers only redoubled Michael Pollan's interest in the relationship between us, as eaters, and our food. The biological, botanical, and sociological investigations he had already undertaken in his first (gripping) books served as the perfect foundation upon which to erect the tower of food conversation in his four later books.

We spoke more of Wendell Berry and of the quality and flavor of the Chez Panisse offerings. I revealed that I was terribly excited to meet Mr. Berry, a man whom I so admired, except there was one thing that had me scared shitless. Wendell Berry had agreed to speak with me for my second book, and so etiquette demanded that I send him my first book, so he would have the opportunity to see what I was about. Well, if you've read my first book, you'll understand that while the idea of Wendell Berry reading most of its contents would make me proud, there are some rather ribald portions that I feared would offend even a reasonable sailor, let alone this paragon of decency.

Michael grinned and said that he understood my point of view but that I might be surprised. "Sometimes Wendell writes like a preacher, but I think he can appreciate every side of a story." For the record, I took my book to Kentucky with me and handed it to Tanya Berry, Wendell's wife, upon our meeting, along with the tribute of nice Colonel Taylor bourbon that had also been at the suggestion of Mr. Pollan. I did, however, ask her not to read it. Or rather, I warned her that it contained some blue material. If they have read it or not, I have as of this writing received no report. I sincerely hope from their silence that it didn't kill them.

As I have earlier noted, Wendell Berry has achieved his particularly conscious perspective from remaining geographically within his farm, and his farming, for a lifetime. This has allowed him, and his talent for patient observation, to notice all the negligent, blind running our society has been doing dead in the wrong direction. Michael Pollan has lit his torch, partly from Mr. Berry's flame, and brought the conversation down from the mountain into the trenches, where we are all huddled over our smartphones.

Here's what I love about Mr. Pollan: In a time when we civilians are slowly waking, as if from a Twinkie dream, to the reality of what corporate interests have been feeding us—and we have been willfully and ignorantly swallowing, literally and figuratively, for decades— here is a scientifically minded, affable writer who is doing all the research I wasn't even aware I had been wishing someone would do. He has connected the dots for us in a deeper way than the others, partially because he is one of us. Michael Pollan is the nicest valedictorian that ever went to school, because he has done all the homework, *and* he's letting us copy down his notes with impunity.

My best friend, Pat Roberts, without whom I would be lost, has an attractive touch of the conspiracy theorist about him (I am not saying he's not a Freemason). Among the many tips he has given me over our years together, for seeing through the fog of bullshit with which "they" have so artfully covered our eyes and ears, is a documentary called *The Century of the Self*, by Adam Curtis, and a terrifying/infuriating book entitled *Lethal but Legal*, by Nicholas Freudenberg.

The "they" to which I am here referring are the corporations behind food and beverage, tobacco, alcohol, firearms, pharmaceuticals, and automobiles. In *Lethal but Legal*, Freudenberg solidly details the manner by which this group, the "corporate consumption complex," circumvents decency entirely by controlling legislation pertaining to the harmful effects of all these products. American lobbyists (I wonder if any of them are white dudes?) have been shaping governmental policy for decades in a way that allows harm to the health of millions of us sheep, while lining their pockets.

How did this happen? We have certainly been asleep at the wheel, allowing our complacency to seep into every aspect of our lives, where it has taken root with tenacity. Wendell Berry sounded the alarm forty years ago. Eric Schlosser, author of *Fast Food Nation*; Morgan Spurlock, director of *Super Size Me*; and their ilk rerang the bell more than a decade ago. Slowly we have blinked our eyes open, even as we slowly chew our Western Bacon Cheeseburgers, and said, "Oh. Oh, wow. I have a mouthful of garbage." If you're anything like me, you think, "I really have to stop eating this," while taking another bite. We're in trouble, folks.

In his introduction to *The Century of Self*, Adam Curtis states, "This series is about how those in power have used Freud's theories to try and control the dangerous crowd in an age of mass democracy." I was particularly astonished by the work of Edward Bernays, nephew of Sigmund Freud, who brought his uncle's theories to bear upon the public with immediate results. Contracted by the tobacco industry in the early twentieth century to disarm the taboo against women smoking in public, Bernays created a public event at the 1929 New York City Easter Parade. At a preordained time, several debutantes on a float pulled out cigarettes and brazenly fired them up, as forewarned paparazzi snapped their photographs.

The next day, the public was shocked to see the headlines referring to the young ladies and their "Torches of Freedom." This maneuver was entirely successful for a couple of reasons: In later interviews, Bernays explained that he simply applied Freudian psychology to the situation, giving women the sense of having "a penis of their own" to brandish, a powerful incentive given the women's suffrage movement afoot at the time. Even more nefarious, the term "Torches of Freedom" pandered to the public's sense of patriotism, so that if one were to disagree with the idea of women smoking, one could be accused of un-American sentiments. Bernays had practically written the Fox News playbook in one fell swoop.

Our nation had come into a time of manufacturing prosperity heretofore unseen, with a surplus of products available for purchase but a frugal populace that pinched every penny. Edward Bernays was determined to convince people that purchases would make them "feel better," and one of his investors, Paul Mazur of Lehman Brothers, said, "We must shift the focus of advertising from 'needs' to 'desires.' People must be trained to desire; to want new things even before the old has been consumed."

I don't know about you, but I find that information and its clearly successful execution horrifying. Our national obesity and diabetes epidemic, our death rates due to alcohol, tobacco, and automotive- and gun-related incidents, have been ushered along by our friendly corporations entirely on purpose. In 1927, an unnamed journalist said, "A change has come over our democracy, and it is called 'consumptionism.' The American citizen's first importance is no longer that of citizen, but that of consumer." In 1927! That's sixty years before Rogaine even showed up, and forty years before the advent of Doritos! By God, they had our number.

By now, food companies have our string-pulling down to a science. A vast array of popular products on the grocery store shelves and the drive-through menu are engineered to be light on the health and heavy on the flash. Delicious flavor powder! New color, now even greener! Wait'll you get a load of the aromatic gases emanating from these microwavable food envelopes! Advertising has become pure psychology, tugging at our long-conditioned desires. Some modern classics are the McDonald's campaign that gives us images of happy families and their pets, running in the yard and playing sports, to the sugary refrain of "I'm lovin' it," or "We love to see you smile." I fear they may have mistaken my grimace of intestinal discomfort for a smile, but I suppose that's forgivable given the vast viewing distance from the bank all the way to which they have laughed. It now occurs to me that they are merely referring to themselves when they intone, "I'm lovin' it," as they watch us mindlessly gobble those irresistible fries and deep-fried chicken clumps.

"So now what, dumbass?" I ask myself. That's where Michael Pollan's entertaining and illuminating road maps come in. In *The Omnivore's Dilemma*, he breaks down four different meals for us, spanning the spectrum of purity from an entirely fast-food meal to a meal comprised only of ingredients grown, hunted, or foraged. In between, he goes into gratifying detail about what items in the grocery store bear any resemblance to what their labels tell us, and how Freudenberg's "corporate consumer complex" has even commandeered our formerly trusted descriptors like "organic" and "natural." Just the long list of products in the store that are made with high-fructose corn syrup is a staggering wake-up call.

Mr. Pollan can take a complicated biological subject, like how stupid it is to feed corn to cattle, and lay it out for us in digestible layers: Our country had a postwar surplus of corn. The excess corn was fed to cattle. Cattle are literally not built to digest corn, because they are ruminants (they have a "rumen," or extra stomach, for digesting plants that carnivores can't), so corn makes them sick. The beef industry, instead of putting an end to the corn diet, just shoots the factory cows full of drugs to keep them alive long enough to harvest their beef.

This is obviously an oversimplified summation of only one of the many revelatory topics delivered in Pollan's writing, but it should give you the gist. I'd love to see a statistic here in 2015 of how many restaurants and butchers are now touting their grass-fed beef as opposed to corn-fed, thanks to Michael Pollan's benign whistle-blowing. I have recently eaten in classic steakhouses in Indiana and California whose menus were still loudly advertising the "finest in corn-fed steer meat."

Five minutes of research into factory farming will immediately turn your stomach and reveal to you the filthy, and simply evil, production methods of most of our country's meat products: beef, pork, chicken, eggs, salmon, trout, and more. We have allowed these abominations to occur, and we continue to support them through lazily ignoring the truth. Mr. Berry, Mr. Pollan, and others have given us no excuse to remain in our passive denial.

Both of these writers speak very plainly and effectively about the heavy-handed bullying that agri-giants like Monsanto and Cargill have employed in order to legalize their genetically modified organisms, also known as GMOs. Even the acronym seems unscrupulous, its initials softening the creepy science-fictional quality of an organism that has been genetically modified. The truth that Mr. Pollan makes quite plain, that seems to me the point to which attention should be paid, is that these organisms have not been genetically modified to make our food *better*. Is that not the bottom line? Shouldn't a food company succeed because they strive to make *good* food? That these global corporate monoliths have forced these aberrances upon us for profit alone seems inarguable. This is not the first time that man- and womankind have thought they might prosper by outsmarting nature. The Greeks have plenty to tell us in their dramas about hubris, and I'm afraid that historically things don't ever turn out well for the guy or gal, flying too close to the sun, or inventing a "better" corn seed.

We were doing so well just a few generations ago. Among his rules for eating, Michael Pollan tells us to "avoid anything your grandmother wouldn't recognize as food." As I learned from his *In Defense of Food*, in 1977 Senator George McGovern headed up a Senate Select Committee on Nutrition and Human Needs, and they discerned that the solution to America's growing epidemics of diet-related illness could be alleviated if we would consume less meat and dairy. Simple and good, right? Apparently not if you were McGovern's cattle-ranching constituents in South Dakota. They led a firestorm of criticism that caused the committee to reword their guidelines in much softer language, meat-wise, and soon saw McGovern ousted.

Remember the Oprah Winfrey burger debacle of 1998? In the throes of fear over mad cow disease, she merely stated that a guest's remarks about mad cow "just stopped me cold from eating another burger." A group of Texas beef producers sued Oprah under Texas's False Disparagement of Perishable Food Products Act of 1995. Of course, the Texans had their asses handed to them, but to me, the case begs the question: Why would you ever need to enact such a state law in the first place, unless there was something unseemly in your methods? The specter of mad cow had been raised because the factory farmers were feeding their beef cattle *ground-up dead beef cattle*. This is the fact that had these "ranchers" taking the moral high ground? Michael Pollan puts it into perspective very succinctly with his adage, "You are what you eat eats."

In 1910 Theodore Roosevelt spoke at the dedication of the John Brown Memorial (and I am most definitely not saying Brown was not a Freemason). Roosevelt said, "It is necessary that laws should be passed to prohibit the use of corporate funds directly or indirectly for political purposes; it is still more necessary that such laws should be thoroughly enforced. Corporate expenditures for political purposes, and especially such expenditures by public service corporations, have supplied one of the principal sources of corruption in our political affairs." In 1907 the Tillman Act had been signed into law to curtail the very corruption of which number twenty-six spoke, but no federal committee was ever enacted to enforce the new legislation.

Michael Pollan is one of the key investigators today, pointing out the direct effects of this malfeasance running rampant in the aisles of our grocery stores. Food corporations are aware of the harmful effects of their products, so they muscle legislation into existence so that nobody is allowed to say that their food is unhealthy? We are dietetically mired in a morass of advertising falsehood, when all we want to do is feed ourselves and our families delicious and healthy comestibles. How do we get back to the kind of eating wherein good health is simply a matter of course? Pollan tells us, in no uncertain terms. From *In Defense of Food*: "If you're concerned about your health, you should probably avoid products that make health claims. Why? Because a health claim on a food product is a strong indication it's not really food, and food is what you want to eat."

As we were finishing up our delicious chat at Chez Panisse, a restaurant that it seems like Alice Waters started in 1971 just to wait for Michael Pollan to arrive and champion it, the waiter asked if we would like dessert. I scrutinized the menu and declared that I really shouldn't have dessert with lunch, but for the sake of research, I had better order the Epicenter Orchards Apple and Huckleberry Galette with Vanilla Ice Cream. Michael generously offered to help me out with it, and we ordered coffee (for me) and tea (for him) as well.

Just then, the waiter brought out the first dessert on the menu, charismatically entitled A Bowl of Bob's Black Mission Figs and Frog Hollow Farm Warren Pear, as though it's nomenclature had been penned by Mark Twain for a café at Disneyland. Michael said, "Look at this. This bowl is absolutely just simple fruit; it's the ultimate Chez Panisse creation. What they're saying is, 'We can't improve on this.' Some of it's not even cut up . . . it's just *curated*." We shared the fruit, and it was sublime. I mentioned that it reminded me of a recurring theme in the woodworking we do at my shop, particularly with the slab tables: We try to inflict as little ornamentation as possible upon the wood, oil it and polish it, and get out of the way of Mother Nature. Like George Nakashima, of whom you may soon read (in chapter 15).

"Oh, I love Nakashima," replied Michael Pollan. "My parents own a bunch of his pieces." O the serendipity. Hilariously, in fact, Michael remembered going to Nakashima's studio as a kid, and while George sketched ideas for his folks' furniture needs and they browsed among the stacks of slabs to find just the right piece of walnut for their dining room, Michael ran around bored with Nakashima's son, Kevin.

Michael said that he understood my comparison of Nakashima to Chez Panisse: "You're describing the philosophy of this restaurant. If they get the right ingredients, cooking's not an issue." He tells us in his essay "Unhappy Meals": "Even the simplest food is a hopelessly complex thing to study, a virtual wilderness of chemical compounds, many of which exist in complex and dynamic relation to one another." In fact, that too sounds just like the woods we use in my shop. "Fine woodworking" comprises a set of techniques shaped around a respect for the unpredictable and sometimes downright ornery behavior of wood. We know that wood is an organic compound, made up of cells that can behave in mysterious ways, and so we join pieces of the compound together by methods that pay respect to that misbehavior.

When it comes to knowledge, again, I feel that we have been seduced into thinking that total comprehension is possible, because we have on our phones instant access to more *information* than we can cognitively handle. But there is a huge difference between information and knowledge. Tanya Berry said to me that she finds it upsetting nowadays when people look into their phones in the middle of a conversation, first because it's rude, but second because anytime there is a question, people will now just Google the answer. Wendell chimed in and added, "They're losing the ability to use those three beautiful words: *I don't know.*"

Wendell Berry snagged this inbound 1945 quote from Sir Albert Howard, tossed it to Michael Pollan, who then passed it along to me via his writing, and now I'm lobbing it to you, in the hope that you'll resoundingly dunk it through the hoop of public clarity, over the outstretched hands of FDA befuddlement: that we would do well to regard "the whole problem of health, in soil, plant, animal, and man as one great subject." With that wisdom in place, I vote that we try to simplify things as much as possible, starting with our food purchases. Another bon mot from Michael Pollan's deep well: "If it came from a plant, eat it; if it was made in a plant, don't."

The answers to all the confusion about food lie in simplification. Michael Pollan suggests that we simply make our food, and hence our health, more of a priority. If you love your child/spouse/pet/self, then don't feed them fast food or processed products that you know are unhealthy. Make your meals important enough that you simply take the time and effort to pack a lunch rather than depend on what is offered by retail food locations near your work or school.

Seek out local sources, like a farmer's market or CSA (community-supported agriculture), which will deliver fresh produce to you weekly.

"Pay more, eat less," says Pollan. It sounds antithetical until you realize that cheap food has not been created for your health or quality enjoyment; it's been engineered to be cheap. I am still working on it, but since I first started reading Michael Pollan's food/cooking books, my wife and I eat exponentially better, and we feel great, and she looks great. I still look like me, but I did go down a size in jeans. Suck on that, McDonald's. I'm smiling wide, but you can't see me.

PART 3

MAKERS

The Toolmaker

13

THOMAS LIE-NIELSEN

If you are the type of person (excellent nerd) who is obsessed with the shaping of wood using hand tools, then you are my kind of lady or fellow. If you enjoy discussing the difference between a half-blind dovetail and one that is fully sightless, then you and I could hang out, so long as you can tolerate a beefy feculence in the immediate atmosphere and the occasional ripping report announcing the refreshing of said funk. If you are so into your wedged tenon that your coffee grows cold awaiting your attention, then you are undoubtedly the sort of initiate who is aware of the "Cadillacs" of American hand tools, that is to say, the ones that are made at Lie-Nielsen Toolworks. If you are not my sort of weirdo, then chances are you remain ignorant to these sublime, finely crafted implements. Let me inform you.

(Note to youngsters: In my day, the Cadillac was an automobile made by the General Motors Corporation that was considered the "top of the line," and so to refer to any member of a given classification as the "Cadillac" was to employ a figure of speech indicating that it was "the best." To this day, they continue to make a fine, quality ride, but I no longer find that metaphor to be in popular use.)

Actually, let me back it up another degree. Have you heard of Maine? If you drive east to, say, Boston, then take a left, after nipping off the corner of New Hampshire, you'll find yourself in the magnificent state of Maine. This is the rugged locale of the Lie-Nielsen Toolworks, as well as the WoodenBoat School and countless other inspiring individuals. (Check out Robert Shetterly's painting series Americans Who Tell the Truth.)

Thomas Lie-Nielsen, born in 1954, is the son of a Norwegian boat-builder who had immigrated to the United States in his teens, where he skippered local boats and eventually ran a handful of wooden-boat shops. Having grown up in the skilled atmosphere of these shops in the relatively remote area of Camden, Maine, Thomas then went to school at Hamilton College to study English before moving to New York City to seek his fortune. He took a job with a tool mail-order company called Garrett Wade in the late 1970s, once again exposing himself to the types of tools he'd grown up around. The company offered a variety of items, including the finest hand tools available for woodworkers at the time. Trouble was, "the finest available" didn't always necessarily mean anything that great. It's just that there were very few companies in the world making these specialized tools. (GarrettWade.com is still a source of tools and other swell implements, where I often shop for gifts.)

Interestingly, WoodenBoat magazine had begun publishing in 1974, and Fine Woodworking magazine had just fired up its presses a year later in 1975. These were the result of our nation's tool purists wanting a better education and community in support of crafts like heirloom furniture construction and wooden-boat building. Nobody in the States was making high-end woodworking tools in any substantive way, because there was not yet a noticeable demand, and companies that were making tools were cranking out tens of thousands of them per week, which didn't leave much opportunity for quality control.

In the Garrett Wade catalogue, there was a small hand plane called an edge trimming block plane that was an adaptation of the Stanley #95, handmade by a machinist named Ken Wisner in Freeport. Mr. Wisner decided to retire from producing this plane, and Lie-Nielsen recognized an opportunity. As I mentioned, the planes and chisels available at the time were generally mass-produced, and so they lacked the level of detail and finishing that we have come to appreciate in today's hand-tool market. Thomas understood that these catalogue tools were not remotely up to snuff; in fact, they were downright shitty, and so his gut told him to take quite a plunge.

He contacted Mr. Wisner in Freeport and acquired the tooling, plans, and components necessary for producing the #95 himself. Moving to a blueberry farm in West Rockport, Maine, he began producing these planes in a small shed, successively delivering his first product to Garrett Wade by 1981. Lie-Nielsen Toolworks was born. Thomas was twenty-five years old.

After a few years of this, he added a second tool, a skew-angle block plane, so he had to move to a bigger shed on his farm. Things were going well—two sheds well. In 1988 he moved to an actual eight-thousand-square-foot building in Warren, Maine, and then expanded into an additional thirteen thousand square feet in the mid-nineties.

The company is now producing more than twenty thousand individual tools a year and still growing. And you have probably never even heard of a skew-angle block plane, but take it from me—among block planes, Lie-Nielsen's is the Cadillac.

On January 2, 2015, my pal Jimmy DiResta and I drove to deep Queens, New York, to a Lie-Nielsen Hand Tool Event. If you're not yet familiar with my friend Jimmy, throw this book out the window and go plug his name into YouTube. He has his own channel where he posts his top-drawer homemade videos on making all sorts of items with tools. They are as gripping and impressive as he is handsome (they are quite gripping). When I'm on the East Coast, if I'm doing anything fun in the realm of making stuff, I can usually be found riding shotgun with Jimmy and his equally talented lady pal Taylor Forrest, who works wonders on metal, leather, wood, denim, and Jimmy.

We walked into the enormous and butt-ugly (gorgeous), old brick warehouse where the event was being staged. It was rather frigid, and the "show" occupied two large rooms, where five or six toolmakers had their wares displayed around woodworking benches, for the trying out of the tools. The air smelled of sawdust and mold, as well as the fumes from the generator that was powering the only lights, as the building's power had been shut off the day before. The air was filled with the sound of men and some women, mind you, chatting about tools and stuff, and, of course, the incessant, sweet noise of saws and plane blades zipping through wood, as prospective buyers tried out these luscious hand-crafted tools.

As Jimmy immediately dove into the playpen (he was in the

market for a big joiner plane), I scanned the room, and across the expanse I spotted . . . no, it couldn't be. I wandered closer. He was performing a little card-scraper workshop for a few rapt pilgrims. Good Christ, it *was* him. Gary Rogowski. One of the greats. Shit, I had learned *all* my biscuit tricks from that soul-patched sum-bitch twenty years ago! He runs his very own kick-ass woodworking school in Portland, Oregon. What was he doing here? Slumming, it turned out, between speaking engagements, trying to unload some books and DVDs. He was very generous with us plebeians, and I learned three better ways to sharpen my scraper in about twenty seconds. Here was a master, and a jazzy one, at that.

Then I wandered into the next room and was double gobsmacked. There was Matt Kenney from *Fine Woodworking*! One of the finest! I had known Matt for a few years, having run into him at another gathering of chisel freaks, but here in this crappy brick room in Queens, it was as though I had just pegged Strider sitting in the Prancing Pony, although Matt is inescapably sweeter in countenance than Aragorn could ever hope to come across.

We spoke about what a neat get-together this was, and he had this to say about Lie-Nielsen: "During the last ten to fifteen years, there has been an explosion of high-quality, American-made woodworking hand tools. In fact, it's not unreasonable to say that we're living in a golden age of hand tools. And I believe that Thomas Lie-Nielsen is largely responsible for this."

I replied that I was really enjoying being around a bunch of other folks in Carhartt jackets, none of them clean, except maybe mine, their hands dirty with tool oil and calloused with work. My actor hands were easily the softest paws in the room. Matt had been studiously hogging out an edge dado with a Veritas plow plane when I approached. As he minutely adjusted the implement's depth, he said that he "had been brought up with the understanding that a man or woman should be able to maintain and operate any object that he or she might own." That's something that woodworking with tools like these allows us to hang on to, in a world where I open up the hood of my Audi wagon and it might as well be an X-wing starfighter.

The presence of luminaries like Kenney and Rogowski was a testament to the strength of the woodworking community. It is truly a band of brothers and sisters sharing knowledge and, when necessary, muscle, and sometimes after that, a delicious brown beverage, or at least a sandwich of savory meatstuffs.

Finally, I got to the man who was clearly in charge of this hoedown, a rugged, muscled chap in a Lie-Nielsen shirt. He agreed to answer a few questions, so we stepped into the back room. He told me his name was Deneb, after the brightest star in the constellation Cygnus the Swan; last name Puchalski, a name I believe to be of merely human derivation, although I failed to ask him.

Deneb turned out to be the son-in-law of Mr. Lie-Nielsen, and also his greatest salesman. These hand-tool events were his baby, Deneb explained, conceived when he realized that the larger-scale tool shows had rather too much of a carnival atmosphere to accommodate their small niche of hand tools for woodworking. They came up with these much friendlier "local get-togethers," at which there were no power tools in sight. Which was good, because there was not so much power, either.

Interestingly, Lie-Nielsen footed the bill for the event but then invited the other local tool-making artisans to set up their displays all together. "That seems counterintuitive," I stated, to which Deneb replied, "No, there is not enough of a market for us to really be competitive with each other. If we can continue to inform the community about the quality of our goods, well, a rising tide raises all boats. Our *competition* is Apple and Sony, anybody who is going after people's disposable income."

Well, this was something new to me. A business that invites its fellow retailers to participate in a small, well, festival, I guess, knowing that any of their sales will help the common cause. This sounded swell, but could the business model hold up?

I later put this question to Robin Lee, from Canadian toolmaker Lee Valley/Veritas Tools, another top-notch North American firm. He said, "This is going to sound trite—but there is an honesty/integrity that seems to be common to people who work with their hands for enjoyment. We both recognize that woodworking is something that people will do for decades, if not for their entire life. We both assume our customers are coming back at some point . . . and do everything to ensure that happens."

These two refined companies, Lie-Nielsen and Veritas, are like if a town had two excellent restaurants on either side of it, and the chefs loved each other's cooking in a way that it inspired them to make new, better dishes themselves. Lee said, "At the same time as we compete—the two firms are really quite complementary. I often describe Lie-Nielsen as 'classical,' where we're 'jazz.' Tom's line is based on executing the time-tested designs of Stanley tools to a quality level that Stanley never achieved. Our designs are based on a reboot for each plane—taking into account changes in methods of work, available materials, and the capabilities of modern manufacturing." I was very charmed by this generosity of spirit that is reflected in the tools fashioned by these folks.

When Deneb started working for Lie-Nielsen fourteen years ago, there were thirty to forty employees. Today there are 100, and they make more than 350 individual tools. This circumstance is peculiar given the fact that they are completely committed to quality over profit. Normal business sense would lead such an outfit to look for places where corners could be cut, or lesser materials substituted, in the way that so many plastics have been introduced into your average automobile, for example. Thomas Lie-Nielsen launched his business with a burning desire to fabricate hand tools the way they ought to be made, and he's not about to forget it.

Before I left the tool show, I asked Matt Kenney for an official quote for my book, and he did not have much trouble coming up with a firm opinion, almost as though he reads books: "We should count ourselves fortunate that in the late 1970s [Thomas] recognized a need for better hand tools, and that he was audacious enough to start making hand planes to meet it. And we should admire the determination, focus, and force of personality it must have taken to develop those early efforts into the company that Lie-Nielsen Toolworks is today."

On top of such a commitment to quality, Lie-Nielsen tools also carry a 100 percent lifetime guarantee. That an American company could grow in this way while maintaining an inarguable level of quality and customer satisfaction thrills me to no end. By the way, I should point out that when they say "Made in America," that is completely what they mean. I was not aware until Deneb informed me that a retail item requires only 60 percent of its labor to be performed on US soil in order to receive that coveted label, which feels like bullshit to me. So much mediocrity has seeped into the regulation of our American integrity that even "Made in America" is only 60 percent true? So some CEO can make a buck, or millions of them? How many of our "American" products are being mostly fabricated in Asia, or Mauritius, or the Philippines, only to have the shoelaces installed in Alabama, so we can pay premium prices?

Robin Lee added, "A healthy manufacturing base is the foundation of a solid economy. It keeps much of the value generated and the resulting employment at home. If your friends and neighbors are out of work, you have no one to sell product to!" In a world where so many commercial strings are being pulled in curtained chambers beyond our control, one place we *can* exert our power is in the open market, namely, where our money goes. I can think of no better place to spend my American dollars than on the tools, and the people, of Lie-Nielsen Toolworks.

14

NAT BENJAMIN

One theme that has repeatedly bobbed to the surface in this book is boatbuilding. From Theodore Roosevelt to Frederick Douglass to Thomas Lie-Nielsen, everyone seems to have taken a swing at building wooden boats. Even your author is not exempt—should one choose to pursue the craft of woodworking, it's only a matter of time before your matriculation runs squarely into the prospect of either boatbuilding or lutherie (making stringed musical instruments such as guitars and ukuleles), if you're the right kind of goofy. You've conquered all the ways to join wooden components at every combination of angles, with or without fasteners, with a mastery of square, level, and plumb. You have spent Gladwell's ten thousand hours on sanding alone. Your fancy now begins to ponder the daunting undertaking of objects that contain no straight lines whatsoever. Impossible? Definitely.

Still, you subscribe to *WoodenBoat* magazine and drift through the pages, finding yourself growing half erect (ladies too) at the merest advertisements for spar varnish. Although you've been using it your entire life, you only just now realize that the "spar" in that nomenclature refers to the horizontal wooden poles on the mast of a sailing rig. When you begin listening to Stan Rogers's "Barrett's Privateers" on repeat, it's over. Notify your significant other that he or she should stock up on good reading material because you'll be building a wooden boat.

When I was overcome by this particular spell in 2001 or so, I was at the airport, and I realized I needed a book for my flight. As luck would have it, I happily happened upon a paperback in the doorway of the bookstore entitled, simply, *Wooden Boats*. Fantastic! I devoured it on the plane and learned about a pair of wooden-boat builders named Nat Benjamin and Ross Gannon on the island of Martha's Vineyard, off the coast of Massachusetts. Their story was as fanciful as any fairy tale to this aspiring woodworker who grew up in the very landlocked region of Illinois.

Unless this riveting book by Michael Ruhlman was a fabrication, there were actually men and women living in this great land of ours, building boats out of wood, using tools, know-how, and of course, gumption. With this hard proof that the construction of a seaworthy wooden hull was not beyond the realm of possibility, I sallied forth in my own small endeavors, which have to date produced a watertight four-foot cradle/tender and two eighteen-foot canoes. I have mentioned it elsewhere, but it bears repeating: Traveling across the water in a boat that one has fabricated oneself holds an eldritch magic that cannot be described. There is wizardry embroidered into the whole of the act.

As the years went by, I saw successively greater triumphant achievements from Gannon & Benjamin Marine Railway (the name of Ross and Nat's company) in *WoodenBoat* magazine, as well as in a beautiful coffee-table book entitled, simply, *Schooner*, by Tom Dunlop, which details the construction of *Rebecca*, a magnificent sixty-foot craft, and then my favorite piece on them, the documentary *Charlotte*, from Jeffrey Kusama-Hinte. Highly recommended, if you enjoy things like life and beauty. Basically, by that point, Nat and Ross had become, to me at least, the rock stars of American wooden-boat builders.

I have traditionally found that the greater the craftsperson, the stronger the self-deprecation, and Nat was no exception. His response to my e-mailed request for an interview included, "You're really scraping the bottom to consider the reprobates at Gannon & Benjamin." I took my two talented "maker" friends, Jimmy DiResta and Taylor Forrest, with me to Martha's Vineyard to meet reprobate number one. Even a couple of days after Christmas, Vineyard Haven Harbor had several beautiful antique wooden yachts bobbing in evidence, as we came in on the ferry.

We met Nat at the shop, aka the railway, named thus for the actual steel rails that run fifty yards into the water, upon which a boat of a weight up to dozens of tons can be rolled into and out of the harbor's water. It was amazing to see in person the old barn in which I had remotely viewed and read of so much mastery. As in all my favorite shops, the tools and machines were ancient and brown and heavy, thickly squatting upon their cast-iron bases. Our foursome immediately launched into the classic shop-geek rap, admiring exceptional examples of band saw and planer and lathe (pre–World War II!).

A good boat shop will have a gargantuan band saw known as a

ship's saw, upon which one can cut a curve on an enormously long and massive timber, like for the keel of a boat, while simultaneously slanting the piece through the saw on what's called a rolling bevel. Considering the modern cost of the tropical hardwoods preferred for such a task, such as angelique, it's a cut that must be undertaken with a lot of care and no small amount of gumption. Jimmy and Taylor and I admired the ship's saw in Nat's shop as he apologized for Ross's absence. "He doesn't come out on weekends," he explained. Sounds like a smart family man. Nat said, "You should most definitely include him in your assessment. He has been my business partner, cofounder, and friend for forty-plus years and is equally blameworthy for the relative success and accomplishments of our boatyard."

The pair felt very fortunate to have secured the somewhat ramshackle (read: charming) shop, not only because it sits right on the water, in the perfect location to execute their watery railway transactions, but also because the site very nearly became a fast-food restaurant instead. When Gannon and Benjamin met in the early seventies, as fellow wooden-boat geeks, and gradually determined that they would like to establish a "groovy, casual shop" where wooden-boat enthusiasts like themselves could repair and maintain their charismatic vessels, they set their sights upon the idyllic location where the shop now resides. Unfortunately, a little hamburger concern known as McDonald's had also just plied their troth to the landowner, to build a restaurant complete with a drive-through.

Eventually, the discerning residents of Vineyard Haven, who counted among their number some luminaries of literature, entertainment, and politics, came to the rescue and crushed the burger chain's dreams, leaving the property available to house the Marine Railway. If only all communities could be so sensible. Wooden boat shop or McDonald's? Think carefully, America.

According to Nat, people had always told them they were crazy to specialize in wooden boats, when fiberglass hulls were all the rage, not to mention cheaper to mold and maintain than wooden watercraft. Fortunately, Nat and Ross knew, intrinsically, that despite the superficial advantages of a plastic boat, it just didn't feel as good as wood. It's like swinging a plastic baseball bat or, in my opinion, reading a book on a tablet versus holding the real thing in one's hands. Sure, the newer model has its selling points, but the convenience can't outweigh the solidity and presence of reading off the page for me.

I asked Nat himself why one should choose wood over any synthetic hull, and his answer was most satisfying: "Sailing a wooden boat is a symphony of sound above and below deck as the sea rushes by. She also talks to you—a creak here, maybe a groan or two when driven hard. The glow of varnish, salted-down wooden decks, bronze patina, and the structural timbers and fine joinery—all the lovely details give us a visual feast of grace and beauty. And a wooden boat smells so good."

There's an important distinction to be made here: The people who inspire me never seem to be looking to maximize profits. They have an understanding that life's rewards are to be found much more in the difference between sanding, say, white oak and sanding fiberglass and epoxy. Interestingly, these artisans and freethinkers still manage to lead a life of richness and sometimes even prosperity. I must admit that the more my woodshop relegates itself to solid-wood craftsmanship versus fabricating cookie-cutter items out of man-made "wood" products like medium-density fiberboard, the better we seem to feel.

Of course, in Nat's case, he happens to carry onboard a surplus of immense artistic talent to back up his skills on the spokeshave. While the boat shop houses an ever-shifting roster of craftspeople—joiners, caulkers, sailmakers and riggers, welders and carvers, there is an arcane skill that must come into play before any of these other talents can be employed: that of lofting. "Lofting" is the term to describe how a hull's shape is described by means of its "lines." If you can imagine the lines of latitude and longitude on a globe and then apply similar lines of sectioning to the shape of a boat, these are the lines with which lofting concerns itself. Enjoyably, the corresponding lines on the curving, slanted stern, or rear, of the vessel are known as buttock lines, which goes a long way toward explaining why your average wooden boat is rocking such a sweet caboose.

I could spend an entire chapter describing the process, and you would be asleep by the first sentence, so let me try and nutshell it for you. First of all, Nat has to bring his historical knowledge of boat shapes to bear upon his imagination. This is the culmination of centuries of design, making improvements incrementally, builder by builder, across different cultures and different types of sea, river, or lake, until by now the craft has achieved a relative ideal. Nat understands how the shape and the weight of the hull relate directly to its performance and durability. Bear in mind that there are zero straight lines on this complex shape, and every piece will be made of wood in a way that it will keep the water on the outside, with any luck. As he says, "A boat is a piece of furniture you take out on the ocean and throw around."

Once he has conceived the general design, he sketches it out, and if it is a commission, he then discusses it with his client until everyone is happy with the concept. At this point, the lofting begins. Determining a series of those segmenting "globe" lines, using math and, apparently, sorcery, Nat then transfers those lines, full-size, onto an open floor, from which the shape and dimensions of each individual part of the ship can then be determined. Despite Nat's humility in this area, he is truly considered one of the greatest living wooden-boat designers. To say that his craft involves an element of sorcery is actually an understatement. Combine that nuanced ability with the manner in which he and Ross Gannon seem equipped to solve any problem whatsoever that can be solved by tools, elbow grease, a hunk of mahogany, and an inbred understanding of simple machines, and you have the makings of the finest wooden boats that money can buy.

Mr. Nat Benjamin grew up in the small Hudson River town of Garrison, New York, and vacationed at the Pleasant Bay Camp on Cape Cod, where he fell in love with sailing the eighteen-foot Baybird, designed by W. Starling Burgess. He was destined for a life on the open water, and his passion eventually found him crewing boats up and down the Atlantic Seaboard, until at age twenty, an offshore delivery took him to the Virgin Islands. It was there, at Saint Thomas, that his eyes feasted upon a fleet of old wooden masterpieces from the drawing boards of Alden and Herreshoff, Sparkman & Stephens, Fife, Camper & Nicholsons, and Rhodes, noted virtuosos from the golden age of yacht design. Beyond the hypnotizing lines of their boats, Nat was also taken in by the people who owned and sailed them. "They were crazy, but in a good way. They knew how to get the most out of life."

Called upon to skipper the delivery of such fine wooden yachts across the open Atlantic and back, between the Mediterranean, the Caribbean, and the American East Coast, a young Nat Benjamin grew to thrive on such adventure. Returning in a ship from Malta on one such voyage, Nat found his boat in bad shape ("It was what they called a sinking feeling"), so he pulled ashore in North Africa for repairs, "and these guys were good. We ripped off some planks and replaced them, and that's when I first became fascinated by the work of the shipwrights."

Jimmy, Taylor, and I understand, as we were then flatly astonished when we cruised across the road to the larger build shed, in the yard of which were several boats being stored for the winter (including sloop *Sally May*, Nat's first design, built for James Taylor in 1980). Inside, there was a Herreshoff yacht from 1905, undergoing pretty intensive repairs, which I would normally have considered a massive job, had it not been dwarfed next to an enormous Hong Kong schooner built in 1957 to a Sparkman & Stephens design.

The vessel was stripped down to the frames and planks of the hull, and it was mind-boggling as Nat walked us through each piece of the puzzle and how it would fit back together. That's always an important key for me when I consider any project "impossible"; I first consider the fact that, "well, somebody has done this already, so it *can* be done." Then I remember the advice of Ted Moores, my teacher in canoe craft—you don't have to build the whole boat at once; you just have to make the first piece, and then you make the second piece, and so on. Still and all, this stem-to-stern overhaul that Nat was undertaking would make a grown man weep. Even, perhaps, a grown woman.

We asked Nat what price an overhaul like this would run a person, to which he replied, "About a million." As we stood, blinking and nodding with false understanding, as though we hadn't just shit ourselves, he continued. "That's considerably cheaper than building new." Okay, so wooden boats aren't the cheapest investment out there, but then when I stack it up against a wooden-slab dining table from my shop that goes for ten thousand dollars, it seems rather a bargain. The table has maybe ten parts, and most of that price is the labor and the cost of a large slab of tree (usually around two or three thousand dollars). A boat certainly has more than a hundred times as many parts, all of them curved. In boatbuilding, fine-furniture making, and home building, if anybody's getting rich, it's generally not the men and women swinging the mallets. So what is it that drives these goofy boatbuilders, if not the almighty dollar?

Part of it, for Nat, is simply knowing that he and his shop mates do things in the best possible way they can be done. Their techniques may be centuries old, but they are becoming largely lost to us in this modern era of mass-production and computer-generated 3-D printing. On top of which, he told us that, with old boats, it was just worth it to some people to maintain a masterfully built classic rather than spend that fortune on something new. His theory is not at all unlike the way Thomas Lie-Nielsen makes his tools. It is the adherence to the importance of quality in all parts of life, I feel, that protects us from the creeping tentacles of consumerist thought.

Nat described to us the technique of steaming wood so that large planks can be bent around the curves of a hull. In a long box, large enough to encompass the plank, steam is pumped from any primitive kettle arrangement (steam is easy to make), and the wood is steamed for one hour per inch of thickness. Nat was talking about a clipper ship, the *Charles W. Morgan*, which had recently taken skilled wrights seven years to rebuild at Mystic Seaport. The planks on her were three and a half inches thick and forty feet long, which means they would require three and a half hours in the steam box. "So many skills have been totally lost," he went on. "I mean, they used to build clipper ships much bigger than that up and down the coast here; in every backwater creek they used to crank those things out in ninety to a hundred days, from lofting to launching, finished. What people do these days is a joke compared to the work Herreshoff did on his yachts."

We spoke further of the dearth of valuation for hand skills in today's society, and what a destructive and dangerous attitude that is. Nat described the joyful sight of seeing the native children in third world situations strip a palm leaf of its fronds (leaving a paddle-shaped stem), jump into a dugout canoe crafted by their fathers, and paddle into the ocean with aplomb, as happy as clams at high tide. One of the most inspiring books I've read on the topic of such lost skills is John McPhee's *The Survival of the Bark Canoe*, which details a young Maine man's quest to keep alive the noble Native American craft of building a perfect canoe with only ingenuity, a knife, a match, and products that one can glean from the woods.

I think that part of what defines *gumption* involves a willingness, even a hunger, for one's mettle to be challenged. Just like Wendell Berry, Nat finds no use for a computer in his work, especially when it comes to designing and lofting, even though most modern designers have switched to CAD programs. The familiar note here seems to be that people with gumption will bristle when *less* is required of them. A part of human nature tends toward laziness and comfort, which is the part being so lucratively exploited by corporations, but there is a more noble part: the portion of the human spirit that revels, not in ease, but in having *its capabilities tested.* These estimable characters know the profoundest, bone-deep satisfaction of having themselves challenged by the world, and, relying only upon their human capabilities—their gumption—they not only win the contest, but they infuse those around them with the inspiration to shine as well.

Nat pilots sail-powered boats across the ocean, navigating primarily with the celestial bodies and a sextant. He and Ross and their boatyard have produced more than sixty substantial vessels, most of them born of his pencil, not to mention a veritable fleet of smaller craft. He holds a license from the US Coast Guard to captain a ship up to a weight of one hundred tons. Standing in his chilly shop in December, surrounded by all the tools and sawdust, Nat Benjamin said to me with a slight grin, "I find that I have friends that are retiring, and I think, 'Gosh, have they had such lousy work that they want to retire?' . . . If they told me I couldn't go to work, I would be pretty upset."

Echoing the subjects of so many previous chapters—Wendell Berry, Eleanor Roosevelt, Benny Frankles: If you don't love your work enough to have a good time doing it, then maybe you're showing up at the wrong job. Nat Benjamin, most assuredly, is not.

The Woodworker

15

GEORGE NAKASHIMA

Hey, look, it's a Japanese American! And his redoubtable daughter Mira—that's a Japanese American woman!

Talk about the American dream. George Nakashima was born in 1905 in Spokane, Washington (home of the best boot company, White's Boots. Made in America! [The 100 percent kind!]), to a newspaper reporter descended from samurai lineage named Katsuharu Nakashima, and his wife, Suzu, qualifying him from the get-go as an heroic American citizen. Boom.

A bright young pisser, George graduated from the University of Washington with a bachelor's degree in architecture in 1929, then went on to earn his master's degree from MIT in 1931. He moved to New York City and worked as a mural painter and architectural designer. Bingo.

Feeling pretty tall, he hopped a ship to France, where he undoubtedly ate the hell out of some crepes and snails while kicking about the country for a year like a hotshot young American architect. His tour continued to North Africa, and finally Japan, where he got a job with an American architect, Antonin Raymond. In 1937 George volunteered to design and supervise the construction of a religious sanctuary in Pondicherry, India, where he underwent "a deep transformation of consciousness" so profound that he was given the Sanskrit name Sundarananda, which means "one who delights in beauty." Bango.

Nakashima's work thereafter was inculcated with a religious zeal, even as he created his first furniture for the ashram dormitory. He believed that "it was necessary to remove the desire to promote one's individual ego from the creative process and to devote work each day to the divine," a notion quite contrary to Western culture, but one that would inspire him to great heights nonetheless. Bongo.

Returning to Japan, young George canvassed the island nation, absorbing the subtly alluring details of traditional Japanese architecture, and met Marion Okajima, also born in America, who would become his wife. Walkin' tall, eh, what, Georgie? A groovy Sanskrit name and a foxy bride on top of a winning disposition and a surplus of talent for design? The lovebirds moved to Seattle and opened a furniture workshop in 1940, and Marion gave birth to a beautiful daughter, Mira, in January of 1942, and everything was peachy kee— (sound of tires screeching to a stop!). Oh. Dang. Pearl Harbor.

You youngsters may not be hyperaware of this little speed bump in our great nation's track record regarding civil liberties, but if you'll recall from chapter 7, when the Japanese attacked Pearl Harbor, ol' FDR pooped his presidential drawers and, under the pressure of his advisers, issued Executive Order 9066, which yanked about 120,000 Japanese Americans from their (mostly West Coast) homes and plunked them unceremoniously into concentration camps.

"Say what?" you say.

"That is accurate reporting," I reply.

"No shit?," you add.

"That's a negatory on the shit," I persevere.

"That is fucked up," you conclude.

"You don't say. Read on." This next part is juicy and shameful.

We (white folks) tossed the Japanese into camps, despite the fact that two-thirds of them were US citizens, like the Nakashimas. This action was undertaken out of sheer racism and fear. Classic white-guy move. We tucked the "Orientals" out of sight, just to be on the safe side, while we were firebombing Japanese cities in preparation for a massive attack of the Allied forces on Japan. Remember, this is mere decades after the "Yellow Peril" was the commonplace term for our civilization's fear of some sort of Asian invasion.

World War II, to me, is best represented by a group of boys of varying races, playing with their toy guns on a playground. They are shooting and seriously wounding one another, taking sides with their allies, and seeing who will dare to push the game the furthest. One kid with a weird, tiny mustache is playing like an asshole, like he owns the playground, so he is subdued, and it seems like things are going to wind down, except that Japanese kid is refusing to give up. He lands a couple of good shots on the American kid, just on his elbow, but still, it smarts. So the American kid pulls out a nuclear bomb and *nukes* the Japanese kid. The playground is stunned. Nothing remains of the victim but a white shadow on the side of the school building.

Like it or not, if you end a war by being the biggest asshole (by far), you are not really a "victor." You're the biggest asshole, who had the last word, and the reason nobody retaliated is not because the other nations think America is the best. It's because there is not another world power willing to be such a dick on the playground. Knee-jerk "patriots" who proclaim our country's obvious superiority are ignorant to the fact that, while we are indeed superior, it's actually as bullies that we have established our dominance.

The Manifest Destiny was our nation's presumptive attitude in expanding west across the continent, with the absurd aim of "democratic conquest," declared (by us) justifiable, based upon our virtue. You ask, "But who could bestow such a privilege upon this particular group of white people?" Why, the answer is God, of course. That's the Christian God. The same white-bearded fellow who approves of our playground "diplomacy" in the Middle East, for how much difference is there, really, between the Yellow Peril and the Muslim Terror? The same deity, we were told (by George W. Bush), that put George W. Bush in the White House, despite his losing the election—a miracle indeed.

I really like the teachings of Jesus, by the way. They are beautiful and profound and morally unimpeachable. I only wish, like Wendell Berry, that so many of these gosh-darned *Christians* felt the same way. Mr. Berry is classy and respectable, and I admire him powerfully, but he's not here right now, so I'm going to go ahead and assert that the vast number of Americans who claim to follow Christ and yet support actions like our imperialistic tendencies, including slavery, "internment" camps (sounds more gentle than "concentration"), genocide, "police actions," torture, and "collateral damage" . . . well, you're clearly full of shit. Now, let's talk about a goddamn nice furniture maker.

Despite their lemony incarceration at the hands of their cool, white captors (and fellow Americans), the Nakashimas made lemonade quite handily. While imprisoned, George met (and began to assist) Gentaro Hikogawa, a fellow inmate who was trained in traditional Japanese joinery. This style of joinery employs no fasteners, relying instead upon cleverly mating puzzlelike components that are designed to remain dependably conjoined for as long a time as the wood timbers themselves do. Once again, we are presented with a discipline that chooses beauty, quality, and patience over speed and profit.

Nakashima wrote, "The decline in quality of modern furniture is probably due in part to the use of the quick, easy and cheap dowel joint. The decline of modern domestic architecture can be traced to the popularity of the stud wall put together with hammer and nails, a type of construction calling for no joinery at all. By contrast, the early American house and barn with their excellent joinery still represent the best we have produced and will greatly outlast contemporary buildings."

Nakashima took to this ancient joinery style like a televangelist to your grandmother's pension dollars, and when his family was sprung from the Idaho camp after being "sponsored" by their white pal Antonin Raymond, they set up a home in New Hope, Pennsylvania, where Raymond lived. The young family had to start over very much from scratch, and they spent a rough couple of winters getting their domicile together, literally stacking the stones from the property into walls.

It wasn't long before George was crafting what would become his signature style of sculptural tables, chairs, benches, and cabinets in his Pennsylvania studio. The Nakashima table style can best be described as employing a large slab of wood—made from one vertical slice of the tree—which has been flattened and smoothed on its faces but retains the organic, natural outer edges. In the beginning, he used no power tools, mostly because there was no power. As a purist student trying to emulate his work, I always felt conflicted when employing electricity upon any step of a Nakashima piece, until I read this: "As much as man controls the end product, there is no disadvantage in the use of modern machinery and there is no need for embarrassment. . . . A power plane can do in a few minutes what might require a day or more by hand. In a creative craft, it becomes a question of responsibility, whether it is a man or the machine that controls the work's progress." Boy, that was good news. I was further tickled to discover that George would drive a couple of large screws up through the bottom of his tabletops into each wing of the famous butterfly keys that he installed along cracks or seams. Screws!

He applied his philosophy of gentle curiosity to the wood, revering the material with a most Eastern sensibility. "I have always been interested in meditation and mysticism," he said. "I think I've always been that kind of seeker. But I am also Japanese enough and pragmatic enough to want to give this spirit physical expression." I suppose I can't blame him for citing his Japanese heritage after being, you know, thrown into a concentration camp with his wife and infant daughter, but I hope that we Americans can evolve our country into someplace where George would not mind flying his flag.

We certainly have a long way to go. In a 1962 manifesto, George said this: "In proportion to the flood of consumer goods, we are probably at one of the lowest ebbs of design excellence that the world has seen. It requires a genuine fight to produce one well-designed object of relatively permanent value." Now, reader, I'll let you figure out if we've improved matters since then, or if we've made them worse. If you need to hunt for the answer, you'll want to dig up your passport, because the information you seek lies in China, and at the headquarters of IKEA, and Walmart, as well as piled up for your ready research in the "stacks"—by which I mean the landfills around the globe.

For me, one of the most appealing attributes of Nakashima's ethos is that it requires a slow approach. If you are one man or woman, attempting to make wooden implements that patrons will desire, then it does little good to build a plain bench or table exactly like something that could be purchased more cheaply from a mass manufacturer. By using an entire slice of a tree, one creates a singular, sculptural work of art that transcends the mere notion of "table" and becomes something more. With such work, one is literally suggesting that we choose beauty and nature over industrial produce; that we rise above the human weakness that causes things like internment camps. As George put it, "In a world where manual skills are shunned, we believe in them, not only in the act of producing a better product, but in the sheer joy of doing or becoming."

Despite the success and acclaim he received, he strove to keep his shop from growing. He insisted that he and his fellow woodworkers maintain their focus on quality and pure artistry, never quantity. The popularity of his furniture grew incrementally, servicing neighbors and more distant customers alike (like the parents of Michael Pollan) until 1973, when New York governor Nelson Rockefeller ordered two hundred pieces for his new house in Pocantico Hills, New York. From that point on, Nakashima's work began to be highly collectible and is now gracing many major museum collections around the world.

I reckon gumption, then, in the case of George Nakashima, would be located in his ability to bear the indignities and damages inflicted upon him by the sad white people whom he only wanted the right to call "neighbor"; to look inside himself and the trees beneath his hands and find a deliverance to a more peaceful life. In 1981 George published his book *The Soul of a Tree*, which instantly became required reading for any aspiring woodworker. In this gorgeous book, dripping with his philosophy and his work in equal parts, he wrote that he strove to discover each wooden slab's ideal use, to "create an object of utility to man and, if nature smiles, an object of lasting beauty."

George passed away in 1990, at eighty-five years of age, but his charismatic daughter, Mira, has taken up the mantle of the craft, to continue his life's work without abatement. The studio is still turning out work as gorgeous as ever to this day, if not more so, since it now has gained the advantage of a woman's perspective. Speaking of her own assistant, Miriam Carpenter, Mira said, "She's been with us for six years, basically doing what I did for two decades, being the understudy. With one big difference: When I did a drawing that Dad didn't like, he would just go in and change it. When I feel I need to change something, I explain why."

I am thus delighted to discern a gorgeous vein of gumption running through the George Nakashima Woodworker studios even now.

16

CAROL BURNETT

The thing about Carol Burnett is . . . she's kind of a goddess. There will be some of you younger types who may not be as familiar with her variety program, *The Carol Burnett Show*, which ran for only *eleven years*, from the late sixties into the late seventies, so I would suggest you treat yourself to some of those on the YouTube. Once you have committed to your viewing, however, do be prepared to cut yourself off cold turkey, as the typing in of that show's particular moniker produces a staggering 166,000 results, many of them full episodes, of which they made some 278-odd. Mind this rabbit hole of raillery; it is rather bottomless, and your sides may actually split should you fail to heed my counsel. Rib-tickling to the point of bruises is guaranteed.

I arrived at her lovely home near Santa Barbara, California, to pick her up for lunch. I had met her twice before, once when she was a guest on my wife's talk show, and once when we sat together at a Broadway play, and she had already set me at ease by treating me like family from the get-go. She has the generous ability to make everyone she meets feel like they're the apple of her eye. Regardless, I was nervous to spend time with her on my lonesome, because I can be clumsy.

She let me in the front door (French oak with copper details) and bid me wait while she fetched her purse. I looked to my right and noticed the door to the powder room upon which was the sort of sign plaque that would normally read RESTROOM or LAVATORY. Carol's read: EUPHEMISM. My tension left me immediately.

She has won accolades for decades, or "decaccolades," if you insist, and much has been (justly) made of her ridiculous comedy chops. She has been as good at winning laughter and awards as my beloved Chicago Cubs have been at not winning pennants, a tall tally of praise, indeed. (Next year, you son of a bitch.) So many laurels have been wreathed about her comedy offerings, I fear that another most significant virtue has been sorely overshadowed: Carol Burnett is *foxy*.

Sure, she makes me laugh. I am a human mammal, which is the only requisite to finding her hilarious to the point of leaving couch puddles. But her face and body language also contain such a surplus of heart and earnest; her smile, such a proliferation of beauty; and her fulsome songbird's voice (when not mangled for a laugh), such a bewitching lilt that I must confess I have been in love with her for forty-some years.

There have been other great beauties in my life, sure, and funny ladies? Shucks, I've been lucky enough to befoul quality programs *lousy* with them. Nonetheless, Carol somehow combines her self-deprecating charm with a natural charisma that makes her the queen of the bunch. (Lest I be suspected of infidelity, I should reveal that my wife, Megan, feels much the same as I; in point of fact, Carol has politely but firmly declined our seventeen entreaties—as of this writing—to join us in a three-way.) Not to mention, she got there decades before the funny ladies to whom I now bow, establishing herself as an intrepid pioneer in a field where few ladies had been allowed to do more than possess bosoms. Gilda Radner, Catherine O'Hara, Molly Shannon, Lisa Kudrow, Julia Louis-Dreyfus, Amy Poehler, Tina Fey, Melissa McCarthy, Rachel Dratch, Kristen Wiig, and now Jenny Slate and Ellie Kemper are all luminaries who have followed in Carol's footsteps from the world of sketch comedy to the top of show biz mountain (to paraphrase Ms. Poehler).

On top of her legendary comedy program and her extensive work in film and on Broadway, not to mention a veritable Thanksgiving feast–level grocery list of awards—Golden Globes, Emmys, People's Choice Awards, and many others (a menu long enough that you had best fix yourself a sandwich if you want to settle in for a scroll down her IMDb page)—Carol Burnett has also published three bestselling books. So pervasively is her mojo workin' that not only did she receive the 2013 Mark Twain Prize for American Humor and the Kennedy Center Honors in 2003, but she was also awarded the Presidential Medal of Freedom in 2005.

When I look back at the aplomb with which she delivered all her delicious performances, the decorum with which she comports herself when not onstage, and all the gales of laughter with which she and her partners in comedy caused our house to be filled, I am inclined to imagine Ms. Burnett as one of those lifelong champion types; the kind of person who wins the preschool lemonade fund-raiser; who earns every scouting badge until they make her up a new badge simply for "badge earning"; and who mercilessly dominates the seventh-grade spelling bee. (In Minooka, she was called Tracy LaLonde.) It's easy, then, to imagine my surprise when I learned that, on the contrary, she had a pretty traumatic childhood, raised primarily by her mother's mother, on relief in a low-rent Hollywood apartment. That fact makes all the more impressive the demeanor of elegance and class she has effortlessly maintained throughout her career, even while falling down a set of stairs.

Her folks were both plagued by alcoholism, starting with her dad when she was just a wee girl in San Antonio. Her mom and dad had aspirations of "making it" in Hollywood, so they moved to Los Angeles, where they ended their marriage in divorce and unloaded young Carol on her grandmother, although her mother still lived down the hall from them. Burnett said that her mother would get mean under the influence of drink, so young Carol took to hiding herself behind a screen and drawing while her mother and grandmother had it out. For a time, she thought she might even pursue a career in drawing, perhaps aspiring to one day illustrate fairy-tale books. Comedy is often the best therapy, however, and so it's no surprise that Carol's famous Eunice character bore some strikingly similar elements to her mother during these fits of rancor. At Hollywood High School, Burnett did perform in some school dramatics, but nothing caught fire, and so she found herself drawn more to her job editing the Hollywood High newspaper.

Finally, at UCLA, majoring in theater and English (because they had no journalism program), she found herself thrust reluctantly onstage in a required freshman acting class. Cast as a hillbilly, she reached into her (heretofore untested) bag of tricks and let rip with a lengthily drawled, "I'm bayaaack." The audience, as hers tend to do, erupted in laughter, and just like that, everything changed. According to Carol, "All of a sudden, after so much coldness and emptiness in my life, I knew the sensation of all that warmth wrapping around me. I had always been a quiet, shy, sad sort of girl, and then everything changed for me. You spend the rest of your life hoping you'll hear a laugh that great again."

She became obsessed with performing and writing for the theater. Her newfound acumen onstage made her popular on campus, an entirely new sensation in her life. Teenage singing sessions, harmonizing with her grandmother and mother (who would also play the ukulele), had revealed to her that she had a strong, leading voice. After a few years at UCLA, armed with this arsenal of talents and a satchel full of gumption, she lit out east for the territory of Broadway, figuring onstage would be where her best shot at success resided. This plan did not align with that of Carol's mother: "She wanted me to be a writer. She said, 'You can always write, no matter what you look like.' When I was growing up she told me 'to be a little lady,' and a couple of times I got a whack for crossing my eyes or making funny faces."

In this one formative anecdote, strongly smacking of Eleanor Roosevelt, Carol was told that she "didn't have the looks" to succeed as a beauty, even as she was stockpiling the clown's ammunition she would eventually come to brandish in her lifelong campaign to make us smile.

She made it to New York, took a room in a boardinghouse for

aspiring actresses, and got a menial job as a hatcheck girl. After a slow first year, she began scoring appearances on a couple of different children's and variety television shows. Burnett even did a season on Buddy Hackett's short-lived sitcom, *Stanley*, playing his girlfriend, but when the show got canned, it was back to the hustle for her. She spent a couple of summers working the Adirondacks vacation circuit, which turned out to be a great boon, as she and her community of talented cutups were able to hone their skills and workshop their sketch ideas before presenting them in the big city.

It's worth noting that throughout her twenties, despite her enormous talent, Carol Burnett really had to bust her hump. I am always hugely inspired (and personally relieved) to learn of the hard work that was required of any of my heroes before they could arrive at the level of mastery for which they ultimately garnered renown, not to mention the redoubled sweat it cost them to *maintain* said level. I copped this axiom from Tom Waits's toothsome cut "Little Man," but apparently the Roman philosopher Seneca was first credited with "Luck is when opportunity meets with preparation," and Carol was loading her plate with a healthy serving of just that: preparation.

The opportunity part came into play, with resultant luck in tow, when she scored the lead in the Broadway musical *Once Upon a Mattress* in 1959 (a show that had been workshopped in the Adirondacks). Since when it rains, it pours, she was then simultaneously hired to work as a regular on *The Garry Moore Show*, a live television variety program that she would shoot live on Fridays before hustling over to her eight P.M. performance of *Mattress*. She was nominated for a Tony for the Broadway musical and two years later won an Emmy for the TV show! Not a bad stretch for a young charwoman yet to see her thirtieth birthday.

Sitting at lunch with Carol Burnett on a beautiful Southern California afternoon, my head was swimming a bit with a heavy dose of how-the-hell-did-I-get-here. Hearing her first-person account of hijinks from the set of her show, and imagining her and Tim Conway and Harvey Korman and the rest trying to get through some of those live sketches with a straight face was the most delicious part of the meal. As we ventured into her earlier history, Carol unfolded a couple of anecdotes that I can't help but pass along:

1. While working on *The Garry Moore Show*, a junior writer she called Doc Simon (Neil Simon) wrote a sketch called "Playhouse 90 Seconds"—a send-up of the popular *Playhouse 90* dramatic television series. As she describes it: "Durward Kirby was in a hospital bed with his head bandaged, I'm his wife or whatever, and he's a doctor. I say, 'How are you, darling?' 'Oh, Jill, I don't feel too well.' And I say, 'Oh, Jack, why'd you have to go up the hill?' And he said, 'Well, I just felt I should fetch a pail of water. Look what happens.' And then Garry [Moore] comes in and says, 'It's not good. What are you gonna do, Jill?' I say, 'Well, I'll just go tumbling after.' And then I dived out of a window. So the producer said, 'Do you know how to dive out of a window, Carol?' I said, 'Oh, sure! No problem.' . . . We're getting on the set during blocking, and so I didn't know what I was gonna do. I just knew I was gonna sail out of that window. I said, 'Well, I'll just go tumbling after,' went out, and I landed on a mattress, and I sat up and said, 'Oh gosh, guys, thanks for the mattress!' I guess I thought I was just gonna go splat! I didn't even think to check."

2. Carol's double schedule in *Once Upon a Mattress* and then rehearsing and performing on *Garry Moore* left her with only Monday nights off. The musical, based upon the Hans Christian Andersen story *The Princess and the Pea*, requires the princess (Carol) to try and go to sleep upon a pile of mattresses. Even though she had the bloom of youth on her side, the heavy work-load still caught up with her during one Sunday matinee, and she was out like a light. She thinks she must have been asleep for only twenty or thirty seconds before the stage manager was able to awaken her with panicked whispers. The moral of the story is either "Too much gumption can land you in trouble with Actors' Equity" or "The employment of gumption requires adequate rest, at the risk of great peril to the gumptionator."

"It never occurred to me to be cynical. . . . I didn't know that I couldn't do certain things, so I did them." Carol Burnett said that of the pluck it must have taken to pull off this seemingly impossible schedule. Ignorance can indeed lead to bliss. I said that.

She struck up a lifelong friendship with Julie Andrews (another fervid boyhood crush of mine), when Andrews guested on *Garry Moore*. In 1962 the pair of luminous ladies appeared in a television special together, *Julie and Carol at Carnegie Hall*. The two had such a magical appeal together, like perhaps a young Aubrey Plaza and Amy Adams, if you combined them with Bambi.

Nonetheless, the (typical) CBS executives were initially reluctant to green-light the idea, as they believed Andrews was not sufficiently famous, and what with Burnett's weekly presence on Moore's show, the public would not be excited enough to tune in. Until one night after a CBS promotional event, when Burnett was unable to hail a taxi. The executives in question offered to wait until she was safely away, but Burnett told them not to bother, because a truck driver would appear shortly to pick her up. Almost at once, a trucker screeched up and did just as she'd predicted. Burnett received a telephone call from CBS immediately upon arriving home. Paying homage to her clear display of bewitchery, they approved the special, which went on to win an Emmy for both the show and Carol herself. The secret!

Despite her televised success in the variety format on *The Garry Moore Show*, Burnett kept thinking,

I'm not really television, I really want to be Broadway. But the television became more fun for me because we still did music and we still had comedic sketches, with the advantage that it changed every week. So I was able to learn how to do different characters, and to be different people, as opposed to being the same person on a sitcom every week, or the same person eight shows a week on Broadway. This was like doing a little Broadway revue every single week, and that became what I liked the most because it gave me, as we say, variety.

Meanwhile, she continued to knock down tall accomplishments like so many bowling pins, as she befriended the likes of Ms. Andrews, as well as Jim Nabors, Mike Nichols, and Lucille Ball. CBS signed her to a ten-year deal, and Lucy, an obvious mentor and producing magnate with her company Desilu Productions, offered Carol her own sitcom called *Here's Agnes!*, which sounds like a pretty hilarious idea based solely upon imagining Burnett as any "Agnes" that might be presented so. The title almost carries with it an implied addendum, as in *Here's Agnes! (Good Luck)* or *Here's Agnes! (With Apologies)* or *Here's Agnes! (God Love Her)*. No matter how they might have played it, the idea was stillborn, because Carol Burnett had her heart set on a sketch and variety show.

CBS was not immediately sold on the idea, as they felt like this arena was not ideal for a person of Carol's gender. As she remembers, "Are you kidding? I was told by CBS that comedy variety shows were a man's game, that it was the domain of Sid Caesar and Milton Berle and Jackie Gleason." Nonetheless, she had a thirty-week guarantee in her deal with the network to try out just such a show, so try it out she did, thank the sweet baby Jesus.

This wasn't the first time Carol had run into staunch opposition on the basis of her gender. It's in that arena that I really sit up and notice her gumption. Burnett tells a story about having wanted— scratch that—having dreamed of attending UCLA: a sheer impossibility for her, as the tuition for one semester in 1951 ran to an exorbitant forty-three dollars. She and her grandmother, existing on welfare, were paying thirty dollars a month in rent, relegating her collegiate aspirations to the realm of fantasy.

Her grandmother, with six marriages under her belt, suggested that she "learn to be a secretary and then you can 'nab the boss.'" Carol, unwilling to pursue her grandmother's questionable career advice, had no options, until she was astonished one morning to find a mysterious fifty-dollar bill in their pigeonhole mail slot. Apparently, somebody had thought she was worth a shot.

Now, let's back up a second and renew our gaze upon our United States. You may or may not (I sincerely hope it's the former) have heard of a notion called the Equal Rights Amendment. To nutshell it for you, it was proposed in 1923, so almost a hundred years ago. The amendment simply states that men and women shall have equal rights in this country. That's it. The amendment still hasn't passed. "What? 'Women's lib' happened in the seventies, playa!" That's as may be, Vanilla Ice (that was Vanilla Ice chiming in—special thanks), but governmentally, here in 2015, we are still shitting the bed. This is the Carol Burnett chapter, so I'll amend that to pooping the bed. You know what? Out of respect for dear Buddy Hackett, let's do sha-pooping the bed. See how easy it is to amend things?

Of course, our government can take a hilariously long time to accomplish things. In fact, somebody should write a comedy program about the glacial pace of . . . oh, they did. *Parks and Recreation*. I'm given to understand it's a quality program. But ninety-two years is maybe a bit much, no? To simply state—well, let's let Ruth Bader Ginsburg say it better than I could: "If I could choose an amendment to add to the Constitution, it would be the Equal Rights Amendment. . . . I would like my granddaughters, when they pick up the Constitution, to see that notion—that women and men are persons of equal stature—I'd like them to see that it is a basic principle of our society."

Okay, that's powerful. On a side note, how badass is the Ginsburg household that they have the Constitution just lying around where grandchildren can pick it up and peruse it? Back on point—our government was founded by a bunch of white dudes. It was a crazy Anglo-Saxon sausage party, and the new nation that they forged has done a great deal of good, as it continues to do. However, they naturally filled the inaugural documents with a lot of language like "all men are created equal" and "to secure these rights, governments are instituted among men."

Well, at the time, it at least made more sense, since women were still many dozens of years away from being allowed to vote. But to allow the condition to persist in this day and age strikes me as rather egregious. I wouldn't blame the ladies one bit if they described the penis bearers with the same words our Founding Fathers used in reference to their own oppression at the hands of Great Britain: "They too have been deaf to the voice of justice and of consanguinity." Man, those sons of bitches could write. "Consanguinity," by the way, means "from the same blood," or, more simply, "kinship."

We get it, guys. You're dudes. If you let the ladies into the club, you're going to have to stridently rein in the farting. Believe you me, *I get it.* By the way, it's not just the bros standing in the way of our female counterparts; it's also, sadly, some real asshats who happen to presumably wield vaginas. One of the most effective of said asshats in the effort to squelch the ERA was named Phyllis Schlafly, a conservative Republican activist who ran for a congressional seat in Illinois, my home state, to my shame. She made a very big stink on behalf of traditional gender roles, arguing that this amendment could (gasp) cause women to be drafted into the military and lead to unisex public bathrooms!

Such a dipshit sounds laughable now, I agree, but when she was spouting this tripe in 1972, it had an effect. Another piece of propaganda targeted "unskilled housewives" who would "risk losing their alimony" if the amendment were ratified. This was the climate into which *The Carol Burnett Show* was launched, which made it an incredibly powerful statement on behalf of women's equality.

When asked later if she considered herself a feminist, Carol replied, "I really didn't at the time, until the ERA came about. And the person who got me very interested in the ERA was Alan Alda. He's a feminist, and he took my husband and me out to dinner one night and he started talking about the ERA and what it was about. I was rather apolitical then, but I said, 'Well, that's not right. Women should be equal in the eyes of the law.' So I got on the bandwagon."

She added, "It was a threat to a lot of women who thought, 'Well, then my husband won't open the door for me'; everybody thought women were going to run around smoking cigars. I mean, how stupid."

My pal Amy Poehler, who has logged an amount of hustle, chuckle, and triumph similar to that of young Carol, sets a great example for all of us by wielding a sunny feminism with a focus on positivity. In fact, she runs an outfit called Smart Girls, which is a great "online community for young girls and the young at heart, which encourages women in volunteerism, activism, and cultural growth." Amy substantially tips her cap to the inspiration Carol provided her: "There was something very generous about her that came across when she performed, a certain female energy. You knew it was her show, and she was running it, but she ruled with an open fist."

I can attest to that, on the part of Amy, as I spent seven rewarding years working not under but alongside the open fist of Amy herself. *Parks and Recreation* won a lot of nice attention for its strong female story lines and positive depictions of women in leadership roles, and with good reason. But when I think about Carol Burnett on her show, or Amy on our show, or my aunts and my grandmother running the farm, or Linda Gillum and Lisa Ragsdale running the Defiant Theatre, or R. Lee running Offerman Woodshop, or Jill and Stephanie and Jess and LeeAnn at Dutton Books running the editing and collating of these very lines, or Megan running me into goodness—wow, this is a great sign of progress: A lot of my life is being administrated by ladies!—I don't think about feminism, or even that they're women. In all these contexts, they are just people. People who are good at their jobs, doing good work.

Thanks to the example set for us by people like Carol Burnett, who hasn't logged her victories by shouting or campaigning but by simply doing what she does best, we can begin to understand that women are *already* leading us. They always have been, despite what the white guys wrote in the history books. They gave birth to each and every one of us, and so there is no denying their majestic power. Shouldn't they be earning the same wages, then, as the rather less magical dudes? It wouldn't be special treatment. It would be simply treatment. When we as a nation can finally deal fairly with people of every gender, wherein all the people are receiving the same *treatment*, then I believe one of the benefits will be that we'll have more time for laughter.

The Troubadour

17

JEFF TWEEDY

If you look him up on the Wikipedia website, the entry begins like this: "Jeffrey Scot 'Jeff' Tweedy (born August 25, 1967) is an American songwriter, musician, record producer best known as the leader of the band Wilco." I don't recommend you do look there, as there are two perfectly good books about Jeff and Wilco, and I would always encourage you to eschew the computer in general, not to mention— that website is weak and yields inconsistent information.

First of all, the grammar is for shit. Somebody who can tolerate monkeying with computers, please go in there and put an *and* in front of *record producer.* Number two, they are burying the lede by a country mile. Jeff Tweedy is really nice. Jeff Tweedy is really smart. And Jeff Tweedy is really, really cute. He's what the young ladies of a bygone era would refer to as a "dreamboat." For my money, he's also the preeminent American singer-songwriter of my generation. Finally, I would add that I am in love with him. We are getting married. The end.

Just kidding, guys. Just joshin' around. But not really.

He is already married to a champion named Sue, and I am also already married, to a champion named Megan. Plus, Jeff and I are heterosexuals. Strike two. If it weren't for these formidable obstacles, then we would probably be together already and be very happy, but I guess since that's not in the cards, I will have to be satisfied with writing this chapter about him and also being his pal.

In the late 1990s, my friends Pat Healy, Paul Adelstein, and Pat Roberts were three veritable gold mines when it came to turning me on to music that thrilled my bucolic blood. You see, I was (and still am) a very slow and methodical student when it came to learning anything new in our culture. That is why Roberts was able to hook me on Pink Floyd twenty years after they blew everybody else's minds. These three estimable mates caused my CD rack to brim with Ween, Radiohead, Gillian Welch, Beck, the Beastie Boys, Will Oldham, Björk, Ben Folds, and a lot of early Bob Dylan records. Once they were added to my shelf already sagging under the expanse of Tom Waits, Neil Young, Johnny Cash, They Might Be Giants, Laurie Anderson, and Nick Cave, we had the makings of a well-tuned young hedonist, not to mention a swell hoedown.

Like most humans, I am very moved by music. It can rile me up or make me incredibly happy, or it can move me to tears, all with a commensurate amount of relish. Music shared among friends and family, I have found, is one of the most powerful bonding methods we have as monkeys who can wear jean shorts and press "Play" on our music devices with our handily opposable thumbs and fingers. So when Pat, Pat, and Paul brought me Wilco, in the form of their first two records, *A.M.* and *Being There*, I was born anew. Jeff Tweedy's music spoke to us, and much of the eared world, with a compelling relevance. It was clearly *our* music. How did he do it? How could he see inside me? Little did I realize that I was enjoying the song stylings of my future husband.

As I had recently moved to LA from Chicago, the town that Jeff Tweedy has called home for twenty-five years or so, his lyrics inspired in me a strong tendency toward nostalgia for my recent years in the Windy City, which had been immensely satisfying on an artistic level. At the time, I was still very good at smoking, so the lines "When you're back in your old neighborhood / The cigarettes taste so good / But you're so misunderstood / You're so misunderstood" really pushed my fond-memory button. With good reason, it turns out, as Mr. Tweedy grew up in a geographical circumstance quite similar to my own. His hometown of Belleville, Illinois, was proximate to St. Louis in the same way that my village of Minooka, Illinois, was close to Chicago. We both felt out of place, or "Misunderstood," in our conservative communities, and so we turned to the arts as an escape route to the world at large.

In the late eighties, Jeff met his future wife, Sue Miller (just the sort of charismatic lady you want to be in charge of things), when she was booking bands at the Cubby Bear in Chicago. Sue subsequently operated the legendary rock club Lounge Ax in Chicago's Lincoln Park, which quickly became the premiere venue for taking in the most enervating new indie rock acts, including Tweedy's band from Belleville, Uncle Tupelo. My pals and I enjoyed the bar for the killer music (like Adelstein's band, Doris) and the cheap, cold longnecks, so there's a good chance that Jeff and I spilled beer on each other at Lounge Ax in the early nineties, although Cupid was clearly not ready for our two hearts to beat as one just yet.

Tweedy, like Dylan, has the knack of composing and delivering his poetry so that *everybody* feels as though it's about him or her personally. When his album *Summerteeth* came out in 1999, with the particularly dark poetry of "Via Chicago," we couldn't stop playing it over and over again at the house in Silver Lake we called Rancho Relaxo (cribbed from *The Simpsons*). Wilco's subsequent records have only served to deepen my discipleship.

The music of Wilco, once they distanced themselves from the slight Uncle Tupelo flavorings of their penetrating first record, *A.M.*, has been delightfully mercurial through the years. It changes and transmogrifies, much like, well, a maturing human personality. One noteworthy peak across the ridge of the Wilco mountains is the story of their 2002 release, *Yankee Hotel Foxtrot*. Sam Jones made a swell documentary film about this juncture in the band's career, called *I Am Trying to Break Your Heart*.

Jeff Tweedy and company were making some excellent new noises with the exploratory songs on the record. Unfortunately, the new bosses at their label, Reprise Records (a division of AOL Time Warner) were not remotely looking for any adjectives like "new" and "exploratory." Despite the fact that Reprise had paid Wilco to produce the record, it looked like the band might get dropped. Industry insiders were astonished at this bullheaded corporate move, as Wilco had become one of the last great original American bands—the kind of trailblazing artists who would attract other acts to Reprise if they played their cards right. Well, as you might have guessed, Reprise shrugged, dropped their drawers, and took a shit on their cards. At the last second, having gotten wind of the bad PR that would be generated by their split with Wilco, they gave them back the rights to *Yankee Hotel Foxtrot*, free of charge.

Tweedy and the band reached into their reservoir of gumption and made the album's tracks available online at a high quality, so that it wouldn't be pirated in a lower-quality audio file format, a canny move, which yielded a great deal of traffic. Wilco then set out on tour and found that, not only were they selling out, but fans were singing along to the new tracks, evidence that their gambit had struck pay dirt. Once news of this reaction got around, labels were lining up to sign the band and release the record. Jeff ended up choosing None-such Records, a small label that happened to be under the very same AOL Time Warner umbrella. Nonesuch agreed to purchase the new record, meaning that the noble troubadours of Wilco had produced an exciting, new, and creative rock-and-roll album, paying no heed to current fashion or radio popularity, as they never have, and they got AOL Time Warner to pay them for it. Twice.

That kind of happy ending doesn't seem to happen to artists who are striving for fame and fortune. By sticking to their creative guns, Wilco ended up being rewarded exponentially more than they ever would have had they been trying to produce radio hits or merely cap-italize on their cute faces. Especially Jeff.

There was a point in time, before television—so, like, back in Jesus's day—when the population paid much more attention to poets and playwrights and essayists and fiction writers. One of the only sources of entertainment or enlightenment was through the verses that came in the form of pamphlets or were delivered orally in the theater or the village square. In the arid climate of contemporary cul-ture, so many American boys and girls regrettably seem to eschew reading of any sort if they can help it. Our grandparents were made to memorize entire poems or Shakespearean sonnets for school, against their wills in most cases, sure, but still they were instilled with an understanding of poetry.

Popular music nowadays is frequently quite vapid. It's fun, sure, and conducive to jiggling one's fanny, but the same platitudes are regurgitated in hit after hit, with all the pop and flavor of a fine sugared breakfast cereal, and with about as much sustenance. "Tonight's gonna be a good night," "I love you, especially your prominent hindquarters," "Let's get ripped and party according to our rights as free fans of country music" are just a few examples, *verbatim*, of songs that are making their authors millions of dollars on the music channels right now.

A band like Wilco, however, can provide similar feelings of blood-rushing elation with the added bonus that their songs stimulate one's imagination. Both in the beginning and today, I try to take in a Wilco concert for my birthday whenever I can. I recall saying to Pat Roberts when we saw them at the Wiltern in LA a couple of years ago that the thing I love about Wilco live is that their poetry and melodies are so pleasing and penetrating, but then they say, "Oh, now would you like us to crank out some throbbing, evocative rock and roll in which you can lose yourself in waves of bodily pleasure?" And then they deliver exactly that.

But as much as I love feeling the visceral rush of rock and roll through m'blood veins, it always comes back to the lyrics, which recalls Wendell Berry's adulation of the human brain's ability to embroider words and images in its imagination more poignantly than any sensation that can ever be grasped in the light of day. So many of Tweedy's verses are wrought of an inscrutable poetry that leaves the listener no choice but to interpret it personally, which leads to inspiration and a much more personal, mutual experience between author and recipient. A favorite of mine:

Remember to remember me
Standing still in your past
Floating fast like a hummingbird

So now you should have a pretty clear idea of my admiration for this artist. Perhaps you're considering your own strategy to ensnare him in a marriage of your very own. Get in line, sailor.

Imagine, then, if you will, my excitement when Jeff Tweedy came to work on *Parks and Recreation*, in an episode I was directing, no less. We met. In fact, we embraced. Jeff was a little nervous about acting on-camera, which makes sense. Ask him to perform any piece of music and he'll tear into it like a seasoned cleric, but take away the security of his superpower—music—and he's understandably more uncertain about what to do. Luckily, he had two beautiful super-friends to guide him through the scene, in Amy Poehler and Chris Pratt. After a couple of warm-up takes, making us laugh behind the camera, he was confidently nailing his bits.

In a sublime example of what made Chris Pratt such a genius on that quality program, he was to sing a song in the scene and play guitar, then get Jeff's character to join in on the song. Well, naturally, Jeff warmed right into the singing and even began to harmonize with Chris, which was one of the dreamiest scenarios I could ever have imagined: Jeff, Chris, and Amy being hilarious, then Jeff Tweedy starts singing just like Jeff Tweedy, and they'll just keep going until the director yells, "Cut!" except the director is *me*, so we'll do this all night! Magnificent! It's good to be the king!

Except . . . every time Jeff would chime in, Pratt would immediately stop the song and say, "No, no . . . wrong. Listen to me." I would think, "Agh! Chris! Jeff is singing! I would like to hear him! Singing out of that hole in his beautiful face!" But at the same time it was so goddamn funny that Chris's character, Andy Dwyer, would unwittingly commit such a sacrilege. He even became visibly frustrated that Jeff "just couldn't get it right." Perhaps Pratt's general secret was that he would simply discern what would be the one thing that his Andy *shouldn't* do in a given scenario, and then he would do exactly that thing, with the relentless enthusiasm of a puppy. Whatever the source of his alchemy, I could never get enough of it, and it certainly served that night to allow Tweedy (and all present) to enjoy himself.

That was the night Jeff and I became friends. I have had the pleasure of his company on several occasions since, most gratifyingly whilst directing a music video for Jeff and his older son (from his current marriage to Sue Miller, as Jeff and I have no kids of our own), Spencer. They have a two-man outfit called Tweedy, and our little video film was for their catchy ditty "Low Key." Really the first project that I have directed all by myself, the video turned out quite satisfyingly, and so I would recommend you view it on the YouTube computer channel (a rare ilk of computer session that I can condone).

Like so many of the troublemakers in my book, Jeff turned out to be incredibly nice. Like a goddamn sweetheart type of nice that I like. I mean to say I like it, which is why I put a ring on it. I can't help but admire his commitment to his family, for one; to his bandmates and other crew, for two; and for three, to his home in Chicago. Sitting at the kitchen table in the Wilco loft, where the Topo Chico mineral water flows like translucent shavings from a Lie-Nielsen hand plane, I met the members of Wilco. They are handsome to a fault, as sweet as a piece of pecan pie, and I trembled to shake their hands, from nervous excitement, but also in fear that I would somehow clumsily injure the phalanges that spin such glorious noise.

They drifted away to continue variously transforming mere air molecules into Willy Wonka's sound waves, as Jeff and I tucked into a rap session. When I began to describe to him the objective of my book and some of the themes I wished to explore, he quickly revealed himself to be a kindred spirit, only except more perceptive and less reactionary and more smarter than me.

Jeff said that "young people are trying to discern who they are, figure out their identity solely through the products they consume, which is the message the corporations are selling us. That's exactly what they want us to do." I replied that young people and also not-young people have me somewhat worried when I think about the consistency with which we Americans seem to fork over our hard-earned incomes to gargantuan corporations for goods that (a) we don't need, (b) are poorly made, (c) in Asia, without thinking. In the same way that Wendell Berry reminds us to simply acknowledge our complicity with rapacious coal mining every time we turn on a light switch, I want us to remember, every time we click "Buy" on our seventh pair of garishly colored Nike sneakers, the American workers who are not getting to make shoes, and the all-but-enslaved Asian children and their parents who are. Oh, sorry—Mauritius! Every choice we make in life can either support our own homes and communities or deny them.

One of the topics that we found mutually fascinating was the proliferation of smartphone use among young people, but really, by now, people of all ages. I know the gadgets are handy, and they may be here to stay, but there are a couple of issues that need addressing.

Firstly, people have quickly come to be perfectly comfortable with asking a person whom they view as good quarry, for a picture. The picture is rarely desired because the supplicant wants a nice picture of someone they admire in some way. Instead, the photograph's value is to be redeemed, as quickly as possible, upon a social media site like Twitter or Instagram or FacePlace. It is as though our civilization is in a giant scavenger hunt, and a photograph of a person with any degree of celebrity has a point value, to be hurriedly logged, tabulated, and then left to descend in the user's "feed," as the hunt for more slivers of fame continues, dogged and never ending.

The rub is this: It's nice to meet fans. I love it. Fan interaction is almost always nice (unless a meal is interrupted—please don't be that douche bag), because it's a reminder from the world that I have a very lucky job. I love my vocation of making people feel better somehow through entertaining them, and so it's gratifying when they tell me that my efforts are succeeding. My favorite interaction is, unsurprisingly, a resolute handshake with eye contact, followed by an exchange of names and perhaps a pleasantry. However, when the focus is shifted, as it so often is, to the photo, the artifact of the interaction, then that is plainly demeaning and sad to me. This instantly objectifies me, in your eyes, transforming me from a human being worth countenancing to a brass ring or chit to be snatched and cashed in, like any roadside attraction. I have often thought that I might as well send a cardboard standee of myself, for all the interest people have in human interaction here in the age of the selfie. My new policy in auto-graph lines is to insist that phones be put away.

The second issue involves brandishing one's phone at any sort of live event, or while taking part in any audience. It saddens me to have to include such an admonishing tone in what has been, for me at least, a pleasant sojourn together so far, but if you pull out your phone at a live event, then you are an asshole. Whether you're taking pic-tures or recording or whatever else your cool apps can do now, you are decisively not playing well with others. With your selfish action, you are degrading not only your experience but the reverie of all those many people in your periphery who have no choice but to wit-ness your gadget and your egregious lapse of attention and respect.

When we purchase a ticket to participate in the audience of a film, play, dance recital, musical performance, or any other live show, we enter into a tacit agreement, along with the rest of the audience, that we will behave with all the decorum appropriate to the genre. This *never* includes holding up an illuminated screen in the purview of all the audience around you.

In the film of his Sunken Treasure tour, Jeff addresses the audience at one point with frustration (for people in the back loudly talking during the songs) that quickly mellows into eloquence about experi-encing live entertainment. He said, "You feel yourself being in a roomful of people, with all their hearts beating, and all their thoughts and feelings, and you're a part of it—you're not just you. . . . It's a really wonderful thing to be a part of, but you have to pay attention to it. . . . You don't set yourself apart from everybody . . . you're a part of something, and it's wonderful."

It's a great concert film, more of a tour film, actually, and I was very moved by that testimonial. Jeff went on to persuade his audience to experience the sensation of remaining completely silent as a group for a time, and the intense hive focus is palpable even in the film, so it must have been utterly fantastic in the room. I am grateful to Jeff for reminding us of the magic that can be achieved in a roomful of people, which is what I have always loved expressly about performing live theater: If you're not there, then you don't get to feel the magic. Attempting to capture a piece of that essence on your phone device is antithetical to the whole point of buying a ticket and sitting in a seat. You *can't* preserve the magic of the medicine being exchanged between performer and audience. Yes, it works both ways—we performers need you to be there for us just as much as you want us to give of ourselves to you.

Holding up a phone or, God forbid, a tablet, is merely the surface of the crime, but the core of the matter is philosophically more rotten. I'll let Jeff take over with an anecdote from a show:

I was really proud of myself because . . . I thought I had come up with the most exquisite way to express how I was feeling and I actually told the person in front of me—I said, "I do want you to film this and I want you to put it on YouTube—you're surrendering your memory to an imperfect medium. Your memory is already imperfect, but this is worse. This is worse. It's never gonna be as good as being here with all these people, losing yourself and at the same time finding yourself a part of something

bigger than yourself. You're never going to experience that in that thing."
And it's the only thing I've never seen on YouTube.

I said, "You are the best husband I have ever had." And he said, "What?" And I said, "Nothing."

One thing I love about being married to Jeff is that, at moments like this, he can calm me down, by now with just a glance, after all we've been through, but even back then, he simply stated that he also meets a lot of kids by whom he is really inspired. First of all, let's take a minute to highlight the Tweedy lads, Spencer and Sam. Both top-drawer young men, refreshingly smart and talented.

Spencer is a rock drummer with a classy sense of panache, already playing with his dad, not to mention Mavis Staples and other major acts for whom Jeff produces records. The first time we chatted, he gave me a comprehensive overview of Chicago politics, in particular how they applied to some current school funding issues, all the while showing me hilarious videos on his phone. Plus, he's got excellent manners, and the deadpan of Buster Keaton. We have spoken on many topics, and I'm usually the one getting the education.

Receiving such lessons from a teenager gives me hope for our future, indeed. Jeff also mentioned that his kids and their friends were really curious and learning to do things that we would never have done as kids, like getting together to make pasta for a handmade pasta party; one kid raises chickens in his parents' basement, which he then barters for guitar strings and other sundries. If I was worried about future generations, pasta and basement poultry make a good start toward assuaging my fear. Jeff adroitly pointed out that kids spending all day in front of the TV, computer, or video games or delinquently committing crimes is a newsworthy story, as in "What is to become of our nation's youth?," but when kids are engaged in satisfying, old-fashioned work or play outside, it's just not a story, so we don't hear about it with nearly as much frequency. The silence doesn't mean the good stuff is not happening.

Sam, the Tweedys' youngest, has a winning demeanor once you get his attention, which can prove to be an elusive prize. Once you get it, though, you are aware of a sharp customer staring out from under his bangs. He's the kid whom all the parents would have had programming their VCRs back in my day. Sammy knows how things operate. Forgivably young, he is still in school and so has appeared less around the scene, but Jeff and Sue operate with their boys in evidence whenever possible—not on display, but as participants in their lives: the hallmark of a family of quality doing it right.

Talking to Jeff about religion, big surprise, we again came down on the same side of the bunk (is that the saying?) regarding any sort of evangelical proselytizing on the part of *any* faith. With his dreamy face, he said, regarding religion's supposed benefit (the removal of ambiguity in one's life concerning the big picture), "I would rather have people happy than sad and coping in some way, but to me the best thing— I don't get to make the rules, but if I [did], everybody would work really, really hard at being okay with not knowing. Everybody would just put their heads together and hug each other and say, 'We don't fucking know.' So let's dance."

I was recently walking across Manchester, England, to go see Jeff and Spencer and some friends play a show at the Ritz. I passed a smartly dressed, handsome young fellow at a corner, handing out a beautiful colored pamphlet with a blue whale on the front, and—what's that? Across the top of the cover was printed the question "Was Life Created?"

"Are you a creationist?" I asked him.

"No, Jehovah's Witness," he replied, as friendly as could be.

"Wow. I would very much like one of those, thank you! This will most assuredly make it into my Jeff chapter!"

He was puzzled by this, but his conditioning won out in the end as he bade me a cheerful good-bye.

This was *fascinating* to me. Here I was, a freewheeling Yank in northern England, and a young chap randomly hands me this bullshit. I read the thing, and the basic objective of the writing is to convince the initiate that "science" is not as reliable a resource for describing the physical world, including all life thereupon, and its creation, as the Christian Bible. They were also quick to point out that the Jehovah's Witness interpretation of the Bible as scientific truth was much less bat-shit crazy than those of other, more fundamentalist sects.

Here's what I want to try to get across to you, and them: I want you to think about why it is, *really*, that your church has you out on that corner. Is it really because of your concern for me and the rest of the uninitiated public? Us non-witnesses? If the contents of your brochure held even one sentence that was not meant as propaganda, like, say, the hard, cold information that we know as science, still fallible by the way, but way more honest, then why would you need to be recruiting others to your cause? Can you understand that your belief system is based upon a book written by human men, describing a creation story that is made up almost entirely of supernatural elements? And so, subscribing to that story as "the truth" requires, by definition, an act of faith. That is why we often refer to religious beliefs as "faith." That's fine and dandy. All who subscribe to your faith are welcome to believe that the world began in any way you like. In fact, our Constitution explicitly states that you may so freely believe.

I would also just like to point out that there are no *scientists* handing out any brochures on any street corners, hoping to convince people that their version of creation is actually true. The scientists are at the pub watching a sporting match of "footie" whilst enjoying a pint with their mates. The difference between their relative confidence and your uncertainty, Bible-brochure-hander-outers, is that they can prove the facts of science (to put it very simply), and you can't prove the first phrase of your claims. Please think about that. Why do you suppose some guys who wrote a Bible had the "God" character in the Bible recommend that *you* convince all the other people to sign up for this program? What if we pagans happen to be the absolutely most Christlike Samaritans on the planet, but we don't believe in God? Is that not okay with you? Think about it.

By the way, as Jeff pointed out, as well as Wendell Berry, we *don't know*. Scientifically or biblically, we can never actually know everything, ever. Those big questions are what we call "mysteries," and they're a really cool and irrefutable part of life. Instead of denying them or embroidering religious myths around them, let us simply respect them. Democrats, Republicans, women, men, in-betweeners, Americans, earthlings, let's all try to respect the mysteries that make us all just people. We're complicated; we defy really any absolute categorization beyond that of "human."

Jeff was there to reassure me. He said gently to my whiskered face, "'What do I have control over and how can I take [my] power back over the actual things that [I] have control over? What would make the world a better place based on what I'm actually able to do?' And what would make the world a better place, if people followed my example, would be if they made shit instead of destroying shit. If they spent more of their day being squarely on the side of creation versus destruction. I say [it] all the time [when asked]—'What do you think politically, where do you stand as an artist?'—Art is its own country. It's its own state, and I don't need to have a political view—What I do is political . . . squarely, on the side of creation, there's a place for you . . . you invest yourself. That's what it is."

I walked into the empty Ritz theater in Manchester where Jeff stood alone onstage with the vintage Gibson J-200 that he calls Buck, getting ready to sound check. He was performing Neil Young's song "The Losing End," and he smiled and nodded when he saw me. He sang:

Well, I miss you more than ever,
since you've gone
I can hardly maintain.
Things are different 'round here
every night,
my tears fall down like rain.

I thought the same thing that every fan thinks when it seems as though Jeff Tweedy is singing to him or her alone: "I will have you for my husband."

The Humorist

18

GEORGE SAUNDERS

I need to come clean here. I'm afraid I must level with you. A big part of my attraction to this project, if it's not already perfectly obvious, has been my selfish desire to meet some of my heroes. My editor, Jill Something, and I were discussing the loose shape of this undertaking, when it occurred to me: I could exploit this "book project" to serve my own nefarious motives. We quickly amassed our list of thirty-eight or forty Americans, starting with mostly historical, or "dead," individuals, and then there were some obvious living figures who were proffered by Jill, knowing me rather well after editing my first effort at a "book project" (the canoe one).

"Wendell Berry," she said.

"Duh."

"What about Carol Burnett?" she lobbed.

"You read my file. Two for two."

Then it got fun. Running through the greatest hits of my life, in any cultural arena—it didn't matter—to land upon citizens with gumption. I began piling on actors and filmmakers and musicians and artisans, but a deficit occurred to me: I didn't really have a modern luminary of literature on the list. Wendell Berry and Michael Pollan don't count, because calling Mr. Berry a writer is like calling Gandalf an igniter of fireworks, and Mr. Pollan is straight-up nonfiction.

"George Saunders," I said.

"Ooh, yes," she affirmed, always the mollycoddler, but also a smarty-pants, so she knows what's good.

Jill wrote to George's editor (they belong to the same font club) and passed along this tiny note from me, a similarly personalized version of which I sent to each of my hopeful subjects:

> *Dear Mr. Saunders,*
>
> *Hello! My name is Nick Offerman, and I am an actor and woodworker and writer. I am working on my second book for Dutton over at Penguin Random House, a book that will comprise a list of "Great Americans"—each person selected for his/her exhibition of a spirit of rebellion or muckraking or revolution with regard to the way we are evolving, particularly in America, toward decency (or not). I sincerely hope that the book will contain more humor than that last sentence.*
>
> *Other subjects will include some "founding father" material, focusing on how this whole American experiment took wing, or hoof, as well as many other political and cultural firebrands. A couple of Roosevelts, Theodore and Eleanor, Frederick Law Olmsted, as well as some modern-day achievers, like Yoko Ono, Michael Pollan, and Wendell Berry, and other artists, woodworkers, activists, farmers, and a couple of boatbuilders.*

I want to examine some of the good and bad effects of "progress," from the Europeans' conquering of North America to the plight of modern advertising/television, and how we continue to succeed or not at becoming more decent people whilst surfing a massive tsunami of technology, information, and media saturation. Looking at religion, technology, human rights, nature, guns/war, tobacco, hand-crafting, advertising . . . hopefully with a chuckle. Hilarious, right?

I am quite besotted with your fiction, for its humor, intelligence, and social criticism. As such, I'd love to include you in my next humble book effort. What that would entail depends upon your willingness, but I would cite parts of your writing that support my themes, and then ask you some pertinent questions about the ideas therein. I could do it by correspondence, but I would prefer to sit and chat if possible, perhaps over a coffee or plate of ribs.

I am happy to conduct this conversation in any setting you may prefer, and I am conveniently commuting between New York and Los Angeles for the balance of 2014, to perform husbandry upon my bride of 14 years, Megan Mullally, an exceptionally talented and beautiful lady. She will be performing in a Terrence McNally play (It's Only a Play) from September through January 4. If you'd like to come as my guest, do simply holler.

I would also relish springing for any meal or diversion in which you might like to partake during our chin-wag. Perhaps I could row you across the Hudson in an historic Whitehall skiff, and that is not a joke. I know a guy.

I am happy to provide any references you might like to investigate, and also my first clumsy tome, Paddle Your Own Canoe, *upon which I can't wait to improve.*

Sincerely,

Nick Offerman

P.S. Perhaps we can work in a jaunt in the park?

Long-winded? You bet. That's my bag. Surely that has dawned on you before now. But I had to be sure that the sincere tone of my proposed book (this one!) was sincerely communicated, while simultaneously putting across my sense of humor. Furthermore, I wanted to make the idea seem as painless as possible so that the inconvenience of spending an afternoon with me wouldn't seem like a clear deterrent.

Imagine my excitement, then, when this showed up in my electronic mailbox *the next day*:

Dear Nick,

Loved your letter and would be very happy to get together. We're big fans of your work and of your wife's work around here. I think it might be best for me to try something in the fall—am cranking away on a new book for the remainder of the summer, with a quick trip to LA to see our daughter. Would be fun to see the play, if that's possible. Thanks for reaching out and for reading my stories and all of that too.

George Saunders

P.S. Ok, but no carriage rides.

He was a peach! This was no minor deal—as a person who works in show business and lives in Los Angeles, it so happens that sometimes I get to run into people I admire, and sometimes they are not nearly as swell as I would have hoped. The disappointment can be crushing. Usually, though, it's just surreal, like the time I pulled up next to a nice convertible, I think a Bentley, at a light. I looked over to see Dustin Hoffman at the wheel. He looked at me and slowly nodded, as though to say, "That's right, son," before zooming away. That Dustin Hoffman shares this plane of existence and (presumably) wields a driver's license makes my head swim.

To receive a reply in such a generous fashion from someone like George Saunders was a thrilling surprise, to say the least. I do believe I may have giggled, and it's likely that I performed a portion of a jig. We struck up a correspondence, George and I, and soon discovered that we had a lot in common when it came to our developmental years, a fact that would prove to engender an easy camaraderie between us. He's been teaching creative writing at Syracuse since 1997, which is in a particularly gorgeous region of far upstate New York, redolent of maple, walnut, cherry, and sycamore trees, among other noble deciduous favorites.

As it happens, we finally made a date for December 19, 2014. George was going to be in New York City, and I cleared my day, reread my favorite stories, and planned our itinerary. Despite his reticence, I looked into a carriage ride. It would have been so cozy!

Upon the day, I arrived at the brownstone that Syracuse maintains on the Upper East Side. George stepped gamely out into the cold air and we exchanged a friendly embrace. I've noticed that this is happening more recently—people hugging openly instead of the handshake or weird, extra-hetero "bro" handshake/half hug/back pat. Maybe it's just occurring within my own circle of artistic love, but I recommend it to you, this technique of hugging, no matter where you may reside. It really lends an immediate sense of camaraderie and trust that is not fully conveyed by the more circumspect handshake. I am also traveling so frequently these days that each such meeting with a valued compatriot has become that much more precious, as in: "Good God, let us sit and talk together and try to do some good, because I fly out for Topeka in the morning."

We went to a classically New York, or "crappy," diner (perfect) around the corner and took a little table for two halfway back along the wall in the shotgun layout of the joint. The waiter came quickly, took our orders for coffee, and moved on. I started my recorder and we dove in, but not before the waiter came back to take our food order. It being nine thirty A.M., we had both had our breakfasts. This coffee was intended to serve as the prologue to a very special lunch date.

"If you're not gonna eat, you can move to the back, or you can be quick!" barked the all-business bacon slinger.

"We'll be quick," said George.

I didn't want to be quick. I wanted to be slow and comfortable so that my interview with George could be as good-written as possible. He is good of writing, and I wanted him to see that I could also, too. Also, plus, my journalism is still additionally maturing, so I really needed time to take in the details of my surroundings, like a sponge, you know, that starts out dry, but then you get water on it and it gets wet totally. It "absorbs" all the "wetness." Metaphor. You know, so I could squeeze, then, the water of some stark truth into my "piece." All over it.

I inhaled, squinting with peepers, through my nose holes like in a sleuth simile. I looked left. Nothing of details would escape my looking. Salt . . . pepper, what's up? Sugar and other sweeteners in paper squares but longer than a square, like so many small-ass, monochromatic, or "one-color," flags from the nations of Diabetes Town. Their valor is weak, as evinced by the Eastery color choices of yellow, pink, and green fading, like the sense memory of my eyes sensing the colors in Aunt Dee's powder room in 1983, except she also had a shitload of lavender.

To my right, a row of fucked-up toadstools, except the stems were steel and the caps were like cushions for sitting on, like a seat stool stuck in the forest floor, except this was a real floor with linoleum covering like a really spread-out hat.

"Goddamn," I thought. "I'm gonna write the shit outta this thing."

I slipped the waiter a twenty and said we'd be staying for a bit. His apron pocket sucked up that bill like a northern pike inhaling a night crawler. That's a fish. Eating a worm. But figurative. I felt like I had pokered in playing that dicey hand, "New York style," and the nice thing about a book deal is I can write that twenty dollars off, so I guess the joke was on you, Joaquín.

When George Saunders puts away some coffee and begins to rap, you had better pay attention. As he says himself, his thoughts come very quickly and explosively, and they'll turn on a dime. Given the level of creativity at which he operates, that made for an extremely intense conversation that was more delicious to me than many

Reuben sandwiches I've known. I mean to say his language was god-damn delectable.

I would expect a person packing the horsepower of intelligence that is exhibited in his story writing to be arrogant. I would also expect that person, in a dialogue with me, to eventually, or, well, soon, arrive at con-descension, no matter how pure their motives at the outset. Mr. Saunders exhibits neither arrogance nor haughtiness. He is a sweetheart who hap-pens to have a surgically incisive talent for writing, especially satire. Sorry if I'm blowing your cover, George, but I'm a writer, and I truth it up like in a way that I can't help it, because of that's how I play.

George grew up in a suburb of Chicago called Oak Forest, Illinois. It's hard to imagine a community name that conjures a more charis-matic image than Oak Forest, unless you want to throw maybe the Shire, Rivendell, or Wildwood into the ring. He attended Oak Forest High School, approximately thirty-five miles east of my Minooka High School, which explains our mutual love of the Chicago Cubs, but not the garlic-buttered, chopped-steak sandwich known locally, in my area, as the poor boy. George's neighborhood had a chipped beef sandwich, but it was sadly bereft of any colorful moniker.

Like myself, young Saunders took to the stage of the Catholic church as a lad, where he found he quite enjoyed the captive audi-ence, who, as church etiquette demands, must politely consume whatever it is you read from the big, gospel-y book, howsoever you choose to deliver it. George enjoyed "getting up and milking the mike," as he put it, in his parish's newly constructed and acoustically pleasing meetinghouse.

But that's plenty enough about this writer guy, wouldn't you say?

Let's take a look at something very nice George said to *me* about what he sees as the core of the matter concerning what makes my character, Ron Swanson, work on the quality program *Parks and Recreation*. "The first time I saw you, I thought, 'I know that guy.' And you have a whole legion of people behind you . . . the way that you had crystallized your knowledge of where you came from was evident and it represented more than just you. You're bringing a world that isn't normally represented correctly."

Now, of course this was a nice thing to hear from George, but I can pretty swiftly deflect a healthy portion of the credit to the fact that, as Ron Swanson, I am merely the embodiment of a rich collaboration. Without the writers and my castmates and the rest of the crackerjack crew, I would be much less effective. Unlike Mr. Saunders, who is doing his magnificent work all on his lonesome.

He continued. "Your physical bearing and the way you work, it brings out something of America that—I thought, 'Oh, my God, there's a whole part of my life that just opened up in the way he looks onscreen.'"

Again, "the way [I] look onscreen" is more thanks to my parents (for the genes), the costume designer, and the hair and makeup crew, not to mention the grips and electricians, who illuminate me *and* the edifice of a hairdo we call "the Full Douche." The reason I have done myself the favor of pointing out these nice observations on the part of George is to point out George's propensity for nice observations. Every character he introduced into our conversation had enjoyed a similar attention from his affectionate eye: "He had enormous forearms"; "she was one of those sexy, bottle-waisted, middle-age types"; "he's got a really strong Chicago accent"; etcetera.

I *would* like to flatter myself so far as to acknowledge that we recognize something of kin in each other, the kind of folk who know their way around a can of suds, a tire gauge, and a potato fork (hipsters, please don't appropriate those as your next accessories). We have both worked as roofers. George also worked in a slaughterhouse, an experience I don't envy him, but the simple fact of which gives me an idea of his tenacity.

Don't get me wrong—these are not boasts. The familial feeling is born of, quite conversely, an understanding that we have simply endured the parts of life that a person doesn't brag about and have come out the other side with ten fingers. Each. Nonetheless, I have to cop to this: George Saunders paid me some compliments, and I have repeated them in my book, which makes me a jerk, and no amount of equivocation can dilute that. Moving on.

His stories have been compared to Kurt Vonnegut's, for their seriocomic timbre, and I suppose that the freshness of his prose must bear a similarity to the whimsical strangeness Vonnegut presented when he was new on the scene. If you have yet to enjoy George's stories, you're in for a delectable treat, and not just a dessert, like pie, but the kind of dessert that makes you think. Like three hours of pie with a Zen koan written out in the crust.

Take, for example, this bit from a CNN interview on the eve of the millennium in 1999:

I don't think much new ever happens. Most of us spend our days the same way people spent their days in the year 1000: walking around smiling, trying to earn enough to eat, while neurotically doing these little

self-proofs in our head about how much better we are than these other
slobs, while simultaneously, in another part of our brain, secretly feeling
woefully inadequate to these smarter, more beautiful people.

George Saunders says that, as a young man, he knew somewhere deep down that he wanted to be a writer, but he wouldn't realize it for some time. He studied the guitar instead, playing in different bands and determining that he would become known as a virtuoso. He doggedly learned an extremely difficult classical piece (*Capricho árabe*, by Francisco Tárrega) with which to impress his teacher at community college. He worked and worked until he felt cocky, and when he went in to perform it, he played it better than he ever had before. He ripped through it with intensity.

When he'd finished, he cracked his knuckles and waited for his mentor to tell him that he had "the goods."

His teacher, apparently moved, said, "I want to tell you something."

"Yeah?" said George.

"If you don't change your life, you're going to be a very unhappy adult."

What he then explained to George was that, sure, he had mechanically nailed going through the motions of the song, but without paying any attention to how it *sounded*. The teacher told him that he had a certain talent but that his tone was no good. Tough love, to be sure, but George and I agreed that many of today's youth could use just such a dose, because for all its toughness, it is still love.

One might thank the guitar teacher for his timely admonition, since the work George has done since finding his true calling (although he is still a wicked guitarist) is veritably dripping with tone.

In any case, that was more or less the end of George's musical aspirations. He found himself somewhat adrift until his high school biology teacher, Joe Lindblom ("You would love him—he's a sailor. Your feeling toward woodwork? He's got about sailing"), gave him a copy of Ayn Rand's *Atlas Shrugged*. Reading that novel (and libertarian treatise) cracked open a door in George's imagination that he hadn't previously noticed. He began to realize that he was a thinker.

To wit: "It made me think I could go to college. I had this kind of comic vision of myself, like, in a sweater with some girls, talking philosophy. Just walking across campus talking about the big issues."

Saunders couldn't read music, but he applied to Boston's prestigious Berklee College of Music and was denied. Same for Notre Dame. Huh. Joe Lindblom came to his rescue once again and hooked him up with the Colorado School of Mines, Lindblom's alma mater. Because of his former teacher's faith in him, George buckled down (with gumption) and completed the community college hours he needed to be accepted, and even then, it took a personal vouching from Joe Lindblom to seal the deal. Thus was Saunders saved from the ignominy suffered by so many young people who just give up on having any ambition in life through a combination of apathy and ignorance. Thank you from afar, Joe Lindblom, and I believe George was right. I love you plenty.

That was 1976. George took to the work and graduated with a degree in geophysics. Over the next several years, he "beatnik'd around," working in Asia, Los Angeles, Illinois, and Amarillo, still casting about for his entrée into his true calling: "I think it was basically a process of not being that great at being an engineer (and the queasy feeling that went along with it) and not being quite bright enough to go directly for what I liked (ie, reading and writing)."

After such beating about the bush, Saunders finally decided to go for it as a writer—"all or nothing." He applied to himself a work ethic over a few years that was more about finding a method and a rhythm: "I didn't make much progress, except it suddenly started to seem doable—like a series of choices that led to other choices. Wrote a weird story that got published—sort of a precursor to the stories in *CivilWarLand*—and used that to get into Syracuse. So, to paraphrase Fitzgerald or Hemingway: 'Gradually and all at once.'"

When George first arrived at Syracuse to study creative writing in graduate school, straight from Amarillo, he had the impression that his unusual, more rural background would be valued by the mostly urbane, Ivy League classmates among which he found himself. He was mistaken.

They derisively would say things like, "Amarillo? Aren't there a lot of currency exchanges there?"

George said, "I kept trying to get it through to them that, like, these are people living [in Amarillo]. There's real life going on there." To me, he added, "It was never anything but a joke to them, but to me it was hurtful. I said, 'I know I'm right. I know that they're blind to this whole part of the country.'"

And so, indirectly, the Ivy League snobs helped George along as well, by influencing him to galvanize his vision of the America he would feature in his stories; those living in the not-inconsiderable acreage between the cities of "tastemakers" on either coast. Despite the erudition evident in his writing, one can't help but feel his feet (and his point of view) rooted among the people of Amarillo and Illinois and Colorado and so on. The People.

His gift for effective storytelling involves an uncanny ability to examine all sides of every question without judgment. I don't know about you, but I'm a human being, so my default setting is to absolutely come down on one side of any issue, depending upon how the question affects my well-being. I believe that's called human nature. Because he loves us, George Saunders respects every opinion, leaving his own ego out of it, which makes even his scariest scenarios palatable.

Another topic upon which we spent a good deal of Joaquín's twenty-dollar table time was a mutual appreciation for our redoubtable fathers. George shared this story, which seems to me to have laid the foundation for his ever-expanding generosity toward the human race: At Oak Forest High School, in the 1970s, the food was apparently terrible. "They had the hamburgers in the plastic bags that you would microwave and whatnot." So the students decided they would organize a walkout. "We were very much in the thrall of Abbie Hoffman and the whole thing [re: the 1969–70 Chicago Conspiracy Trial]." So everything was set to stick it to the man on a Friday morning, but the Thursday night previous it occurred to George that maybe he would tell his dad about it, just in case. So he did. He honestly told his dad they were planning a walkout because the food was so bad.

"'Oh, yeah. Sure, that's great,' said Dad. 'Could I ask you something, though?'"

George said to me, "Just like Columbo."

"'Just one thing. You've let the principal know that this food is an issue, right?'"

"'Nah, he wouldn't listen.'"

"'Oh. Okay. Although you're kinda setting yourself up a little bit. Because if you walk out and you never tried to solve the problem . . . Anyway, just think about it.'"

The next morning, George went in to speak with the principal, Toby Hightower.

"'George, uh, what? What's goin' on?'"

George hadn't known that Principal Hightower even knew his name. He soldiered on and explained that the food in the cafeteria was really bad.

"'Well, that's not acceptable. I'm gonna appoint you head of a commission. Now, I want you to go out to— Would five days be enough? Five different school districts, every Friday you go out and— Pick a panel, three or four kids—and we'll send you out to these schools. You tell us which one you like and you wanna hire.'"

"Anyway," George said, "that little move that my dad did there was like—don't assume your enemy is beneath you."

Pretty badass dad skills right there. I began to understand how such a man as George Saunders could come to write stories with such a sincerely fair and balanced perspective, not to mention a measured examination of modern American society that requires backing up only the slightest step before the purview shows us to be clearly hilarious, heads buried in our phones, scrutinizing who might "like" us, fashion trends swinging recently from "heavily tattooed and stretching irreparable holes in the earlobe with gauge rings" to "lumbersexual," which apparently entails growing a beard, wearing flannel over pre-distressed work dungarees, and posing for photographs with an axe of any stripe. (I have been mortified to be even tangentially mentioned by "the press" in association with this, or any such fashion trend, but I can rest easy. I looked like that twenty years ago, and I'll still look like that twenty years from now, if my luck holds.)

At this point in our chin-wag, George and I left the scrutiny of Joaquín's hawklike gaze and set out across Central Park. No locomotion by carriage, sadly, just perambulating. I greatly enjoyed the commingling of my subjects, rambling with Saunders toward the west side of Olmsted's park, under the beneficent Dakota windows of Yoko, as George revealed to me that not only was he a Wendell Berry fan, but he had set one of his poems, "The Wild Rose," to music! Reminder to self—score that track for audiobook. (I actually said to George, "We may have to lay that track down," and he said, "Yeah, lay it down and cover it up.") We arrived right on time for our lunch at the newly refurbished Tavern on the Green, the history of which I delightedly explained to George as we sat to steaks and beer and fellowship in the former sheep barn for Olmsted's pacifist flock.

As it so often does with me, the subject turned to religion. It's funny—I have been on the receiving end of a good deal of knee-jerk reactions from followers of various Christian denominations regarding my religious material. They don't seem to comprehend my commentary, a blindness that is, I suppose, the way of the zealot? What such critics don't seem to glean is that I am probably thinking about their religion much more than they ever have. The religions of the world are generally founded upon deep wisdom and beautiful notions that have been carefully wrought. Much as I have done for our founding governmental documents, I would just like to suggest that we always continue to freshly examine the truths at the foundation, rather than just accept our televangelists' interpretation at face value. Sometimes when I speak to people about Wendell Berry, they ask, "Don't you know he's religious, though?" I answer that, yes, he is my favorite kind of religious person: one who knows what the hell he's talking about. You won't catch Mr. Berry blindly following the *people* who are leading their flocks in all sorts of disparate directions, some few of them decent. Mr. Berry also has enough respect for his fellow man and woman to refrain from attempting to recruit us into his church. By removing these confusing modern church habits from the conversation, he is able to shine a light on the heart of the matter: the writing. It's not the text of the Bible that's troublesome (with a few notable exceptions—please see my previous book), but what people are doing in the name of that text that bothers me, as well as Wendell Berry.

George Saunders agreed that such blind adherence to rote dogma creates the false impression among church folk (and political parties) that matters of the soul (or government) can be rendered neatly in black-and-white terms. The thing I love about these great thinkers by whom I am inspired is that they understand the *imperative* of coming from a place of ignorance, which will never change. The mysteries of the universe can literally never be decoded, and so the task before us is not in the solving but rather in accepting the ambiguity in the parts of our world where unknowable magic, also known as nature, resides.

George started out Catholic, as discussed, but was soon disillusioned by that brand of solace. Now he is a practicing Buddhist, and it shows.

He said, "What I'm trying to understand is how Christianity—if you could be sitting with Jesus, okay, the guy. You know, that guy . . . How did it then [go from that] and become, like, no swearing and no fornication? . . . Well, I do know how. The culture said, 'Hey, that's good. Let's lay *our* shit down there.'" Wendell Berry just published a new book of essays in which he addresses the folly of such an approach—by refusing to consider the whole of all the complexities of human life as one and instead having the hubris to think that we can control individual actions like premarital sex or blasphemy as though they can be separated cleanly from the whole organism. Should these indiscretions be the recipients of some of our focus? Absolutely. No question. But to simply, flatly forbid these inexorable acts of nature takes about as much smarts as the enacting of Prohibition did, and we all know how that turned out.

Mr. Saunders (hell of a good rib eye at Tavern on the Green, by the by, plus local craft brews) made yet another perceptive point. He said, "Somehow it's weird that all these thousands of years of human thought have gravitated toward those questions and those approaches, and now here we are with not much, really. We're extreme materialists. So I've just been trying to figure out a way to think about those things. I say that in a positive way, meaning, as your doubts come up—totally allow them in the room." Allowing one's doubts to exist "in the room" requires courage. These religions have flourished, in part, for centuries exactly so that we don't have to stay in the same room with our misgivings, our elemental comprehension of what

H. P. Lovecraft illuminated so succinctly: "The oldest and strongest emotion of mankind is fear, and the oldest and strongest kind of fear is fear of the unknown."

This has really become a refrain with so many of the great scholars profiled in this book. Own your doubts. Recognize our fallibility as humans, admit we can never possibly know even half of everything about the natural world, and so then embrace the unknown and, thereby, embrace one another. There is comfort.

George continued. "It's funny to go back to the Catholic stuff with some of that in mind. They had a beautiful thing that they kind of covered in crap, and if you could tear all that [dogma] off, there are incredible principles at the center of it. But it's almost like if I was gonna give you a gift, and I put it in the middle of six rooms full of Styrofoam. [You] would be like, 'What's all the Styrofoam for?'"

An excellent point that I would reiterate. Most all religions have terrific and valuable principles at their centers. The owner's-manual quality of the values they have to teach us is sublime, or it can be. But by the time you get down to simply meditating upon the principle, you have had to slog through a great number of self-serving, man-made rules.

George: "It's that people get habituated to certain ways of thinking and they associate, for example, Christianity with a legitimately positive feeling they've had in church or whatever. But then it gets locked in, so they take all the Styrofoam as well. They accept it. So the enemy becomes the habituation."

He talks good, this George Saunders. Super good. We agreed that this conundrum is very similar to the state of politics in most households as well. Habituation sets in, and we citizens no longer feel the need to stay on top of every issue coming down the pike. Thanks to the "Styrofoam" around our political leanings, we can simply (and lazily) vote down party lines and never miss a wink of sleep. George pointed out that it's just like Wendell Berry's take on the programs of optimism and pessimism—our "programs" put us in the dangerous position of complacently siding with "our kind," whether it's Catholic or Muslim, Democrat or Republican, Caucasian or Cherokee.

George and I reemerged into the park after lunch, enjoying a bracing stroll as he walked me to the subway, but he had thankfully not quite finished chewing on his theme. That is (to paraphrase him), that these habituations that have become deep ruts in which all our wheels will run without a need for steering are a sort of philosophical slavery. Quoting Abraham Lincoln (yes, he's like *that*, and what's more, he later sent me the full quote for accuracy), he laid this on me as we arrived at Columbus Circle: "As I would not be a slave, so I would not be a master. This expresses my idea of democracy. Whatever differs from this, to the extent of the difference, is no democracy." That guy Lincoln also talked pretty good.

From this, I would suggest that since many of our politicians are by now being rather openly paid by corporations to shape our nation's laws to serve their profits above our individual rights, we have all become slaves of a different sort. Are we not slaves (me included) to the messaging that controls much of our prodigious consumption? How else do we explain our insistence on blithely purchasing an endless stream of unnecessary goods, sending each previous generation of disposable purchases to the landfill?

In 2006 George was hired by *GQ* magazine to write a series of pieces about the contentious border situation between Mexico and the United States. He loaded up his car and began to drive along that imaginary line, and, as he puts it:

> *It was so amazing because every time I'd start [writing] with some idea, usually a liberal idea, then go in, and in the first couple of days of reporting it was totally destroyed. [I] come back and start writing them, and [I'm] like, I'm not going to write according to some notion. I'm gonna see what my best bits are, polish them, put them together, and then see what light comes off. That's the closest to the truth, and it's always gonna be contradictory. . . . By the end, I couldn't think of a thing to say, and I thought—that's the truth. Right there. The individual things are all true but the truth is the composite of all those with [me] not choosing.*

You should buy all of George's books. They are immensely enjoyable but also rife with food for thought in the vein of the topics in this chapter. His most recent book of stories, *Tenth of December*, is a masterpiece of prescient social commentary, packed with the uncomfortable laughter of self-recognition.

I'll end by recommending to you his smallest book, *Congratulations, by the Way*, really just a printed version of the convocation speech he delivered to the graduating class of Syracuse University in 2013. It would make a great stocking stuffer or certainly would be well received by any graduate in your own life. He takes the opportunity, in addressing the shiny, hopeful, collected students, to advise them, above all else in the impending adventures of their lives, to practice kindness. That's it. The fact that this very successful, richly lauded writer chose that sentiment as the focus of his address—be kind—moves me profoundly. As I say good night, George, let's end with a lovely excerpt from that address:

Find out what makes you kinder, what opens you up and brings out the most loving, generous, and unafraid version of you—and go after those things as if nothing else matters. Because, actually, nothing else does.

19

LAURIE ANDERSON

As it turns out, I'm writing this chapter in Istanbul, which used to be called Constantinople—a turn of events that is melodically described in a swinging number by the Four Lads, later covered by one of my all-time favorite bands, They Might Be Giants.

I have often expressed my gratitude to those friends in my life who have been responsible for pointing me in the direction of "the good shit," in terms of books, records, plays, and films. One of the most formative instances of this benevolence occurred in 1989 when my dear pally Joe Foust sold me on They Might Be Giants. Their first few records, in fact, could serve as the soundtrack to my personal transition from ignorant but curious small-town athlete to ignorant but curious college theater student with better taste in music.

Joe hooked me specifically by using their cover of "Istanbul (Not Constantinople)" as the front-of-house music when he did a college production of *Constantinople Smith*, by Charles L. Mee, the self-same prolific fellow who wrote *The Berlin Circle*, the play in which I met my wife. Near the end of that show, the entire cast sings the Beatles' "All

You Need Is Love" in German ("Alle Brauchen Liebe"), bringing me around to Yoko. I do so appreciate such turns of serendipity, and I like to notice when the strands of life connect in such a fashion.

On their albums *They Might Be Giants*, *Lincoln*, and *Flood*, the band displays myriad examples of musical styles, rendered with the whimsy of the most sublime jesters. With lyrics hilarious, strange, and educational, backed by instrumentation ranging from baritone sax and xylophone to accordion, to literally the kitchen sink and a refrigerator being struck with drumsticks, the charismatic Brooklyn duo of John Flansburgh and John Linnell funded our young, burgeoning imaginations with artistic possibilities both richly detailed and patently absurd.

On their third release, *Flood*, considered to be their definitive recording (although they have many varied and excellent subsequent records), track six stood out to me as something special. "Your Racist Friend" is sung from the point of view of a partygoer who refuses to stand by while another reveler engages in racist language. It's a catchy tune with a thoughtful heart: "This is where the party ends / I can't stand here listening to you / And your racist friend." This was an eye-opening moment for me—a song from a fun, weird band that I loved could also have a powerfully relevant social message? Say. I liked where this was going.

This epiphany, it turned out, was merely the appetizer for the work of another artist who was about to change the trajectory of my creative development. Mr. Foust and the rest of the gang who would go on to form Chicago's Defiant Theatre company with me took me to see a woman on tour at the University of Illinois's magnificent

Foellinger Auditorium. It proved to be one of the most astonishing live performances I have ever witnessed. The tour and album were called *Strange Angels*, and the woman's name was Laurie Anderson.

When performing live, especially in that era, Laurie Anderson loved to employ technology, or as it became in her hands, toys. Please bear in mind that in 1990, technology was not remotely as advanced or ubiquitous as it is today. The Sony Discman was cutting-edge, and computers were generally still monstrous hard drives with a TV monitor—and not a flat-screen TV, but the kind that was as deep as it was wide. An entire rock concert of the day, replete with projections and video components, probably used less memory than your iPod Nano.

There was a large video screen hanging upstage at Ms. Anderson's show, and she stood at a keyboard, or set of keyboards, with other doohickeys in evidence, technically speaking. There were three microphones, side by side in a row. I'm writing this from memory, but what I remember is that through her groundbreaking use of technology in performance, she bent and stretched our little midwestern minds before fully blowing them when she picked up her electric violin.

The central microphone worked normally, but each of the two side microphones piped Laurie's voice through a filter, so one sounded like a somewhat truculent, authoritative man (an alter ego who has come to be known in later years as Fenway Bergamot), and the other mike filtered her voice into a harmonizing chorus. The videos on the screen alternated between abstract beauty and short vignettes in which she was playing the man character, complete with mustache,

and shot with some sort of fish-eye lens, creating a somewhat dwarf-
ing, fun-house-mirror effect. Her electric violin looked like something out of *Tron* that might also emit a lightsaber's blade, and I also
recall a bit where the lights went dark and the only light was inside
her mouth, intermittently visible through the opening and closing
iris of her lips.

Those futuristic effects were merely the garnishes of an aural feast
that served course after course of poetry and song, alternating effortlessly between humor and beauty and erudition, sometimes all in one
verse. The artist herself was, and is, the definition of puckish. She
casually wields a beautiful, fairylike face, augmented by hair sculpted
into spikes of mischief. Her singing voice, unadorned, is lovely and
plaintive, given to chewy consonants and popping stop-plosives when
her voice goes into character. The combination of her violin and the
computer/synthesizer/keyboard at her fingertips provided a veritable
onslaught of musical sound, running the gamut from a quiet, ambi-
ent shower to a crashing monsoon.

Can you tell I was smitten? I was, in case that's not made clear by
the intensity of my recall some twenty-six years later. Just imagine,
you take that whole package in a dark theater, bring up some interesting, minimalist shafts of green and blue light, strike a few sustained
chords like a tired calliope, and then hear her speak:

I met this guy.

And he looked like he might have been a hatcheck clerk.

At an ice rink.

Which, in fact, he turned out to be.

And I said,

"Oh, boy. Right again."

Let X=X.

You would have been equally enamored. As was my habit, I began to search out everything she had done that I could find, which turned out to be a great deal, as she has been an accomplished visual artist, composer, poet, photographer, filmmaker, electronics whiz, vocalist, and instrumentalist since the 1970s.

There was another song that first night that stood out to me in the same way that "Your Racist Friend" had struck a chord with its social consciousness. This time, the track was "Beautiful Red Dress," and the theme was not racism but feminism.

I'm sure that I was distantly aware of the 1970s ERA of Carol Burnett and other heroic ladies, but with the much more imperative subject of baseball on my child's mind in small-town Illinois, it did not occur to me to perform any arithmetic around the topic. So when Laurie Anderson spoke these words to me and my fellow audience members during the bridge of that song in 1990, it was very much my awakening as a woman: "Okay! Okay! Hold it! I just want to say something. You know, for every dollar a man makes, a woman makes sixty-three cents. Now, fifty years ago that was sixty-two cents. So, with that kind of luck, it'll be the year 3888 . . . before we make a buck."

It was hard to miss the point, when she put it like that. Here I was, absolutely besotted with this ethereal talent and the plying of her wares, but when I heard that particular line—that was the moment I understood Laurie Anderson to be heroic as well as intoxicating.

Contemporary research reveals the gender wage gap to be a bit of a moving target. President Obama cited the ratio at seventy-seven cents to the man's dollar a few years ago, but that has been discredited. It's difficult (for me, anyway) in this age of the twenty-four-hour news cycle and the endless websites devoted to "the truth" to ferret out any purely factual information, unblemished by some party's agenda. Regardless of the precise number, the gap perseveres. I do find it satisfying that the situation is improving, but the glacial pace of coming equality could use a goose.

It's been 240 years or so since this nation was founded by an elite group of white men, which seems like it would be a decent enough amount of time to find a balance in the way we reward folks of either gender, as well as those whose genders reside somewhere in between male and female.

As I have said, throughout my life, women have been in charge of a significant portion of my own little universe, beginning with my grandmother and aunts running the farm business in roles somewhere between CEO and CFO (not to mention driver, cook, laundress, and card sharp), followed by the directors and artistic directors of the Defiant and Steppenwolf Theatres.

Five excellent female persons make up more than half the staff of eight at Offerman Woodshop: Lee, my shop manager, is a small but mighty lady of talent and mirth without whom we would founder. Michele is a fearless surgeon and effervescent giggler, armed with chisel, *dozuki*, and block plane. Krys (gender nonconforming) has a three-year streak going for best smile and staunchest labor. Jane brings light to the shop, literally, with her intrepid lamp creations of wood and steel, and she also runs the shipping office with Sally, our sage and sometimes mother hen. (Apologies to white dudes Josh, Matty, and Thomas. While I love you equally, this is not your chapter.)

In the film and television business in Los Angeles, Amy Poehler springs to mind as a shining example of a person with talent, integrity, ambition, class, and gumption, whom I consider one of the best bosses I've ever had. Nicole Holofcener, as well, is a maverick filmmaker for whom I love working, and Beth McCarthy-Miller is a legend of a director. The splendid talent Diablo Cody. Superheroic Lake Bell. Legendary beauty and famously nice Courteney Cox on her show *Mix It Up*.

Oh. That's only six ladies. Out of dozens of producers and directors with whom I've played. Oops. Thar she blows. The White Guy Whale of Unfairness! B'Christ, mateys, she eludes us yet! We've nary a choice but to keep on her, even round Cape Horn if that be what it takes. We'll not rest until we are warming our chapped white hands by the flames of her oil, and this metaphor is beginning to erode a bit. . . .

The point is, we must needs keep at it. Hillary in the White House will be a profound, although long overdue, step forward. I'm not here to argue the better or worse of it all (it will be better) but simply add my voice to the momentum. If a group of American people, in this case, the ladies, is not receiving a fair shake, then that is a deficit that must be remedied. The great thing is, like the Super Friends, Mighty Morphin Power Rangers, or Voltron, we can grow stronger as a nation only by utilizing all the powers on the team.

Laurie Anderson is just the sort of person I'd like to see in charge of some decision making, but she will likely remain too wise to be caught wearing any such mantle. I think the reason I am so inspired by her work is because of the sublime balance she strikes between mischief and benevolence. Her voice and her melodies are generally very loving, which makes the social criticisms therein very easy to swallow. On top of this "spoonful of sugar" approach, she also refrains from pedantic language, making us instead engage with her in the arithmetic of her phrasing. She is a storyteller, first and foremost, wrapping her anecdotal morals in showmanship and delight.

Speaking of language, another of her early refrains that has always stuck with me is the phrase "Language is a virus." Referencing a line from that institution of American letters and Anderson collaborator known as William S. Burroughs, "Language is a virus from outer space," this simple declaration stuck with me, which I suppose has also had something to do with the fact that a lot of my own work involves writing and speaking words carrying the very same virus, as it were. In her song of that title, she speaks the lines:

Paradise is exactly like
Where you are right now
Only much, much better.

This assertion moved me. It contains wit, it reminds me of something Mark Twain might have said, but it also inspires me to consider words in general, and their accepted meanings, and the effect they have upon thought. The abstraction of "paradise," for example, can conjure anything from a vision of the Christian heaven or Garden of

Eden, to a tropical island getaway, to an empty room containing nothing but a fine steak, a glass of Scotch, and *The Bridge on the River Kwai* on the tube.

I am reminded of a dinner in the Offerman household, circa 1982, when I broached the question that was surely on everyone's mind:

"Mom, why is it okay to say 'crap,' but we can't say s-h-i-t? Aren't they the same thing?"

"Watch it, Jasper," said my dad.

"Eat your beans," said my mom.

There were issues of censorship in the air all around me: the words that weren't allowed in school, George Carlin's "seven words you can't say on TV," Tipper Gore's shamefully overweening efforts to "clean up" the music industry. I became (and remain) a fan of language that is considered profane by the more puritanical factions of society, not because I wish to cause offense, but because its use communicates an adherence to the freedom of speech that is imperative to understanding how all humans can be treated equally. By freely interchanging "shit" and "crap" as a curious kid, for example, I was learning to signify that I was not a member of the vast cabal of conformist thought striving to maintain an atmosphere of oppressive conservatism in the home of the brave (coincidentally the title of another top-drawer Anderson record).

With age, my fascination with the topic of semantics has only grown, because I still deal in language as my stock-in-trade. These very sentences, word by word, I am composing with care to do my best to communicate what's in *my* brain into *your* brain. Neato, right?

Words, though, much like a devastating virus, can be so powerful in the way they afflict a population. For example, there's a six-letter word containing an *n*, two *g*'s, an *r*, and a couple of vowels that is so powerful that my publisher "really thinks I had better not type it," no matter the context. That's pretty crazy, isn't it? What a couple of sounds can signify to a group of people? In a very real sense, I suppose that word is so powerful because it contains the crushing weight of the sin of American slavery. No matter; I don't have a need for that word here today, but I would like to examine a few others.

Let's talk about pussy. Let's also talk about balls. No, things are not about to get pornographic, I'm sorry to say, but hopefully they will remain juicy. There is a deeply encoded tendency in our society to describe negative concepts with female terminology, and vice versa. For example, in the sports locker room we might say to a weak team member, "Don't be a pussy." Conversely, should a woman distinguish herself, utilizing her talents and gumption, we might say of her, "she's got balls." I'm sure you can think of more examples—"Don't be a little bitch," for instance. (The same goes for "faggot" and "gay," obviously, but that's another chapter.)

Every time this sort of imagery is utilized, it subtly but firmly reinforces negative gender stereotypes. This usage must be extirpated from daily use if we are to progress in a substantial way. We have enough trouble with the patriarchal foundations of the language to begin with, without worrying about our naughty bits being misrepresented. For example, a few paragraphs back, I accused Ms. Anderson of exhibiting showmanship, which is anatomically incorrect. However, that's how the dudes who created our words set it up. We don't have the word *showwomanship*. This is clearly bullshit.

One of my favorite pieces of Laurie Anderson's writing (and performance) comes from the song "The Dream Before" on the *Strange Angels* record. Here is the last verse, but you really must listen to it, preferably in a comfortable, meditative state for optimal brain-pan impregnation:

She said: What is history?
And he said: History is an angel
being blown backwards into the future.
He said: History is a pile of debris
And the angel wants to go back and fix things
To repair the things that have been broken.
But there is a storm blowing from Paradise.
And the storm keeps blowing the angel
backwards into the future.
And this storm . . . this storm
is called Progress.

Now, this is clearly evocative on many levels, and when I first heard it on that night in the beautiful auditorium at the southern end of the quad at Illinois, I thought that I would never know a greater feeling of catharsis in my life. Her poetry, combined with the delectable noises by means of which she delivers it, is like an extremely luxurious and pleasurable brain massage, like an opiate that taps into your language facility as well as your pleasure center.

In the verse's first line, she gently emphasizes the "his" in her pronunciation of "history," which was the first time I had been pre-sented with that particular twist. It has been followed by countless similar examples, fertilizing an endlessly growing awareness of such iniquities in place the world over. Just yesterday, Megan and I toured the astonishingly beautiful Sultan Ahmed Mosque in Istanbul (aka the Blue Mosque), where we learned that the men prayed on the main floor, or "the good seats," while the women were required to remain out of sight around a second-story catwalk or behind screens at the back of the main floor, or "the shitty seats." Megan was required to cover her hair with a scarf to be permitted entry, which she excitedly said was "just like Carrie on *Homeland*!," but it was not lost on us that I, as a penis owner, was allowed to bare my tawny locks for all the world to gaze upon.

It's complicated, to be sure. The cultures of the world, including ours in America, are steeped in centuries of tradition and bad habits. Plus, there *are* important, significant differences between men and women that also must be paid fealty, in the realms of health care and childbearing, for example. All we can do is continue to unravel this intricate puzzle in which our patriarchs have ensnared us until every-body is earning a wage commensurate with everybody else. There will always be assholes, and there will always be saints, and both can oftentimes be found within each of us. If we can make things equal based on gender and race and creed, then we can be free to just focus on the asshole/saint ratio.

My first meeting with Laurie Anderson in person was at her apartment in 2014, and she couldn't have been more friendly and welcoming—a good thing, since I was somewhat freaked-out to meet her. I've met a lot of famous folks whom I admire, and I've generally become inured to being starstruck, but as you can tell from the content of this chapter, she was an artist whose work had profoundly shaken up my life in the best way.

We launched into a cordial "get to know ya" chat, and I described the idea of this book and the sorts of notions I was hoping to convey. I'm not certain if she was even aware of her brattiness, or if it is just her nature to be devilishly inquisitive, but my planned interview of her quickly became an interview by her, of me. She kept me at ease while peppering me with questions about my book and my life. Of course, this was very seductive to me, as I would love nothing more than a person I so admired to have any interest whatsoever in my story. It was like a much more benevolent version of Edmund Pevensie's first meeting with the evil witch Jadis in *The Lion, the Witch and the Wardrobe*, wherein she plies the helpless lad for information with Turkish Delight and flattery. Laurie was probably not even aware of my pathetic situation, but I was nonetheless under her power.

"It's a list of Americans who inspire me," I managed. "The kind of people you wish would run for office but are too smart to ever do that."

She told me that I seemed like a pretty all right sort, and that maybe I should consider running for office.

"Um. Okay, thanks," I laughed, "but the book—"

"I'm thinking, like, a depressed American city . . . once great, that you could bring back to its former glory. . . . Huh . . . what about Detroit? I think you would make a great mayor of Detroit. I'll tell you what," she said with a twinkle in her eye. "I'm happy to answer questions for your book, you know, give you an hour or two. But if you would run for mayor of Detroit, I will get fully behind your campaign."

I have to admit to taking a considerable pause to think about this idea before coming a fair distance back around to my senses.

"Well, I had better, you know . . . stick to acting and writing and stuff. I'm probably not really cut out for politics."

"Suit yourself," she replied, her grin as impish as that of Robin Goodfellow. It just occurred to me that she would be an amazing casting choice for Peter Pan, perhaps as adapted by Caryl Churchill.

Our second meeting was arranged after a few instances of passing in the night like ships, one or both of us on the road, away from New York City. I asked Laurie if she could get together in the first week of December, to which she replied, "Hmm . . . I could meet late Wednesday after the Dylan show at the Beacon if you're uptown—should be elevenish—could meet at the top of the Time Warner building where there's a good view at that hour of paper shredding in surrounding offices. . . ."

Done. That Wednesday turned out to be the day that a grand jury decided not to indict New York City police officer Daniel Pantaleo in the choking death of Eric Garner that had occurred on July 17, 2014. The verdict of "no indictment" sparked nationwide outrage and protests, coming as it did on the heels of Michael Brown's similar case in Ferguson, Missouri, outside of St. Louis. Eric Garner's murder-by-cop was the case about which media factions were up in arms—not over how in the world there was to be no trial, but over whether the term *choke hold* was the appropriate language to describe Pantaleo's arm, crooked around Garner's neck from behind in a "hold" that was clearly "choking" him. I say "clearly," because the whole episode was played ad nauseam on news outlets for days, leaving little question as to the officer's unnecessary violence, which the grand jury blithely exonerated.

As I made my way on foot up Eighth Avenue toward my meeting with Laurie, I found myself wading upstream through ten blocks of marching protestors chanting "I can't breathe! I can't breathe!" (Garner's final words as he was dropped to the sidewalk by police) and "Hands up! Don't shoot!" (in reference to the Michael Brown case). It was an intense reminder of how incredibly racist certain aspects of our society can still be, particularly in the relations between some black civilians and white police, particularly concerning these two cases, in which all apparent evidence, of which there was no shortage, pointed to malfeasance. Yet both cases were dismissed without further investigation.

Laurie's phrase "meeting on top of the Time Warner building" had conjured images of sheltering from the wind in the lee of large air-conditioning units, trying to light our cheroots with our last remaining wooden matches. Fortunately, the rendezvous she had in mind was of a considerably more indoor nature, in the swell lobby bar of the Mandarin Oriental hotel, located on the thirty-fifth floor of the Time Warner building. The windows of the room look out across Columbus Circle to Central Park, delivering one of the finest views of Olmsted's (and Vaux's!) masterwork for the price of a cocktail and a couple of sliders. (Note to the management: The sliders used to include three small burgers with varied cheeses and sauce, but they are now only two in number, with standard toppings on both. Please return to the original, vastly superior preparation.)

We got a sweet table right by the windows and ordered: bourbon and grilled cheese for her, sliders and Lagavulin for me. Moving through the topics of Bob Dylan, Wendell Berry, and boatbuilding, and Laurie's rendering of a relevant joke—"Why is there no woman on the dollar bill? 'Cause it'd only be worth seventy-seven cents'"— we finally came upon the quarry of my seeking: Laurie's ideas.

> *I think parents should buy their kids a house. They should go to college later—I think right now, they spend all their time, the first ten years of their lives working up to knowing what they want to do, so they can get a job, so they can get a house. Give 'em a house . . . it's pretty arbitrary to go to college . . . to do what?*

We agreed that in most American neighborhoods, you could get your kids a fine house for the price of one year of college at a high-end school, or four years at most state colleges. In a very Wendell Berry turn of conversation, we discussed the prudence of one getting one's feet underneath one before committing to the debt that comes with a college degree that often ends up useless.

The talk turned to the protest down on the streets of Manhattan, and Laurie said, "I'm glad people are realizing—I don't want to say something mean here, but the police are really brutal. They're really entitled, you know?" I agree with her. The thing that frustrates me is the inaction, the seeming helplessness of the people. Two clear cases, representing a great many more similar episodes of injustice, have outraged the public and caught the nation's attention for a lingering moment. Both cases have been stridently protested but then summarily dismissed. The white guys are apparently not going down without a fight.

This talk provoked more treasure to spill forth from the fecund imagination sitting across from me. She described an acquaintance of hers who is suffering terribly from post-traumatic stress disorder and is unable to reenter society because of his affliction.

So this is my campaign. What I want to propose is a sort of reverse boot camp. So [the army] believes in indoctrination to kill. Then they should believe in indoctrination not to kill people. When you join the army, boot camp's at least two months, [because] a lot of people really can't just pick up a gun. So the idea is, on the other end is two months, they're still paid, they're still in the army, they're still employed by the US government, and in this boot camp they teach us how to drop *the gun. Drop the gun. Drop the gun and try and pull back into wherever they were coming from.*

My admiration continued to swell. Laurie Anderson has attributes that are reminiscent of other characters exalted in these pages; for example, she always seems to be thinking about how to train her particular weapons of empathy upon some sort of need she perceives in the humanity around her. Part of her technique seems to come from a fascination with the myths that each culture creates to explain the unexplainable parts of the world around us.

Laurie made a very compelling case for religion in general, versus science, pointing out that science redefines its "absolute truth" every six months. She said, "Think of science like Aristotle or somebody. Let's make something really perfect. Let's conceive the universe as thirty-five spheres. Then everything has to happen perfectly, but then Kepler said, 'Guess what? They're not spheres; they're ellipses!' And people said,

'That's not as perfect as spheres!'" Her point being that humanity scientifically craves perfection, but the natural world of course is imperfect; it is not symmetrical. Therefore, the elasticity or ambiguity of myth can more comfortably encompass all our fears and questions. Again, finding comfort is not knowing.

Furthermore, many of my heroes generally eschew the modern fashions of social media and overconsumption of technology-based entertainment; whether it's in the woodshop or writing by the light of day, they lean toward "unplugged." Laurie gets her kicks in the opposite direction—she has been a self-proclaimed "gear geek" for decades. She is responsible for musical innovations like the tape-bow violin, the talking stick, and her special voice filter for the "voice of authority" (Fenway Bergamot), which she refers to as "audio drag." She now carries an iPad that she uses to record music, using a plethora of apps to achieve her various effects. She said, "Yeah, it's more than a studio. Just every instrument ever made, every filter ever made, every groove ever made . . . I love new stuff."

In the middle of our palaver, Laurie stopped short, distracted by something over my shoulder.

"What do you think of that?" she asked.

I looked back at a large, confusing painting on the wall overlooking the bar area.

"It's either really good or really bad," she continued. "It might be a combination."

I pitched in. "My gut reaction is: abhorrent, but then I . . . yeah, I'm gonna stick with abhorrent."

She said, "But it really bothers me. It's not a tasteful painting, but—"

I said, "No, but it caught your attention."

She went on. "You could say that about it. It did, and it really bothers me."

There was a similarly styled second painting across the room that we had to get up and scrutinize. In the baffling details I pointed out the New York Stock Exchange, a picture of a squirrel, and the name Pocahontas. Laurie grew suspiciously silent, but I am not saying that she is not a Freemason.

Our conversation ended up on the topic of love. We did not discuss Laurie's relationship with Lou Reed across the last twenty years of his life. We did discuss my wife, Megan, and the fact that she and Laurie had both performed in the excellent performance space thirty floors directly beneath us, known as the Allen Room. I described Megan's show to Laurie, which included a duet with the late, beyond great Elaine Stritch, as well as other dark, funny, and eclectic song choices.

Laurie said, "I love dark. That's beautiful. And she sang there."

I said, "She did. I'm a big fan. I got real lucky in my marriage."

She said, "Yeah. Being in love is the whole point. It's the whole point."

A sprite to the end, Laurie left an indelible impression upon me in the manner by which she gravitates toward lightness and humor, fueled all the while by the noblest of emotions. Witnessing her acuity and commitment to whimsy firsthand, in addition to my previously cultivated devotion to her cleverly orchestrated glamours, I realized as we said good night that I would be enlarged by the compassionate effects of her gifts for the rest of my days. I was as crazy about her witchcraft then, on top of a building, as I had been twenty-five years ago in the middle of a cornfield.

20

WILLIE NELSON

America, to me, is freedom.

—WILLIE NELSON

If you have not caught up on the quality television program *Parks and Recreation*, I will simply reiterate that I portrayed a devilishly handsome (according to my mom), gruff libertarian named Ron Swanson—a man with little use for modern fashion or popular culture. That is, popular culture beyond the novels of Patrick O'Brian, *The Bridge on the River Kwai*, and the records of one Willie Nelson. The sum total of musical selections we ever heard Ron enjoy, in fact, was comprised of Willie's songs "Buddy" and "Hello Walls." I mention this now, in this context, because the character of Ron had a (hopefully) enjoyable, curmudgeonly demeanor, founded in an obdurate, John Wayne–esque simplicity when it came to his stance on most issues, particularly those issues concerning this great country that we call America.

That a singular American man such as Ron Swanson would choose the music of Willie Nelson serves as a splendidly accurate introduction to not only my vision of the ideal country we live in, but what's more, the nation that America could one day become. He has been a musical and political maverick for decades, one who has often been revealed as quite human, a fact that he openly displays in his lyrics.

Born in 1933, Willie grew up playing music (and football, baseball, and basketball, natch) in the small town of Abbott, Texas, about a half hour north of Waco. His first professional gig earned him eight dollars playing rhythm guitar in a local polka band, and he was hooked.

"That first night I made money making music, I knew that I had succeeded."

Despite his wealth of talent for songwriting and performing, Willie spent years jumping around the western United States, working at a vast variety of odd jobs, with a focus on radio DJ gigs—a position that allowed him to record his songs on the radio stations' equipment. He sold songs here and there, primarily in the flavor of the west Texas country genre in which he had made his beginnings, until he finally made the move to Nashville in 1960.

Despite the successes of "Hello Walls," recorded by Faron Young, and Patsy Cline's famous cover of his song "Crazy," Willie had a hard time finding his niche in the conservative setting of Nashville country music. He had contracts with Liberty Records, Monument, and then RCA across the later sixties, with middling success. His songs would make the charts but never top them, which meant his songwriting royalties would about break even with the cost of tours and living. During this time, however, he began to develop confidence in his own unique sound, along with the likes of pals Waylon Jennings and Kris Kristofferson. Their less-polished, more honest and stripped-down style came to be known as "outlaw" country.

In December of 1970, his house in Ridgetop, Tennessee, outside of Nashville, mysteriously burned to the ground. Willie took this as a sign from the gods to leave the conventional business of Nashville music and head back to the state of his youth.

Austin, Texas, one of the most charismatic American cities—state capital and also "weirdness central"—is where Willie took up residence in 1972. Over the forty-plus years since, he has established himself there as something more than a mayor or royalty. He has become Austin's wizard. I am perhaps in danger of overtaxing the use of "Gandalf" as a high compliment, but I cannot bear to refer to the warlock Willie as Dumbledore, Oz, or Thoros. He demands something more classic.

Willie Nelson is the Merlin of Austin. Yea, and of America, to boot.

By the way, I am sorry to report that I was not able to meet Willie for an interview. Oh, I'm not sorry for you, reader. I mean my sorrow in a purely selfish way—as I should be able to render a serviceable, if not enjoyable chapter from my research and clear ability to opine, for better or worse. But, selfishly, the crybaby in me rears his head back in a tearful squall when I lament that I have not yet shaken Mr. Nelson's hand. I'd settle for clasping either one of his astonishingly nimble dinner plates, those ennobled workhorses with which he manipulates the fretboard and strings of "Trigger," his eldritch, scarred, and seemingly immortal Martin guitar, to disseminate his delectable mix of jazz and country styles, hitting perhaps eleven other genres in between them.

In 1974, Willie was the star of the pilot episode of *Austin City Limits*, the now-venerated PBS show that initially highlighted the music of Texas but has come to represent the finest of contemporary performers across genre lines. Notably stripped down in its production, the "unplugged" quality of the program's presentations often delivers performances that are considered definitive—one of the reasons that the show is the only television program to date to have been awarded the National Medal of Arts. Considering all this, they could not have found a more perfect point man than Willie Nelson.

Once he made the move to Austin, Willie was able to get his feet under himself artistically, a strengthening that saw the advent of his signature style, which we've come to know and love and upon which we depend when we're in need of any emotion from melancholy to mirth. His third record of this renaissance, *Red Headed Stranger*, is my favorite of all his albums. It's got everything: horses, murder, Bonaparte, a piano, a preacher, and "Blue Eyes Crying in the Rain," which provided Willie Nelson the singer with his first number one hit.

That was followed soon after by my next two favorites, *The Sound in Your Mind* (1976) and *Stardust* (1978), and the new independent feeling and flavor of these records would serve to fuel Willie's prolific output, which has included to date more than one hundred records. If you throw in compilations, collaborations, and film soundtracks, that number tops three hundred. It's worth noting that Willie was past forty years old before he saw the kind of success with which we have come to identify him. He'd been selling songs as a writer for fifteen or twenty years, but once he broke free of the constraints he felt in Nashville, his talent and creativity took him to a whole new level, a fact that reminds me of this, one of my favorite Willie quotes: "The early bird gets the worm, but the second mouse gets the cheese."

By the early seventies, Willie was into his third of four marriages, and he has fathered seven children to date, but considering his apparent joie de vivre, I wouldn't cut off his tab just yet. The roller coaster–like undulations in his life's path have undoubtedly played a salient role in Willie's seeming ability to perpetually represent the average American. Even now that he has been a colossal success and icon for decades, the various platforms and causes for which he advocates allow America's working class to feel that he remains representative of their best interests, quite simply because he does.

The bearded and braided man who said, "If you're not crazy, there's something wrong with you," certainly inspires confidence in me. He's another person I think we'd elect to office in a heartbeat, if he was ever convinced to run, although I'm afraid he'd have to be awfully high to entertain such a conversation. Rocky Mountain high. On weed.

With his social activism alone, he's accomplished more for the good of our citizenry than most politicians will in their lifetimes, the difference being that we *pay* the politicians. He's been a very vocal advocate for the adoption of horses, supporting the Animal Welfare Institute (AWI) with a letter campaign urging the public to contact their representatives in Congress about the AHSPA, or American Horse Slaughter Prevention Act, a proposed piece of legislation of which I had not heard, for a seriously macabre situation occurring under the table.

Apparently, a great many horses are being slaughtered (one every five minutes, according to the AWI) by nefarious overseas interests, for human consumption. For obvious reasons, this information is being kept under wraps, but until Congress passes a ban on this practice, horses will continue to be shipped to Mexico to meet the same grisly end. Given his alignment with Habitat for Horses, and the many horses he has personally adopted to his ranch in Texas, this cause is a no-brainer for Willie the cowboy.

There has been a good deal of discussion in this book about the ways in which our society is voraciously consuming the dwindling natural resources on our planet, but there are few examples given as to tangible solutions to which we may offer our support. Willie has actually funded two plants, in Oregon and Texas, that produce biodiesel fuel. Made from mostly soybean oil, this biodiesel can be burned in conventional diesel engines without the engines needing any alterations. Finding an alternative to the monstrous amount of petroleum products and coal that we burn every day will be one of the most important forward steps we can take in conserving our planet for future generations. I personally have no bright ideas for how to do this, as I am a jackass, and so I am extremely grateful to Willie and other forward thinkers like him for stepping up to the plate on all our behalf and taking a swing at it.

Another amazing movement in which Willie has played a leading role is the establishment of Farm Aid in 1985—the annual one-day music festival that raises money and awareness for the plight of the small American farmer. He was joined in this effort by Neil Young and John Mellencamp, as well as a killer lineup of guest artists every year (including Jeff Tweedy and Wilco), and the organization has raised millions of dollars in aid for failing farms, but more important, they have made Congress sit up and take notice of the financial dilemma in which these families find themselves when trying to compete with the corporate giants in "agribusiness."

If you don't normally hear about a celebrity and music legend getting behind groups like horse ranchers and farmers, then prepare to be doubly impressed (or if you are already baked, unsurprised) when I tell you that Willie Nelson sits on the advisory board of NORML, the National Organization for the Reform of Marijuana Laws. It has been reported that Willie was not as pleasant a rambler when alcohol was his main medicine, and so to me, his regular and cavalier employment of pot as a reliever of stress is a consistent representation, decades strong, of the *positive* effects of the herb: "I think people need to be educated to the fact that marijuana is not a drug. Marijuana is an herb and a flower. God put it here. If He put it here and He wants it to grow, what gives the government the right to say that God is wrong?"

Like any other mood-altering substance, of course you should think twice about consuming it before entering a situation wherein you might endanger others, like, say, behind the wheel of a moving vehicle or at work as an air traffic controller. One of the times Willie found himself in hot water with the Texas authorities was in 1994, when police found him safely parked on the side of the road, sleeping in the backseat of his Mercedes. He had been enjoying his luck at a late-night poker game and felt too tired to drive, so he pulled off the road to get some sleep. Police officers found a joint in the ashtray and a bag of weed under the seat and decided to give him hell instead of shaking his hand for doing the right thing by getting off the road. Common sense is often low on the list of priorities when it comes to prosecuting citizens for possession of marijuana. In most cases, the "perpetrator" will just be causing a given scene to become more mellow, a state of affairs that seems like it would behoove the authorities to promote rather than punish.

He has said, "There are a lot of ignorant people who don't know, that have been told it's a drug, and if you smoke it you're going to hell. A lot of the right-wing religious fanatics are the ones who are the most against it, just like they're [for] telling women what to do with their bodies. A bunch of old, ignorant white people that are dying off. And the big deal about weed or gays or any of that—it's going away. It's not a big deal no more to most people."

We can only hope that Willie's sunnily disposed prediction on the matter will prove true. It seems like our population has plenty of conundrums to be more concerned with than those Americans putting on a pleasant buzz. For example, the crooks running the pharmaceutical racket: the real drug lords, who exploit our citizenry with exorbitant prices as they maintain a stranglehold on their pill monopolies. There are many places where our law enforcement tax dollars could be better focused than upon stoners consuming *suspicious* quantities of Rolo candies.

In 2010, Austin appended the name of its downtown Second Street to Willie Nelson Boulevard, and two years later, an heroic bronze statue of the wizard (and Trigger) was added at the corner of his honorary street and LaVaca. Appropriately, the unveiling occurred at 4:20 P.M. on April 20 (4/20), 2012, when, according to the *Austin American-Statesman*, "there was something in the air." It's long been no secret that Willie is for weed, as Willie is for America, and so, by God, I am for Willie.

Now that we have paid homage to the cowboy—the sort our mamas should not let us grow up to be—let us also give praise to his weapon. The aspiring baby luthier in me would be remiss if I did not take a moment to turn the bloodshot eye of my journalism upon Willie's one and only axe for about as many years as I've been alive (forty-four): Trigger.

When it comes to acoustic guitars, Trigger's maker, the estimable C. F. Martin guitar company out of Nazareth, Pennsylvania, has been synonymous with the most desirably crafted American quality since 1833. Although Collings, Gibson, Taylor, Santa Cruz, and a score of smaller makers can give them a run for their money by now, Martin is like the Louisville Slugger or Filson cruiser jacket when it comes to longevity and quality. They are the Zippo lighter of guitars.

The year was 1969, and Willie was playing a gig with his band at the John T. Floore Country Store in Helotes, Texas, when a drunk stepped on his Baldwin 800C classical guitar and destroyed it. Willie's crew sent the mess to their guitar man in Nashville, Shot Jackson, who informed Willie via telephone that the damage was irreparable. However, Jackson had this Martin N-20 classical on hand into which he could transfer the Baldwin's electric pickup. For the price of 750 dollars (5,000 dollars today), Willie acquiesced—and unwittingly entered into a marriage made in country music heaven.

The yellow guitar top is Sitka spruce from British Columbia or Alaska. The back and sides are made of Brazilian rosewood, that precious hardwood that is so ideal for musical instruments that its supply has been almost entirely used up and is no longer available for import or purchase, except in tiny, hard-to-find quantities, like the rarest of pearls. The neck is mahogany, also from South America, and the bridge and fretboard are black ebony from Africa. These precious woods, along with the German brass tuning pegs, are typically ideal for this type of instrument, but Willie Nelson's guitar style has proved to be anything but typical.

Although he first learned to play western swing and polka, as well as cribbing all the Tin Pan Alley hits he could handle off the radio, Willie had been turned on to the playing of jazz guitar master Django Reinhardt early on the professional circuit, and he was spellbound. He immediately recognized that Reinhardt's playing was the wellspring from which had sprung all the other riffs he had previously learned, but the original source material was much more pure and variegated. Willie had been learning from fiddle and guitar players who were emulating Django, but now he was thrilled to find the fuel that would spark the fire in his artistic belly for the rest of his life.

Unfortunately, the Martin N-20 was not designed to tolerate the brutal workout of Willie's fingers, as they mixed Spanish finger style with jazz, blues, and good old-fashioned country strumming, a mélange of techniques that alternated between the use of a pick and just the fingers of the right hand. The pinky and ring finger of his right hand soon wore a hole right through the spruce top, near the sound hole, not to mention the other scars Trigger began to accumulate. Some were accidental, or the result of Willie's hammering pick, but others were of a decidedly more intentional bent, such as the place where Leon Russell signed the top with his knife.

Willie and his stage manager, Poodie Locke, found a luthier in Austin named Mark Erlewine, who gave the Martin a thorough tune-up and refinishing, but he could have had no idea that he was entering into a stewardship that has lasted nearly forty years. Twice a year he repairs the finish and he adds bracing under the top where and when necessary, thereby keeping Willie in the saddle. Willie has surmised that he and Trigger have played more than ten thousand shows together, logging more than a million minutes of playing time.

Over the years, Willie's crew have tried to get him to switch to different versions of the same model N-20, both from Trigger's vintage and newly built "classic reissues," but no guitar ever feels remotely the same to Willie, and so it would seem that Trigger will see him through to the finish line. That sense of loyalty bleeds over into everything Willie does, whether he's helping out an animal shelter or just bringing young talent into the recording studio. He seems to have maintained a pertinent sense of humanity in every undertaking, which I suppose is unsurprising by now. Like a Texan Gandhi, he clearly just gets it: "Anybody can be unhappy. We can all be hurt. You don't have to be poor to need something or somebody. Rednecks, hippies, misfits—we're all the same. Gay or straight? So what? It doesn't matter to me. We have to be concerned about other people, regardless."

Maybe he's so good at speaking for the rest of us because he spent many years as just another one of the people trying to make ends meet until he could see his way clear to making his dreams come true. Whatever the reason, this particular troublemaker has done little but bring music and good times to a lot of Americans for a lot of years. We should all be so lucky as to make such trouble.

21

CONAN O'BRIEN

Megan and I share an e-mail, simply because it's all the e-mail address we ever needed. Like many of you, we often feel oppressed by the amount of correspondence in which our business obligates us to partake, and so it has never occurred to us to update or enlarge our computer-using capabilities. As a married couple, this sharing also affords us a considerable degree of transparency, since every electronic letter that we receive by computer is available for perusal by the household. It's not "my e-mail" or "her e-mail," it's simply: "the e-mail." I like the system for its convenience and its inherent sense of fidelity.

Thus, when an e-mail comes in from "somebody good," we consider it fair game for both of us to enjoy. This explains how Megan came to learn about my secret second family in Spokane (but perhaps that's a tale for the next book). She also read, and subsequently insisted that I include in the book, the following exchange between Conan and myself. Much of my solicitation contains the same language that you have previously seen in my electronic note to George Saunders, so I will cut to the chase wherever possible.

Dear Tall Sir, *8/15/14*

I want to ask you for a significant favor, and, despite our secret, long-suffering passion for one another, I mean to do so with (approximately) the same pomp with which I have petitioned Oprah Winfrey.

I am working on my second book for Dutton Books . . . etc., etc. . . . looking at religion, technology, human rights, nature, guns/ war, tobacco, hand-crafting, advertising . . . hopefully with a chuckle. Hilarious, right?

Since my list of swell Americans must necessarily be quite subjective, I can't help but think of you and your, frankly, carnal dance moves and the sense of humor behind which you proffer a mighty intelligence and gentle compassion. I'll be honest: I intend to lionize you. To supplement my detailed recollection of your rippling abdominals, glistening with sunscreen in the Seattle half-light, I would love to engage you in an interview.

If we can nail down a date, I thought it would be really fun to make some sort of destination or adventure out of our interview; nothing too buccaneering, per se, but someplace we'd like to go and rest our weary hindquarters and enjoy a chin-wag. Fresno, I guess, is what I'm driving at.

It could be a hike, or a rooftop where Scotch is served, or it could also be your household fire pit or the ridiculously opulent hot tub at our new digs.

It's also worth mentioning that, as you may be aware, my bride, Megan, is doing a Terrence McNally revival (It's Only a Play) on Broadway from September through the top of January, so if you're heading east at all and you'd like to come as our guest, perhaps sporting a playwright of your own [Liza Powel-O'Brien is a playwright!], do simply holler. I would relish squiring you to any meal or diversion in New York City as well. The Bull Moose Room at Keens. Perhaps I could row you across the Hudson in an historic Whitehall skiff, and that is not a joke. I know a guy.

Sincerely,

Nick Offerman

It took the sluggard an entire day to get back to me, but I was otherwise rather pleased with his response.

Nick, you insufferable bastard,   *8/16/14*

How much time will you need? Forty seconds? A full minute?

Count me in, old chum. Let's figure out a date and I will disappoint with meandering tales. And I will move heaven and earth to see Megan's play. I would watch that woman read from the phone book and ask for an encore.

On a related topic, we must eat beefsteaks soon at a down-on-its-luck Chop House. It has been too long.

Your steadfast friend,

Conan

I guess the headline here is: We talk to each other like total nerds. Passionately. Unabashedly.

The first time I truly beheld Conan was when Megan was doing his *Late Night with Conan O'Brien* show in New York City, circa 2001 or so. I was nothing short of tumescent to meet this impossibly tall man who had already brought me so much mirth with his televised comedy stylings; a hairdo like Kenickie's wet dream; and brave, high weirdness—weirdness that I would later come to understand as the collaborative goulash of chef O'Brien and his coterie of writers of the highest (silly) caliber, like Mike Sweeney, Robert Smigel, Bob Odenkirk, Louis C.K., Jon Glaser, Brian Stack, and Brian McCann (four of whom have appeared on *Parks and Rec*, as Officer Dave Sanderson, Councilman Jeremy Jamm, Ted, and Freddy Spaghetti), with many others over the years.

Conan's take on *Late Night*, replete with his undeniably fetching gyrations (Try and deny it! You can't!), his masturbating bear (not a euphemism, nor golden sidekick Andy Richter—there was an actual man in a bear suit and diaper pleasuring himself), the ineffably irresistible Triumph the Insult Comic Dog, and Pimpbot 5000, had overwhelmingly become the flavor of choice for my generation. The ever-winning David Letterman, to my way of thinking, would always remain our elder statesman of hilarity who had carried forward the legacy of Johnny Carson as the jocular and sidesplitting uncle upon whom we depended for daily humor and wisdom. Don't get me wrong, Dave's still got it, but Conan behaved in a way that our parents' generation could only have described as "deviant" or "squirrelly," and that, by God, made him *ours*.

Wide-eyed and grinning with delight, backstage in the dressing room hallways of 30 Rockefeller Center, I was also digesting my first of many visits to the art deco wonderland of a building from whence the television comedy legends of *Saturday Night Live* and Letterman had sprung, not to mention straight-up hunks like Phil Donahue, Dr. Oz, and Rachel Maddow. Despite the fact that I was merely the frightening, shaved-headed boyfriend of a beautiful sitcom star named Megan Mullally, who was to appear as his guest that evening, Conan could not have been friendlier or more generous to me, and the same goes for his team of producers and writers—a company of brilliant goofballs; erudite and ribald sweethearts who were tickled pink at being paid to create fresh, challenging comedy on a daily basis.

As we shook hands, cracked wise, and engaged in some general grab-ass there in the hallway, a murmur suddenly ran through the throng: "Make way!/Look at his jewels!/Don't give him no jive!" and the crowd parted to reveal the arrival of none other than Mr. T, grinning and hugging everyone around whom he could wrap the tree limbs that he calls arms. I had always been an ardent fan of the man who portrayed both B. A. (Bad Ass) Baracus and Clubber Lang, all while promoting good manners, generosity, and kindness, especially to one's mother, so I was triply excited at this bonus. In the early years of our marriage, riding shotgun with Megan afforded me a great bounty of such thrilling experiences, but Conan somehow proved to be special, and not just because he looks like a handsomer Ivy League version of something out of *The Dark Crystal*.

Although when measured empirically, Conan O'Brien tops out at nineteen hands of height, or a lofty seventy-six inches with his delicate feet clad in only the finest stockings of China silk, with the additional sheave of flaxen ginger stalks atop his noble pate, he strikes me as much closer to ten feet tall. This suspicion of loftiness is redoubled when examining his early achievements. A pubescent Conando took time out from editing his high school newspaper, *The Sagamore*, to win a story-writing contest held by the National Council of Teachers of English, before wrapping it up by graduating as the valedictorian* of his class (*a Latin-ish term that I think means he was in the top several throwers of the javelin [it's no wonder, with that wingspan!]).

He then attended Harvard University, which I'm told is a "college" school on the "East Coast," where in 1985 he earned his BA (also pretty badass) in American history. While attending "Harvard," Conan was twice elected president of the hallowed parody magazine, *The Harvard Lampoon*, a double distinction awarded to only two other persons in history: the humorist Robert Benchley, in 1912, and one Matt Murray, who most recently worked as a writer on the seminal "television" comedy *Parks and Recreation*. (I am not at all "certain" how quotation marks work.) Conan topped off this trajectory by graduating magna cum laude, which I believe is Latin for "terrific at noisome self-abuse."

The fascination with American history exhibited by young Conan would come to play a pivotal role in my own development. While visiting the amazing New York apartment of Conan and his winning bride, Liza, Megan and I did ooh and ooh, and ooh again, in a prolonged fashion, and *then* we would aah: at the interior design, at the art, at their beautiful kids, who looked like they were prepared by the most talented dressers of Bloomingdale's Christmas window displays, and at the breathtaking view overlooking Central Park from the balconies of the Majestic apartment building, just one door south of Yoko at the Dakota.

In Conan's library, the first thing one noticed (after the thick stench of his pomade, Danger Dan's Dappity Dazz) was his collection of fine guitars—only a handful, but clearly chosen by a player with style, which most assuredly describes this comedian. For those of you who would have (rightly) drooled over such beauties, please adjust the book away from below your spit hole before reading further: There sat a 1963 Gretsch Tennessean, a 1957 orange Gretsch 6120, a 1946 Martin acoustic, and a green-and-gold Gretsch (Bono's model) that was signed for him by the members of U2, so he's afraid to play it.

Once you were done with ogling the guitars, the next detail you noticed about the walls of stuffed bookshelves was the proliferation of books about either American history or the Beatles. As he says himself, "Two-thirds of the books in the house are about weird American historical figures, and the other third are about guitars and the Beatles, and the Beatles' guitars. I actually have a book called *Beatles Gear*. I have two textbooks about the Beatles' amps." Many of the best comedy writers I know or have known are obsessed to inebriation with the music and lyrics of the Beatles, but Conan's preoccupation may be the inebrationest.

My own eye, however, was drawn to a collection of titles about Theodore Roosevelt. A set of substantial tomes which I proceeded to steadily borrow and consume, one at a time, until I, too, was firmly clasped in the former Rough Rider's grip.

"Think about it," Conan said. "We couldn't have a president like this anymore. He was an explorer. He was a naturalist. He read and wrote in several languages. He had served in war and was also a diplomat, and the list goes on and on.

"And you know, the big thing we're always trying to figure out today is 'Who's being real?' Is anyone being real? . . . And, man, you know Teddy Roosevelt was Teddy Roosevelt. He was completely a sincere character, and no one's ever doubted that. He was curious, and I love curious people. I think some of our more recent leaders have not been curious people, and we've suffered for it. I think having leaders today who are curious about other cultures, willing to accept that they don't know everything, but they want to know—those are qualities that were great about Teddy Roosevelt.

"The flip side is that I really believe that he was—he needed to be medicated."

His scholarly knowledge strikes me as another tangible proof that some of our most trusted and relevant televised brains (and their crack teams of writers), like Conan, Jon Stewart, and Stephen Colbert, have a fascination with our nation's history, particularly in the revisionist way it's been spun for the public. I don't know if it has occurred to them cognitively, or if it was just an instinctive choice, but perhaps in this age of the ever-shrinking Candy Crush attention span, Mother Nature understands that we need to receive our important information from people who are less serious (read: boring) than straight news anchors. To wit: It had never occurred to me to study Theodore Roosevelt until professor Conan sold me on him.

After college, Conan and fellow Haardvark, television comedy kingpin Greg Daniels, the creator of shows like *King of the Hill* and *The Office*, and cocreator of the quality program *Parks and Recreation*, were hired as a writing team on *Not Necessarily the News*. Like Mr. O'Brien, Greg is relatively tall and lanky, a fact from which Conan drew a certain amount of neurotic comfort, but sadly, Conan simply could not "deal" with Greg's conventional hairstyle, and it eventually tore them apart. Daniels was never heard from again, outside of some scattered "hit" TV shows and some four Emmys from twenty nominations. I'll gratefully remind you that it was Greg who named my character Ron Swanson.

O'Brien struck out on his own, snagging prestigious comedy-writing gigs on *Saturday Night Live* and then *The Simpsons*, where among the episodes he penned was the beloved "Marge vs. the Monorail." According to the other *Simpsons* writers, had Conan not left to take over *Late Night*, he would have soon ended up show-running that estimable cartoon program that is, by now in its twenty-seventh season, possibly the greatest body of work in the history of comedy. It's either that or Ann Coulter's political parody books. Or, of course, that old bowl o' chestnuts, Leviticus.

Although he had studied at the Los Angeles comedy institution the Groundlings Theatre & School, Conan was not yet really known at all as a performer, so much as he was justly considered one of the funniest writers in the business. That's why it came as rather a shock when NBC announced in 1992 that he would replace David Letterman as the host of *Late Night*. Despite Johnny Carson's preference for Letterman, Jay Leno had been selected by NBC to take over *The Tonight Show* for Carson, prompting Letterman to take his superior comedy stylings over to CBS, where he has reigned as Johnny's successor regardless of his former network's choice. We'll examine this a little more closely when we get to a later anecdote involving a little historical item known as "Leno Shits the Bed."

For now, the relevant point was that *Late Night*'s executive producer Lorne Michaels had seen something in Conan during his tenure at *Saturday Night Live* that made him think this young, gangly protagonist would be able to pull off such a move. As we have subsequently seen from the triumph of Conan's show, as well as Lorne's additionally winning late-night choices of Jimmy Fallon and Seth Meyers, there's a reason that Lorne Michaels has remained the number one arbiter of television comedy talent in my lifetime. Of the unprecedented choice of Conan in 1992, Lorne had this to say:

> *I liked that Conan was young, intelligent, and that he had, like Johnny Carson, good manners. A good host always obeys the rules of hospitality, and Conan has an essential decency and work ethic that were obvious from the start. Sadly, talent and character do not often reside in the same person, but they do in Conan.*

Naturally, it took the completely unknown redhead some time to acclimate the *Late Night* audience from the more folksy timbre of Letterman's show to his newer, younger, and goofier style, but acclimate them he did. After a great deal of hard work over the early seasons, Conan led his show to a long-running string of seasons at number one in the ratings. I am no television expert—far from it, a status about which I am glad—but I know enough about how things work at a network to comprehend that a young unknown stepping onto the stage recently vacated by Letterman, struggling at first to build his audience but sticking to his comedy guns of weirdness, would have had to work his tail off to get his ship righted to the point where it was sailing smoothly. That young man's task would have required guts, stamina, and again, disarmingly provocative dance maneuvers. In sum: gumption.

As it happened, Conan and I were unable to secure time, neither upon a Los Angeles rooftop where Scotch is served nor in an historic Whitehall skiff as I rowed his (gi)raffish profile around the cape of New York. Instead, he and Liza invited me to dinner at their beautiful home. I had made the situation quite clear—that I would see him feted as a gesture of recompense, however insufficient, for the generous gift of his time and his mind and his heart. Liza responded that they had split a cow with another three couples, and so she would prefer to prepare a meal with said beef so as to make use of it (the beef was mightily good—the playwright can cook like she's publishing a book on it).

Conilious (his preferred legal name) and I settled into the living room to rap. I have to say, despite always feeling at ease around him, I was just slightly nervous on this occasion, since we had earlier discussed the fact that the very next day was the last day of shooting *Parks and Recreation* forever. Only one day of filming remained, after 125 episodes over seven seasons, and yet no one had ever mentioned the inescapable fact that my character had purloined Conan's own hairdo. I have appeared on his show several times, just fatalistically waiting for his team of attorneys to step out from the wings to slap me with some sort of cease and desist, but it has not occurred. Before I rest too easy, I do believe that I will look up the statute of limitations with regard to follicular homage.

I described the relative aims of my book to Conan, and we

discussed Theodore Roosevelt immediately, natch, and then we carried on into politics in general. He immediately cheered me by pointing out that, although, yes, our country does seem to be firmly lumbering forward in two ruts—one red and one blue—things are incrementally getting better nonetheless. Still I said, there are many singular news stories by which one can, as the result of their examination, grow despondent at the state of human compassion and decency in America. He replied:

> We're in a very stubborn period and it's really hard to get anything done right now, but look at the Civil War. It was at that point by far the bloodiest thing that had happened on the planet Earth. Before the Constitution was even brought up, from the moment the British left and the treaty was signed in Paris, we were at each other's throats. You know, Aaron Burr killed Alexander Hamilton in a duel. Now, you don't see Nancy Pelosi shooting Chris Christie on the shores of New Jersey and then fleeing in a rowboat. . . . The Civil War—Charles Sumner's beaten practically to death with a cane on the floor of the Senate. We've had really dark, horrible episodes in this country, and we work them out and we keep trudging forward. It's like that Beatles song—"I've got to admit it's getting better. A little better all the time. It can't get no worse." You know?

Conan talked about the popular misconception that things used to be great in this country, like romanticizing the civil rights movement for example, when that was actually a quite messy and unclear period. It was a good sight better than the state of affairs at the time the Emancipation Proclamation was signed, but it's not like you sign a paper, or espouse an idea, and a nation of human animals just auto-matically "gets it." He reminded me of just how complicated we are and how complex and glacial, therefore, our gradual improvement must be. I said that I was cheered by his perspective, and that I felt naïve for wanting the impossible—our nation of people, and ulti-mately our planet, to all treat one another with decency. My mistake was in reckoning this job of work as one that could ever be completed, which it cannot; but as Wendell Berry tells us, we simply must do the work that we are aware needs doing. That is the way.

Despite all the ways in which we're still lousy people, Conan went on to describe a quality about our country that he finds to be one of its greatest strengths: our willingness to air our dirty laundry.

"We're like a family that fights a lot, but it's out in the open. The scarier family is the one that pretends like there's not a problem."

He pointed out, in reference to the recently released CIA torture reports, that while some of the activities our country gets up to may be shameful, he is not comfortable judging people in whose shoes he has not walked, and so it's healthy to "let it bleed. Let it out. . . . That makes our country very unique—I don't know that there's very many other countries in the world where they would say, 'Look what we did.' I mean, the Japanese are having trouble acknowledg-ing sixty years ago in World War II. We're saying 'We did this four, five, six years ago.' . . . I think that's a very positive quality that this country has; the civil rights debates and arguments and violence were all broadcast at the height of the Cold War, and it was an embar-rassment to us, but . . . we let it bleed. We let it out, let people see what we are."

I said, "That's poignant. I'm grateful for your perspicacity."

"I'll look that up later."

"I look up to you a great deal."

"As you should."

"Well, you're tall."

We got to discussing things, like young people and work ethic—one of my favorite harangues—and I have to say: I kept lobbing softballs about which I expected Conan to respond with intelligence and humor, which of course he did, but I suppose I was not expecting the richly gracious humanity that I found beneath his gingery crust. For example, I thought we would merely commiserate about kids always looking at their phones, and the vapid quality of so much of contemporary popular culture, but instead, I was handed:

You also have to remember that there's a ton of young people out there killing themselves to go to medical school and learn how to be radiologists and physicists and to invent a better computing system—we just don't see them, and it can make us feel like the whole thing's going to shit and it's the fall of the Roman Empire, but I think, No, there's a lot of good people out there, they just don't get as many YouTube hits. That's the problem. It's negative selection.

Boy, that cheered me up. As a guy from rural Illinois who now lives and works in the entertainment capital of the world, it's hard to simply even drive to my woodshop without being deluged by billboards and garish messaging. The grocery store also dresses the slut, with the bullshit of tabloid headlines emblazoned in the vicinity of every checkout station (a trend away with which, it seems, some modern chains are doing, thankfully). I mean to say, it's been easy for me to conclude that we have indeed gone to hell in a handbasket, but Conan is right. The technique I need to perfect is changing my paths of travel so that they intersect the empty messaging as little as possible.

One good way to achieve that goal is by choosing to do work with people you like. You won't always agree with them, but I believe that we humans, by definition, don't *always* agree with *anybody*. That's what makes us so goddamn cute. But if you can live and work with people you like, you can get a lot of work done in a way that enlarges every member of the team. If we don't learn to stick together and put up with one another when something unpleasant occurs, then we risk being absent when something wonderful happens. Being alone is rarely any good, which is why we look for work to do that can be best achieved by many hands.

Conan: "In the meantime, we've created a little biosphere. We're employing some people, and it's nice. We've built a little community, and what's the alternative? The alternative is me, here, building a ship in a bottle and probably drinking a lot of red wine and shooting at crows with rock salt. I picture the end of *There Will Be Blood*—you come visit me and I bludgeon you with a bowling pin."

He told me about a time that another new, young writer on a TV show with him complained, "I don't like it that we write this stuff, and then they change it. I don't like that they change my words before they go on the air."

Conan replied, "Oh, you know what's interesting? You know whose work was never changed—they never touched it, and she had complete control of everything she wrote? Emily Dickinson. She wrote it in her attic, and then she died. Probably coughed up blood and keeled over and that was it. And they found [her work] later on, and they never changed a word."

We were talking about understanding the group dynamic, which always involves compromise on every level. That is the cost of working in a group, but it can also be the great benefit of working in one. And Conan pointed out, as he often has, that he understands the marriage of art and commerce; that if you're going to depend upon a company with a broadcast channel to deliver your art to the audience, then that's a relationship that has to be respected, by both sides.

I nodded, because my first impulse has always been to want to bad-mouth NBC because they never really got behind our show, *Parks and Recreation*. We never, ever saw a *fraction* of the incredible amount of promotion they would put behind their annual attempts at new comedies, even when we were winning some very high-end critical acclaim. Year after year, they would relegate us to the back of the line and instead plug their new shows very loudly in the hopes that those shows would become hits and earn them more revenue than our show with not-so-hot ratings, and then maybe they wouldn't be fired for not earning enough revenue. The number of those new shows that came close to achieving that goal? Zero shows.

Focusing solely upon that information can certainly fuel my ire. What I quickly learned, though, partly from the wisdom of my producers Mike Schur, Amy Poehler, and Morgan Sackett, was that although NBC wasn't demonstrably trying to advance our show, they also were not canceling our show, a move which, however distasteful, they would certainly have been justified in making. But they didn't. Oh, they almost did. Several times. There's a story about one of our executives boarding a flight from New York to LA, and when he got on the plane we were canceled, but when he landed there had been a reprieve. But the end of the story is that they let us live.

We made 125 episodes of a show that I think is the epitome of quality entertainment—it teaches us lessons about being nice to one another and finding success in life—by God, it's churchy stuff, but in a much more enjoyable package than any sermon to which I've been party, because it's funny as shit. So, at the end of the arithmetic, my feelings toward NBC are composed of gratitude. Keeping our show on the air, numbers-wise, was not the best business decision for them (which is why they so desperately tried to create remunerative replacements), but nonetheless on the air they kept us. They're still having a hell of a time finding their ass with both hands, in a landscape without mercy, and I don't envy them their task. I wish them well and Godspeed.

I say I don't envy them, because their jobs are made up entirely of commerce. Their concern is the marketplace, which can be a tough place to go to work, especially nowadays, what with technology changing perpetually and public tastes becoming much more diverse as they are presented with so many more options from which to choose when it comes to television programming.

Which has a lot to do with what I see as the cause of the whole *Tonight Show* debacle from 2009.

The whole thing started when NBC gave *The Tonight Show* to Leno instead of Letterman, which was undoubtedly a "numbers" decision. Johnny Carson had given his tacit approval of Letterman by appearing on his *Late Night* show, while he did not visit Leno even though Leno *was guest hosting Johnny's own show.* A few years later, Carson openly said that he had preferred Letterman as his replacement. Now. The fact that NBC either didn't ask Carson's opinion or they did ask but didn't care enough about it says to me that then and there is when they began to devalue *The Tonight Show.* It apparently became all commodity, with no humanity.

Despite the bad feelings that the whole meshuggaas caused, I'm not out to roundly denigrate Leno here. He is a funny man, and he is good at telling jokes. In interviews surrounding this mess, he talked an awful lot about ratings and sounded like very much the company man, which to my way of thinking is the mark of an adequate person for his particular job. The conundrum of network television is that mere adequacy does not breed excellence. A Leno looks good on paper, but if you want your program to be more than adequate, if you want your show to be sublime, then you need a little more creative fire in the belly from your host. You want an adventurous maverick who is willing to just toe, or even caper across, the company line. You want a Carson or a Letterman or a Conan.

When peddling a creative product, a corporation is bound to take missteps. It happens all the time, and unfortunately the creative side of the equation often involves artists being hurt in the process. A corporation, despite the Supreme Court's declaration that it has the same rights as a person, cannot, by definition, watch and enjoy a TV program. A corporation can see only a product, the value of which can be determined for them only by hard, cold numbers. Leno or Conan equals cheeseburger or McRib. This is literally dehumanizing, and so it's up to the creative participants to shoulder whatever indignities might come their way at the hands of the corporation. That's showbiz, kid.

The ultimate boner, then, to my way of thinking, was in Leno's lingering. When the network was still desperately trying to fit two leading men into one late-night Batman suit, they went so far as to try and shoehorn an hour of Leno into the prime-time space preceding *The Tonight Show*. A patently bad idea, about which Jeff Zucker, then president of NBC Universal, made this unfortunate statement:

"Too much on television is the same show recycled. [*The Jay Leno Show*] will be a show that can provide an answer for the changing times we live in."

That's some next-level salesman jive-talking right there.

The only appropriate thing for Mr. Leno to have done at that junc-ture was to walk away. I'm sure that became quite clear to him once the dust had settled and the irreparable damage had been wreaked upon his own image and that of *The Tonight Show*.

In his subsequent interview with Oprah Winfrey, Jay made no concessions whatsoever, pointing the finger of blame in every direc-tion except where it belonged—aimed squarely at his own famous loaf of a chin. "[NBC] said, 'We want you to go back.' I said, 'Okay.' And this seemed to make a lot of people really upset. And I go: 'Well, who wouldn't take that job though? Who wouldn't do that?'"

Uh, I'll tell you who, Mr. Leno.

Conan wouldn't do that.

The clear question to those watching was not "Who wouldn't do that?" Quite the opposite, in fact, the question was "Who the hell *would* do that?"

NBC had made a right mess of things, but they could focus on their hit reality show *The Voice* and limp forward. Leno shrugged, polished his acres of precious vintage cars, and told himself he was a blameless prince. Conan walked away.

This is solely *my* beef, by the way. Conan could not be more Zen about the whole thing, and when I told him that I might mention the topic, he said:

> *I'd be lying if I said I completely understand it, but I think when I'm ninety, there'll still be moments of "What the hell was that all about?" . . . But mostly I feel like, you know, grateful. . . . I was dealt a series of cards and I played them as well as I could and I feel like I did the right thing by my people and my fans, and so I'm at peace with all that and really grateful that I get to go out there and do my thing every night. You know? And do it my way.*

Just then Liza came into the room to deliver two large Ziploc bags of fresh beef for me to take home. If there's a finer hostess than her, show her to me, and I'll eat my hat. I also took the gentle hint that it was getting on toward bedtime in the O'Brien household. I said that I would wrap it up shortly, and that Megan was going to be very bummed to hear of our splendid three-way night together, without our usual double-date foursome (Megan was performing on Broadway yet).

Conan said, "You should really play this up like it was the greatest night ever."

I said, "Yeah—'Honey, they had that amazing masseuse Greg Lewis and his friend from the NFL both massaging me while I just ate a few pounds of fresh beef.'"

Liza said, "'And Cartier watches and fine art were given away, and there was lots of dish—a lot of celebrity gossip.'"

Conan said, "'Oh, that's right, they had the greatest story about Ellen. Having diarrhea.'"

We said good night to Liza and wended our way toward the evening's close, as Conan laid into some weighty Irish jazz riffs:

"What we're seeing is just what we've seen again and again, which is, sadly, people our age saying, 'Damn it, this is the way it's supposed to be!,' and being angry about change—and the quality I wish for most in myself, in later age, next to just incredible sexual powers—"

Me: "Sustained erections."

Him: "Sustained—I mean, erections that are just like, you know, you have to put, like, traffic cones around my dick because it's such a problem. Move power lines.

"But that aside, the thing that I would like most to stay young is to accept change; be interested in change."

He spoke some more (I couldn't shut him up, truth be told. Blah, blah, wisdom, blah) about how human nature informs us—when people applaud us, for example, how it's in our nature to think, "Yes, that worked, and I was rewarded! I like rewards, so I'll keep doing that same thing for as long as I can." I'm sure we can all think of examples of performers who have kept on doing "the same thing" for far too long. You can almost see the calcification occurring as they, say, perform that hit song from 1978 one more time.

Instead, my host suggested, we prosper by "keeping our eyes upon our own test or running our own race. By working hard, building things, writing things, making things, and trying to better yourself, trying to be a good person, that is our life's work. That's how you proselytize, is by doing it.

"Everything in your body's going to tell you to hunker down and shake your fist at the sky like King Lear, it's like—try not to go that way. The easy way to go is to say, 'It's all gone to shit,' when the great moral of the story, I think for your book should be, that *It's always been shit.*"

Boom. That's my valedictorian, right there.

I paused and considered that subtitle: *Gumption: It's Always Been Shit.* . . . Hm. It's not bad, but I imagine Dutton might have a different opinion.

Conan said, "It's a very tricky marriage, art and commerce, and I, for the most part, and this includes NBC, had a really great time, and it worked out really well for me. [I] got a lot of attention for this one time when it really didn't work out, and I was very disappointed in the way certain people behaved, but the headline was: 'For the most part, it worked out.' . . . Whenever my life is summed up by somebody, I want [the account] to be very positive: 'That guy got away with murder and had a really good time, and worked his ass off.'"

Jill, let's interpret that as a tacit invitation to pen the biography of Conan O'Brien. I'll call it *Sorrow's Bane: One Handsome Yankee's Dandy Doodle.*

He's like if Tilda Swinton had a threesome baby with a Viking and a stork. He just wants to put on a hell of a show for us, a goal at which he succeeds with great regularity. The moral? "It's always been shit."

Long may he run.

EPILOGUE

Here we are, my gentle, no doubt sleepy reader. What a sweet soiree we have enjoyed—you, me, and twenty-one American heroes.

I am charmed by the thought of such a party—Willie Nelson smoking out Eleanor Roosevelt while Jeff Tweedy teaches Frederick Douglass and Olmsted to sing "California Stars" and Laurie Anderson and Ben Franklin fuck with the lights. Wendell Berry stands at the window, with Yoko astride him, piggyback, as she points out a moonlit cloud and tells him what to do with it. Theodore Roosevelt is wrestling George Washington while Tom Laughlin and George Saunders get into an excited spate of Jungian dream analysis. Michael Pollan lovingly prepares sandwiches of true North Carolina barbecue while Carol Burnett leads the rest of us in an up-tempo "Big Rock Candy Mountain." All the while, Conan just dances up on the coffee table, all sexy like he does. Count me in. By God, I'll do the dishes.

In the arithmetic I've executed for this book, I have certainly learned a great deal about all the different ways that gumption can make a profound difference in a person's life. I came out of this investigation with a much sunnier disposition than the one I wore upon entering, as my subjects repeatedly displayed for me the ready fruits to be plucked from the admirable human qualities of kindness, obduracy, originality, hard work, and flexibility. These accomplishments of my esteemed twenty-one have pointed me squarely in the direction of further good work. As Mr. Berry put it, "I want to deal with people who are at work because they see the real reasons to be at work. That's what I call hope, if they can keep going."

I sincerely hope that my gathering of troublemakers has done you some good and that perhaps we shared a chuckle or two as well. If my luck holds, I'll see you at work.

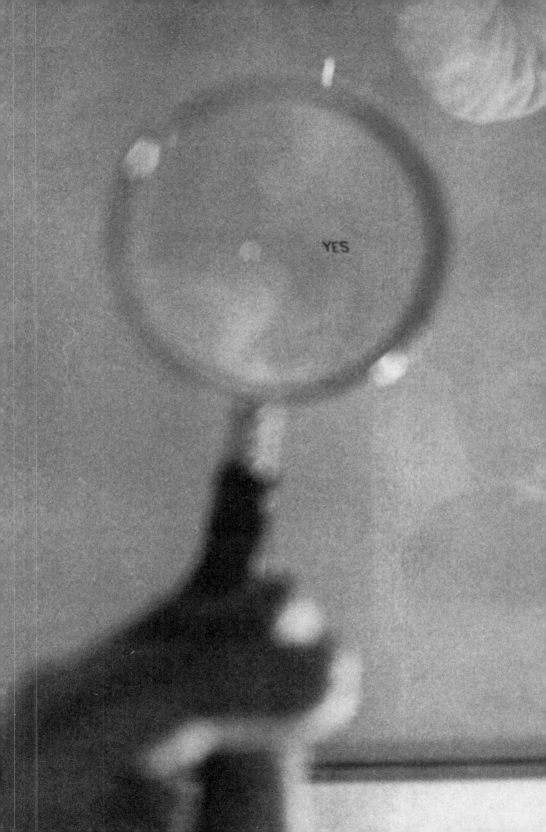

FURTHER READING BY SUBJECT

GEORGE WASHINGTON
Chernow, Ron. *Washington: A Life*, New York: Penguin Press, 2010.
Shea, Robert, and Robert Anton Wilson. *The Illuminatus! Trilogy*, New York: Dell, 1983.

BENJAMIN FRANKLIN
Isaacson, Walter, ed. *A Benjamin Franklin Reader*, New York: Simon & Schuster, 2003.
———. *Benjamin Franklin: An American Life*, New York: Simon & Schuster, 2003.

JAMES MADISON
Broadwater, Jeff. *James Madison: A Son of Virginia & a Founder of the Nation*, Chapel Hill, NC: University of North Carolina Press, 2012.

FREDERICK DOUGLASS
Douglass, Frederick. *Narrative of the Life of Frederick Douglass, an American Slave*, 1845.

THEODORE ROOSEVELT
Hunter, Gordon. *Selected Speeches and Writings of Theodore Roosevelt*, New York: Vintage, 2014.
Roosevelt, Theodore. *Hunting Trips of a Ranchman*, 1885.
———. *The Autobiography of Theodore Roosevelt*, 1913.
Morris, Edmund. *The Rise of Theodore Roosevelt*, New York: Coward, McCann & Geoghegan, 1979.

FREDERICK LAW OLMSTED
Martin, Justin. *Genius of Place: The Life of Frederick Law Olmsted*, New York: Da Capo Press, 2012.
Rybczynski, Witold. *A Clearing in the Distance*, New York: Scribner, 1999.
Twombly, Robert, ed. *Frederick Law Olmsted: Essential Texts*, New York: W. W. Norton & Company, 2010.
Kowsky, Francis R. *Country, Park & City: The Architecture and Life of Calvert Vaux*, New York: Oxford University Press, 1998.

FURTHER READING BY SUBJECT

ELEANOR ROOSEVELT
Roosevelt, Eleanor. *The Autobiography of Eleanor Roosevelt*, 1961.

WENDELL BERRY
Berry, Wendell. *The Unsettling of America*, San Francisco: Sierra Club Books, 1977.
———. *Watch with Me*, New York: Pantheon, 1994.
———. *Jayber Crow*, Washington, DC: Counterpoint, 2000.
———. *Life Is a Miracle*, Washington, DC: Counterpoint, 2000.
———. *Our Only World*, Berkeley, CA: Counterpoint, 2015.
———. *The Memory of Old Jack*, New York: Harcourt, Brace, Jovanovich, 1974.
———. *Fidelity*, New York: Pantheon, 1992.
———. *Bringing It to the Table*, Berkeley, CA: Counterpoint, 2009.
———. *The Way of Ignorance*, Washington, DC: Shoemaker & Hoard, 2005.
———. *Citizenship Papers*, Washington, DC: Shoemaker & Hoard, 2003.
———. *In the Presence of Fear*, Great Barrington, MA: Orion Society, 2001.
———. *Nathan Coulter*, Boston: Houghton Mifflin, 1960.

YOKO ONO
Higgins, Charlotte. "*The Guardian* Profile: Yoko Ono," *The Guardian*, June 8, 2012.
Sheff, David. *All We Are Saying: The Last Major Interview with John Lennon and Yoko Ono*, New York: St. Martin's Griffin, 2000.
Ono, Yoko. *Grapefruit*, New York: Simon & Schuster, 2000.
Cott, Jonathan. *Days That I'll Remember: Spending Time with John Lennon and Yoko Ono*, New York: Anchor, 2013.

MICHAEL POLLAN
Pollan, Michael. "Unhappy Meals," *The New York Times*, January 28, 2007.
———. *Second Nature*, New York: Atlantic Monthly Press, 1991.
———. *A Place of My Own*, New York: Random House, 1997.
———. *The Botany of Desire*, New York, Random House, 2001.
———. *The Omnivore's Dilemma*, New York: Penguin Press, 2006.
———. *In Defense of Food*, New York: Penguin Press, 2008.
———. *Food Rules*, New York: Penguin Books, 2009.
———. *Cooked*, New York: Penguin Press, 2013.

THOMAS LIE-NIELSEN
Becksvoort, Christian. *The Shaker Legacy*, Newtown, CT: Taunton Press, 1998.
———. *In Harmony with Wood*, New York: Van Nostrand Reinhold, 1983.
Korn, Peter. *Why We Make Things and Why It Matters*, Boston: David R. Godine, 2013.

FURTHER READING BY SUBJECT

NAT BENJAMIN

Ruhlman, Michael. *Wooden Boats*, New York: Viking, 2001.

Dunlop, Tom. *Schooner*, Edgartown, MA: Vineyard Stories, 2010.

Gardner, John. *Building Classic Small Craft*, Camden, ME: International Marine, 1996.

Moores, Ted. *Canoecraft*, Richmond Hill, ON: Firefly Books, 2007.

GEORGE NAKASHIMA

Nakashima, George. *The Soul of a Tree*, New York: Kodansha USA, 2012.

Nakashima, Mira. *Nature Form & Spirit*, New York: Harry N. Abrams, 2003.

CAROL BURNETT

Burnett, Carol. *This Time Together*, New York: Harmony Books, 2010.

————. *One More Time*, New York: Random House, 1986.

JEFF TWEEDY

Tweedy, Jeff. *Adult Head*, Zoo Press, 2004.

Kot, Greg. *Wilco: Learning How to Die*, New York: Three Rivers Press, 2004.

Grierson, Tim. *Wilco: Sunken Treasure*, London: Omnibus Press, 2013.

GEORGE SAUNDERS

Saunders, George. *CivilWarLand in Bad Decline*, New York: Random House, 1996.

————. *The Braindead Megaphone*, New York: Riverhead Books, 2007.

————. *Tenth of December*, New York: Random House, 2013.

————. *Congratulations, by the way*, New York: Random House, 2014.

LAURIE ANDERSON

Anderson, Laurie. *Stories from the Nerve Bible: A Twenty-Year Retrospective*, New York: HarperPerennial, 1993.

WILLIE NELSON

Hall, Michael. "Trigger: The Life of a Guitar," *Texas Monthly*, December 2012.

Nelson, Willie. *Roll Me Up and Smoke Me When I Die*, New York: William Morrow, 2012.

————. *The Facts of Life and Other Dirty Jokes*, New York: Random House, 2002.

CONAN O'BRIEN

Babiuk, Andy. *Beatles Gear*, Montclair, NJ: Backbeat Books, 2009.

Spitz, Bob. *The Beatles: The Biography*, New York: Little, Brown and Company, 2005.

Shakespeare, William. *King Lear*.

Robinson, John. *Born In Blood: The Lost Secrets of Freemasonry*, New York: M. Evans & Company, 1989.

ACKNOWLEDGMENTS

Without the thriving partnership of the one-hundred-plus pounds of gumption that is my wife, Megan Mullally, I would still be building furniture with drywall screws (aka "a fool"). My marriage has allowed this book to occur, for which I am deeply grateful, since being in love is the whole point. Laurie Anderson said that.

Secondly, and first and foremost, I have to thank my twenty-one featured firebrands. Each and every one of them has made this work a pleasurable education, even when my body might have preferred a nap to another savory Wendell Berry essay. It has been a sincere privilege to share these muckrakers with you, my readers. I here recognize my audacity in thinking anyone might still be reading this after that uphill slog. Not my first run-in with audacity.

Writing a project such as this one while performing in other jobs and traveling around like an overweight, tipsy jackrabbit has been mighty enjoyable, although perhaps a rather too-ambitious voyage. Without the vigilant and steady hand of Jill Something upon the tiller, I would most assuredly have run aground before clearing the harbor. She handily compensated for my tendency to list to port in heavy seas, assisted by able-bodied seawomen Stephanie Hitchcock on the halyards and LeeAnn Pemberton persuading the capstan in its revolutions, aided by Jessica Renheim, Eileen Chetti, Andrea Santoro, Norina

ACKNOWLEDGMENTS

Frabotta, Dora Mak, and Alissa Theodor. If Jamie Knapp hadn't shown up with her slow match, we never should have fired a single broadside, but she did, and so "confusion to Boney!"

Thayer McClanahan both heaved the log and took dead reckonings with or without a clear horizon every time I needed to know somebody's shoe size, and he spoiled me rotten with his nautical, salty something something from up in the crow's nest. I'm afraid this metaphor is running out of breeze. Oh, the puddening!

I have long admired the intelligence, curiosity, gumption, and, of course, photography of Dan Winters. Shooting this cover with him was a delight and a privilege, made all the more delightful by the redoubtable reconnaissance of Kathryn Winters. I am not saying that they are not Freemasons, nor Knights Templar neither.

My life would be much more giggle-free without the incessant and aggressive humor that Pat Roberts daily gifts to me, which feels like when Uncle Don used to make me eat grass. Fnord.

I thank my redoubtable agents, Monika Verma and Daniel Greenberg, who have been able to hornswaggle the folks at Dutton into paying me for this fun—I mean, work—and then Dutton is also supposedly publishing this thing? That's some good agenting, right there.

Um, so, the folks at Dutton. Thank you for the seventeen-book deal! Two down! Next up, either the Conan bio or that Wonder Twins/Bible hero thing I mentioned with me and Willie Aames. I offer my sincere gratitude.

Special thanks to Ethan Nicolle for his scintillating talent with a pencil. Please look for his hilarious and action-packed *Axe Cop* and *Bearmageddon* titles.

ACKNOWLEDGMENTS

Here follows a list of great American people who assisted me with suggestions and/or aid in connecting with my generous subjects, and/or kept a straight face with me after I cut one in an elevator: CornMo, Stephanie Hunt, Bala Soto, Justin Goldwater, David Schwab, Cooper Holoweski, Burley Coulter, Bob Byington, Karen Jacobs x3, Christian Becksvoort, Mike Schur, Morgan Sackett, Amy Poehler, Nicholas Pollacchi, Laura Dunn, Tanya Berry, Den Berry, Mary Berry, Emily Berry, Tanya Smith, Mart Rowanberry, Lauren Offerman, Tom Waits, Kathleen Brennan, Hagbard Celine, Julianne Deery, Erik Logan, Tyler Jones, Natalie Cherwin, Deneb Puchalski, Matt Kenney, Asa Christiana, Gary Rogowski, Ed Pirney, Tracy Poust, Robin MacGregor, Robin Lee, Wally Wilson, Pam Benjamin, Linda Sundheim, Thacker Hample, Kyle Leydier, Frank Laughlin, Teresa Laughlin, Christina Laughlin, Sarah Vowell, John Hodgman, Sue Miller-Tweedy, Spencer Tweedy, Sam Tweedy, Wilco, Eric Frankhouser, Mark Greenberg, Mary Penn, Helena Fils, Karin Gaarder, Marcus Stuckey, Elmo, Caitlin Clements, Clover, Peryn Schmitt, Troy Schreck, Paul Rudd, Tony Margherita, Jack Shoemaker, Connie Ashton, Joe Goodale, Bonnie Levitan, Mark Flanagan, Largo, Martin Garner, Josie Braymer, Jamie Mandelbaum, Barry Tyerman, Marcie Morris, Nathaniel Bert Smith, Jonas Herbsman, Heidi Lopata, UTA, Adam Siegler, Pete Milsap, Minnie Quinch, Joy Herd, Trina Meliza, Rebecca Lee, Neil Young, John Flansburgh, John Linnell, and Chez Panisse.

CREDITS